THE BASIC
WRITER'S BOOK

Anne Agee
Anne Arundel Community College

Gary Kline
Bowie State College

Eric J. Hibbison, *Consulting Editor*

PRENTICE-HALL, INC.
Englewood Cliffs, New Jersey 07632

Library of Congress Cataloging in Publication Data

AGEE, ANNE.
   The basic writer's book.

   Includes index.
   1. English language—Rhetoric.   I. Kline, Gary,
joint author.   II. Title.
PE1408.A42   808'.042   80-26019
ISBN 0-13-069476-2

© 1981 by Prentice-Hall, Inc., Englewood Cliffs, N.J. 07632

Printed in the United States of America

10   9   8   7   6   5   4   3

Cover design by Miriam Recio
Manufacturing buyer: Harry P. Baisley

PRENTICE-HALL INTERNATIONAL, INC., *London*
PRENTICE-HALL OF AUSTRALIA PTY. LIMITED, *Sydney*
PRENTICE-HALL OF CANADA, LTD., *Toronto*
PRENTICE-HALL OF INDIA PRIVATE LIMITED, *New Delhi*
PRENTICE-HALL OF JAPAN, INC., *Tokyo*
PRENTICE-HALL OF SOUTHEAST ASIA PTE. LTD., *Singapore*
WHITEHALL BOOKS, LIMITED, WELLINGTON, *New Zealand*

Contents

PART TWO   COMPOSING PARAGRAPHS

7   BASIC STRUCTURE OF A PARAGRAPH

8   BEFORE WRITING: EXPLORING

9   BEFORE WRITING: ORGANIZING

10   PRACTICE IN COMPOSING PARAGRAPHS

16   PUNCTUATION

APPENDIX: VERBS

INDEX   409

Preface

In writing, as in speaking, the basic act is choosing. We select the word, tone, structure, and order we want. When speaking, most of us do not think much about the extremely familiar choices we are making. Writing, however, suddenly makes the familiar seem strange.

To help students overcome this strangeness, we have concentrated in *The Basic Writer's Book* on showing the alternatives a writer has for expressing an idea and on exploring the reasons for choosing among the various options.

Why Write?

Many students come to college convinced that writing is a useless activity for them. They believe that writing is being replaced by tele-communications or that the work they will be doing after graduation won't involve writing. They are wrong. For a number of reasons, writing is indispensable.

Writing leaves a record of thought. The earliest writing that archeologists have discovered is business records, and record-keeping is still vital today. The business and professional worlds that students are preparing for live through written records: letters, memoranda, reports, contracts. The information may be stored on microchips in a computer, but it is written out when needed; deals may be made by phone, but written contracts must be signed to confirm the agreement. (Hollywood's L.B. Mayer was right: "A verbal contract isn't worth the paper it's written on.")

When people say they can function in American society without writing, they are boasting they can win a fight with one hand tied behind their backs. Maybe, with luck, they can; but why bother? A "fighter" needs all the resources he or she can command, especially for college, where the written report is often the teacher's only way of judging students' growth toward independence in the fields they have chosen.

However, writing is more than just a utilitarian tool. Early writing was believed to be magic, and writing still does magic. It can help writers discover what they really think, and it can make the thinking better. In writing to persuade someone or explain something, thinking becomes visible, not slippery and hidden as it is in the mind. In writing, everyone can see the strong and weak points; writing can be revised to emphasize the strengths and eliminate the weaknesses. Writing lets a person get a hold on his or her thoughts and improve them.

RATIONALE FOR THE BASIC WRITER'S BOOK

The Basic Writer's Book is frankly eclectic, uniting traditional instruction in the conventions of the written language with sentence-combining exercises and rhetorical considerations of audience, purpose, and style.

Our coverage of the traditional grammatical and mechanical principles is not meant to be exhaustive; we have chosen to discuss certain conventions because of their central role in improving sentence effectiveness. While we have tried to keep grammatical terminology to a minimum, we felt that some terms were necessary to instruct students in the writing conventions and to enable them to share the discoveries they make about the rhetoric and structure of their writing. Instructors may give the terminology the emphasis they feel is appropriate for their students.

We have found sentence-combining an excellent and enjoyable beginning to the mastery of writing. Students are temporarily freed from the necessity of finding something to say and can concentrate on how to present given ideas in the most effective way. Students practice making the choices writers use to construct and improve sentences. In discussing and analyzing these choices, students gain control over what they want to say to a particular audience.

Finally, we have tried in this book to present writing in a rhetorical framework, i.e., as part of a situation requiring consideration of audience, purpose, and style. As much as possible, the conventions of sentence structure and paragraph structure have been presented not in terms of correctness but in terms of rhetorical effectiveness. We feel that reflection on the rhetoric of sentences and paragraphs is absolutely necessary if students are to see writing as a craft that can be mastered, not as an uncontrollable extension of themselves. Discovering that choices exist and learning to discriminate among them are the beginnings of a writer's growth in independence.

We intend the organization of the book to be flexible. Section I concentrates on sentence-combining, investigating various kinds of modification, subordination, and coordination. Section II builds on the principles of coordination and subordination in constructing paragraphs. This section also includes chapters on pre-writing to help students generate the kind of ideas that will make their writing interesting and organize them in a way that will make their writing effective. The last two sections, *Revising* and *Editing,* give students practice in testing the fitness of various grammatical and rhetorical choices for a particular writing situation.

Teachers may follow the format as it stands or modify it to suit the needs of a particular group of students. For example, here is a sample syllabus based on the stages of the composing process:

Pre-Writing

Chapter 8	Before Writing: Exploring
Chapter 9	Before Writing: Organizing

Writing

Chapter 7	Basic Paragraph Structure
Chapter 10	Practice in Composing Paragraphs

Revising

Chapter 13	Word Choices
Chapter 1	Recognizing the Basic Sentence
Chapter 2	Adding to the Basic Sentence
Chapter 3	Coordination
Chapter 12	Coherence
Chapter 4	Subordination
Chapter 11	Unity
Chapter 5	Practice in Sentence-Combining
Chapter 6	Sentences in the Context of Paragraphs

Supplementary Exercises

Portions of chapters 14–16 may be assigned when individual students show a need for practice in the writing conventions beyond that included in the earlier chapters.

ACKNOWLEDGMENTS

We would like to thank our students, whose effort and imagination have fueled our own; Robert Cosgrove of Texas Technical University, Richard Dodge of UCLA, Eric Hibbison of J. Sargeant Reynolds Community College, Richmond, Virginia, C. Jeriel Howard of Northeastern Illinois University, Max Morenberg of Miami University of Ohio, W. Dean Memering of Central Michigan State University, and Ken Symes of Western Washington State University, who reviewed and commented on our work, improving the text at every step; and our colleagues, families, and friends (especially John) whose humor and forbearance made this book possible.

We hope *The Basic Writer's Book* will open up the complex, peculiar world of writing for many students and enable them to delight in it as we do.

Anne Agee
    Anne Arundel Community College
Gary Kline
    Bowie State College

Guide to
Revising and
Editing

ab	Write this word out
adj	Use an adjective (pp. 30–31)
adv	Use an adverb (pp. 15–16)
agr	Make subject and verb agree (pp. 336–40)
cap	Consult dictionary for use of capital letter
coh	Coherence; make connections between ideas clearer (pp. 285–97)
coord	Coordinate these ideas (p. 61)
Comma	Use a comma here (pp. 363–68)
CS	Comma splice; punctuate correctly between sentences (pp. 362–63)
d	Diction; choose a more exact word (pp. 301–2)
dang	Dangling modifier; connect this modifier to the base sentence (pp. 351–52)
emp	Emphasize this idea by putting it in the base sentence (pp. 93–94)
frag	Fragment; make this word group a complete sentence (p. 333)
mm	Misplaced modifier; put this modifier next to the word it describes (pp. 351–52)
org	Improve the organization of paragraph (pp. 223–31)
//	Use parallel structure (pp. 290–93)

passive	Change this sentence from passive to active (p. 26)
pl	Consult dictionary for correct plural
pn	Make pronoun agree with the word it replaces (pp. 341–42)
quote	Put quotation marks here
ref	Make it clear what word this pronoun refers to (pp. 340–41)
run-on	Punctuate correctly between sentences (pp. 359–62)
semi-colon	Use a semi-colon here (pp. 360–61)
shift	Keep the verb tense and point of view consistent (pp. 353–55)
sp	Check this word in the dictionary and then add it to your spelling notebook (pp. 323–24)
sub	Subordinate this idea (p. 124)
tense	Choose appropriate time for the verb (pp. 378–99)
trans	Use a transition (p. 287)
T. S.	Improve topic sentence (pp. 174–75)
unity	Stay with the main idea (pp. 263–64)
val	Use more variety in your sentence patterns (pp. 166–67)
wordy	Say this in fewer words (pp. 307–10)

THE BASIC
WRITER'S BOOK

SENTENCES

PART 1

Ever since you sat in kindergarten and practiced The man ran you've been using sentences to communicate ideas in writing. After writing sentences for so long, you know a lot about them. This book will be building on that knowledge to help you become a more skillful writer.

Being a good writer means knowing how to rework sentences to make them as effective as possible. A good writer can take the first draft of a sentence and expand or tighten it, make its parts more precise, shape and reshape it until it does exactly what is necessary for the situation.

This section of the book will give you practice in working with the basic structure of sentences and in choosing alternative ways of expressing ideas.

The British statesman, orator, and writer, Winston Churchill, claimed that an outstanding part of his education was learning to understand the organization of sentences: "I got into my bones the essential structure of the ordinary English sentence—which is a noble thing." To grow as a writer is to appreciate this nobility.

Recognizing the Basic Sentence

1

[handwritten notes in margin: 3 types — Simple, Compound, Complex]

Every sentence you write creates an impression on your audience. For instance, what impression do you think this sentence would make if it appeared in a job application?

> As a bank teller a possishun wood I like.

Because of its misspellings and confusing arrangement of ideas, this sentence would probably give the reader an unfavorable impression of the person applying for the job.

This sentence would probably create a more positive impression:

> I would like a position as a bank teller.

So, it is important to be able to control the effect of each sentence. To exercise that control, you have to become consciously aware of the information about sentences that you have unconsciously absorbed over the years.

Also, since you and your classmates and your teacher will be discussing the effect of various sentences, it is important that you all be able to use the same terms for the parts of the sentence. This first part of the book will review some basic information about sentences.

The first step in controlling sentences is to recognize what is and what is not a sentence.

Exercise A

Look at the word groups below. Which ones do you recognize as sentences? Put a check next to each group of words that you think is a sentence.

A.

_____ 1. Having a root beer, *Mike listered to the news.*

___✓___ 2. Jean has passed the test

_____ 3. Parked illegally, *the car was towed away*

_____ 4. To give a gift *is not as easy as it seems*

___✓___ 5. The child laughed

_____ 6. Laughing loudly *is not very polite*

B.

_____ 7. The man in the gray coat *was a spy.*

___✓___ 8. They are eating all the candy

_____ 9. All the candy *was eaten by kids*

_____ 10. The truck down the street *is not ours.*

___✓___ 11. The truck raced down the street

_____ 12. The graceful dancers *is a name of a rock'n roll group*

_____ 13. Some hidden passageways *were found in the site*

C.

_____ 14. When I go to Paris *I always bring my dictionary with me*

_____ 15. What she bought *was not so expensive*

___✓___ 16. Kevin will go to Paris

_____ 17. Since it is very expensive *he didn't buy it.*

_____ 18. How they find the time *to do all this work in ½ an hour?*

___✓___ 19. The room became absolutely quiet

_____ 20. After the room became absolutely quiet, *everybody looked at me...*

Exercise B

Copy on a separate sheet of paper all of the word groups you and your teacher agree are sentences. What do all of these word groups have that makes you know they are sentences? They all communicate an idea by giving certain key pieces of information to a reader.

SUBJECTS

For one thing, every group of words that is a sentence names for you the person or thing that is being talked about. In other words, every sentence has a SUBJECT. In "The man ran," *man* is what the writer wants to talk about in the sentence. *Man* is the SUBJECT.

Exercise C

Go back and circle the SUBJECTS in the sentences you just copied. (Notice that SUBJECTS can be either nouns like "the truck" or "Kevin," or pronouns like "they." Both kinds of words can tell a reader who or what is the center of attention in a sentence.)

Look again at the word groups in section A:

to find Subject ask —
What
Who or
Which ones

1. Having a root beer
2. Jean has passed the test
3. Parked illegally
4. To give a gift
5. The child laughed
6. Laughing loudly

Only numbers 2 and 5 tell you who or what is being talked about: *Jean, the child.* In number 6, for example, you don't know who is laughing loudly. Number 6, therefore, is not a sentence because it doesn't give you one essential part of the idea, the subject.

Exercise D

Who or what is the center of attention in these sentences?

Ways to deactivate a verb

1. Napoleon won the battle of Austerlitz.
2. Ms. Barclay hired a new sales representative.
3. New car sales are down again this month.
4. Franklin Delano Roosevelt was elected President in 1932.
5. Few comedians made it as big as the Marx Brothers.
6. Drinking good scotch can be expensive.
7. Television is one of the most profound developments of this century.

1) to + Verb (infinitive)
2) ing word w/o auxiliaries
3) ed en (possibly)

5

8. Some poetry tries to achieve total communication.
9. Agnes, Linda, and Kathy write historical novels under the name of Elspeth Carp.
10. Neutrons allow us to probe the hidden structure of matter.
11. Wild is the wind.
12. Included in the price are taxes and carrying charges.   *are Included*
13. Coiled on the corpse was a hideous serpent.
14. Clinging to the rock were several bright orange starfish.
15. There was a full moon last night.
16. Coming up fast on the outside is Pocomoke Pride!
17. Here is everything needed for happiness.
18. Watching from the castle window was an ugly beast.
19. Here are the specimens for the test.
20. Full, white, and calm floated the moon in an empty sky.

Exercise E

Add a logical subject to each of the following sentences.

1. There are ___*patches*___ in my yard.

2. ___*She*___ waited.

3. ___*My cousin*___ drew up a contract for me.

4. Facing the hunters was ___*the deer*___ .

5. ___*The doors*___ locked up at 5 o'clock.

6. ___*They*___ were stacked on the desk.

7. Planted around the patio were ___*flowers*___ .

8. Here is the ___*man I told you about.*___

9. ___*Onions*___ makes me cry.

10. ___*Cars*___ lay on the parking lot.

VERBS

can be "action V." or can indicate existance"
they also tell when

ways to deactivate on previous page

Presenting a subject is not all that is needed for a group of words to be a sentence. Look again at the word groups in section B:

7. The man in the gray coat
8. They are eating all the candy
9. All the candy

10.   The truck down the street
11.   The truck raced down the street
12.   The graceful dancers
13.   Some hidden passageways

All of the word groups here show people or things that might be subjects. But only numbers 8 and 11 give you the second vital piece of information needed to complete the idea. They are the only word groups in that list that tell you what the subject is doing and that place the action in the present, past, or future: *are eating* (present), *raced* (past). Groups 8 and 11 have VERBS as well as subjects. In a sentence, a VERB shows a subject involved in action taking place in present, past, or future time.

Exercise F

What words in the sentences below show the action that the subject is involved in?

1.   Margaret hit her brother.
2.   Sheldon baked the cupcakes.
3.   The dog swims every morning.
4.   Our class went to the state capital.
5.   Buy a Stratocruiser. ——— *the subject is call "You understood"; it's implied*
6.   I hate strawberries.
7.   She mumbled an apology.
8.   His father said "No!"
9.   Ralph gave the books to Julie.
10.   The boss just fired her secretary.
11.   Wait a minute!
12.   The congregation stood up.
13.   The children squirmed in their seats.
14.   The cat hid in the corner.
15.   The skaters floated across the ice.
16.   Greg lowered the sail.
17.   Open the window.
18.   Marcie ran and skipped all over the yard.
19.   The coach began the drill.
20.   No one paints better than Ted.

Exercise G

By adding a verb, show what each of these subjects is doing.

1.   We _are running_ .

2.   The citizens of the state of Oregon _are Americans_ .

3.   Charles and Don _went to a party_

4.   The new landlord _is too old._ .

5.   Her grandmother _died last summer_

6.   Everyone _was laughing_ .

7.   The papers on the desk _were stolen_ .

8.   Michele _is not my name._ .

9.   Piles of new toys _were brought-in_ .

10.   The tall woman _stood up._ .

11.   A delivery truck _is a need for us._

12.   Heart patients _are generally old_ people.

13.   The supervisor _told him to shut-up_

14.   Several cats _are cross-eyed_ .

15.   The police _asked him a few_ questions.

(Verbs are probably the most important tools of language. They can help you to show meaning in a variety of ways. There is a detailed discussion of verbs on pages 375–408. You may want to increase your skill with verbs by studying and practicing that additional material.)

SUBORDINATION SIGNALS

The basic pattern of meaning that your readers expect to find in a sentence is SUBJECT-VERB. However, not every subject-verb group is a sentence. Look at the word groups in section C:

14.   When I go to Paris
15.   What she bought
16.   Kevin will go to Paris
17.   Since it is very expensive
18.   How they find the time
19.   The room became absolutely quiet
20.   After the room became absolutely quiet

Notice that every word group here presents a subject and a verb, but only numbers 16 and 19 are sentences.

All the other word groups in section C begin with a SUBORDINATION SIG-NAL like *when, since* or *after.* These SUBORDINATION SIGNALS tell you that a group of words contains only part of a complete idea and not the most important part.

For instance, compare groups 19 and 20. The word *after* in 20 is the only difference between them, but that one word signals an important difference in meaning. It tells readers that you haven't given them your main idea yet. The subordination signal, *after,* makes them expect something to complete the thought. Therefore, 20 is not a sentence because of that sense of incompleteness. Read these word groups out loud. Can you hear that some of the ideas are not finished? (Subordination signals are explained in detail in Chapter 4.)

Summary

A sentence expresses a complete thought by presenting

a SUBJECT and
a VERB that shows past,   which are not introduced
present, or future time   by a SUBORDINATION
                                   SIGNAL.

Exercise H

Look again at those word groups in Exercise A that were not sentences. Try to make each word group express a complete idea by adding a subject, or a verb, or a subject–verb unit.

EXAMPLE:

"Having a root beer" is not a sentence. But these are:

                S   V
Having a root beer, *Mike listened* to the news.
                (subject-verb unit added)

  S   V
Miriam is having a root beer.
  S   V
Miriam has a root beer.
         (subject added; verb changed° to show time)

         S   V
Having a root beer is one way to relax.
       (verb added)

° *-ing* verbs and *to* — verbs do not show the time of the action; therefore, they cannot be used alone as the verb in a sentence. You must change the verb to one of the forms that indicates when an action took place—past, present, or future.

3. Parked illegally
4. To give a gift
6. Laughing loudly
7. The man in the gray coat
9. All the candy
10. The truck down the street
12. The graceful dancers
13. Some hidden passageways
14. When I go to Paris
15. What she bought
17. Since it is very expensive
18. How they find the time
20. After the room became absolutely quiet

Exercise I

In each of the sentences you wrote for exercise H, find the subject–verb group not introduced by a subordination signal. Underline that subject and circle that verb.

PUNCTUATING COMPLETE SENTENCES

Most sentences begin with a capital letter and end with a period, a question mark, or an exclamation point. In writing, you use punctuation at the ends of sentences to signal your reader that a new idea is coming.

> Have you heard the news?
>
> The team is so excited.
>
> We won the state football championship!

A group of words that is punctuated as a sentence but is not a sentence is called a FRAGMENT. A FRAGMENT expresses only a piece of an idea, not a complete thought. (For instance, all of the word groups in Exercise H were fragments until you rewrote them so that they had all the necessary elements of a sentence.)

Sometimes, you may use sentence fragments in casual conversation when you are sure that your audience understands the whole idea. But most writing situations demand that you express each idea completely. A sentence fragment in writing may prevent your reader from seeing the whole idea that you are trying to express. This series of fragments, for instance, would probably leave a reader confused.

> Heard?
>
> Excited.
>
> Won!

Exercise J

In the following paragraph, the capitalization and punctuation that mark the beginning and end of each sentence have been left out. Read the paragraph carefully and supply the necessary signals to show where each sentence begins and ends. All the commas and other punctuation marks are correct. Don't change them. Label the basic subject–verb unit in each of your sentences. (This paragraph was originally written as ten sentences.)

America's early settlers built their houses to suit their location. they had to build for the American climate with American materials. they couldn't always have the kind of house that they were used to. In New England, for example, the colonists built longhouses of thatch and bent trees. they couldn't build English-style houses until tools arrived from England. In the Southwest, there was no lumber available. therefore, the Spaniards made shelters from desert clay. In the Southeast, the French raised the first floors of their houses off the ground as a protection from dampness. they also built large open porches to take advantage of any cool breezes. throughout the country, the colonists adapted their houses to American conditions.

Exercise K

In the paragraph below, some fragments have been punctuated as sentences. Rewrite this paragraph making sure that all the sentences present a complete idea with a subject–verb unit. Label each subject–verb unit in the rewritten paragraph.

A baby's first year. Is an expensive year for his parents. New parents may spend up to $4,000. On a child during that first 12 months. Medical costs, of course, eat up a large chunk of the budget. Besides paying the doctor's fee, New parents must also cover the cost of a hospital room, nursery care, laboratory work, And medicines. In addition, the new mother and father must pay for clothing and furniture. As well as food for their child. Finally, the parents must allow for such extra costs as baby-sitting, Impulsive toy-buying and special pictures of the new addition to the family. While parents may look forward to lots of fun with a new baby, They should not be surprised if their budget gets tighter.

WRITING PRACTICE

In five or six sentences, describe your favorite way to spend a Saturday.

Check your writing to make sure that each sentence gives your readers the basic subject–verb information they need to understand your ideas. Be sure that correct punctuation separates one sentence from the next.

I'd like to spend one Saturday alone in my home. Without having my parents or any friends in the house. I'd like to sleep or read in my bed till noon. Then, after lunch, I'd like to watch some T.V.. But after dinner I'd like to go to a party with my friends too.

Adding

to the

Basic Sentence

2

The subject–verb unit, as you saw in Chapter 1, presents the basic information needed to communicate an idea in writing. But writing would be a slow and frustrating process if you wrote only in simple subject–verb sentences, and the communication would probably not be very effective.

Making sure that your reader has the basic information of a subject and a verb is only the first step in writing an effective sentence. Once you are sure that you have shown who or what is the center of attention and what action is involved, you need to fine-tune the sentence so it presents your idea to your reader as accurately as possible. You can make changes in the basic sentence so that it describes the subject and the action more precisely.

MAKING THE VERB EFFECTIVE

Choosing the Verb Form

One way to ensure clear communication of an idea is to make the verb do everything it is capable of doing for you. Besides describing the main action of the sentence, a verb tells your reader the time of that action—whether it is in the past, in the present, or in the future.

For instance, look at these four sentences:

> The secretaries typed.
> The secretaries are typing.
> The secretaries will type.
> The secretaries have typed.

Each sentence has the same subject and the same basic verb. But each sentence says something slightly different about when the typing took place.

In the first sentence, the typing was completed at some time in the past. In the second sentence, the typing is going on now, in the present. In the third sentence, the typing hasn't started yet, but should start soon. In the fourth sentence, the typing started in the past and continues right up to the present. Each verb form places the action in a different time frame. Be sure to choose the verb that gives the time frame you have in mind.

(A full discussion of using verbs to show time relationships is presented on pages 378–99. You may use that additional material to sharpen your skill in controlling verbs.)

In addition to placing action in time, the form of a verb can also show something about the tone of the action. With the right helping verb, a verb can show a tone of emphasis, uncertainty, obligation, or other meaning.

> The secretaries can type. (emphasis on ability)
>
> The secretaries did type. (emphasis on performance)
>
> The secretaries might type. (uncertainty)
>
> The secretaries should type. (obligation)

Each of these sentences expresses a slightly different tone for the action of typing.

The most common helping verbs that express tone are: *can, could, did, does, may, might, must, shall, should, will,* and *would.*

Exercise A

Rewrite each sentence below, changing the time or tone of the verb. Be prepared to explain the difference in meaning between the original sentence and your sentence.

> EXAMPLE:
>
> The members will vote.
>
> *The members may have voted.*

The first sentence shows that the voting is going to take place in the future. The second sentence suggests the possibility that the voting has already been done.

1. The cat climbs.

   The cat can climb

2. The book will fall.

   The book should fall

3. Toni wrote.

   Toni must write _____

4. The knight has ridden.

   The knight will ride _____

5. The doctor operated.

   The doctor will operate _____

6. Arlene scrubbed.

   Arlene will scrub _____

7. Jeff will be promoted.

   Jeff should be promoted _____

8. The lecturer has paused.

   The lecturer might pause _____

9. I walk.

   I can walk _____

10. You can go.

    You must go. _____

Describing the Action of the Verb

Another way of controlling the effect of the verb, besides choosing the appropriate time and tone, is to show the conditions under which the action takes place by using ADVERBS. Adverbs are words or phrases (groups of words) that show when, where, why, how, or to what degree some action is performed.

For example, can you see how adverbs are used in the sentences below to describe the action of the verb more precisely?

Terri visits *frequently*. (*When* does Terri visit?)
Quickly, the truck stopped. (*How* did the truck stop?)
Ed went *to the store*. (*Where* did Ed go?)
I had *completely* forgotten. (*To what degree* had I forgotten?)
Daniel whistled *for joy*. (*Why* did Daniel whistle?)

Notice that *frequently*, *quickly*, and *completely* all end in *-ly*. The *-ly* ending is a good clue that a word is being used as an adverb.

Exercise B

By adding adverbs in the following sentence, show something about the conditions under which the actions occurred.

EXAMPLE:

Clem left. (when?)
Clem left on Sunday.

1. The cheerleaders shouted. (why?)
   because
   ___when___ their team scored

2. The cheerleaders shouted. (how?)
   loudly

3. The picture fell. (where?)
   on the floor

4. The town was rebuilt. (to what degree?)
   almost

5. The tree bloomed. (when?)
   in Spring

6. The soldiers marched. (how?)
   rapidly

7. The soldiers marched. (where?)
   to the field

8. The soldiers marched. (where and how?)

   rapidly to the field

9. Tanya complained. (when and how?)

   Yesterday — — — — — — _angrily_

10. The computer broke down. (where and to what degree?)

    The computer in the library broke down completely

The forms and uses of ADVERBS are presented in more detail on pages 347–49. You may use that additional material to sharpen your skill at describing verbs.

Completing the Verb

A sentence like

> The lawyer presented.

probably raises a question in the mind of a reader: *What* was presented? You could supply that information with another sentence:

> Her case was presented.

But probably you would automatically combine these two sentences to produce

> The lawyer presented her case.

When you use a word or phrase (group of words) to complete the action of a verb, you are using an OBJECT COMPLEMENT. An object complement allows you to show the goal or result or conclusion of the action begun in the verb.

For instance, can you see the complement or completer of the action in each of these sentences?

> Jean found the money. (What did Jean find?)
> The tree crushed Rosita's car. (What did the tree crush?)
> Tanzania closed its border. (What did Tanzania close?)

Exercise C

Combine each of the following pairs of sentences to produce one sentence in which an object complement shows the goal or result of the action of the verb.

EXAMPLE:

Mrs. Burton planted.

Zinnias were planted.

Mrs. Burton planted zinnias.

1. Kelly will deliver.
   The pizza will be delivered.

   <u>Kelly will deliver the pizzas</u>

2. Our congregation built.
   A temple was built.

   <u>Our congregation built a temple</u>

3. The agent has sold.
   The house has been sold.

   <u>The agent has sold the house</u>

4. Alice is singing.
   A ballad is being sung.

   <u>Alice is singing a ballad</u>

5. Writing requires.
   Practice is required.

   <u>Writing requires practice</u>

Exercise D

Combine each set of sentences below into one sentence in which the action of the verb is described by an adverb and/or completed by a complement.

EXAMPLE:

UNIVAC hired.

Dr. Ramirez was hired.

The hiring was done last year.

She was hired as research director.

Last year, UNIVAC hired Dr. Ramirez as research director.

UNIVAC hired Dr. Ramirez last year as research director.

1. The tenor sang.
   His part was sung.
   It was sung during dress rehearsal.
   He sang badly.

   The tenor sang his part badly during the dress rehearsal

2. Dad barbecued.
   A pig was barbecued.
   It was barbecued over an open pit.
   Dad did this dramatically.

   Dad barbecued a pig over an open pit dramatically

3. Vicky plunged.
   A sword was plunged.
   It was plunged through the villain's heart.
   She plunged it forcefully.

   Vicky plunged a sword through the villah's heart forcefully

4. The cat scratched.
   The scratching was wild.
   She scratched the back door screen.
   She did this for five minutes.

   The cat scratched wildly the back door screen for 5 min.

5. The policeman arrested.
   A burglar was arrested.
   She was arrested yesterday.
   She was arrested after a long search.

   After a long search, yesterday the policeman arrested the burglar.

6. The peas were grown.
   Mr. Thornton grew them.
   They grew in his garden.
   They grew last spring.

   Last spring Mr. Thornton grew peas in his garden

   _____

7. The children chased.
   Their friends were chased.
   They chased during recess.
   They chased around the playground.

   The children chased their friends around the

   playground during recess

8. The teller counted.
   The receipts were counted.
   They were counted at the end of the day.
   She counted them slowly.

   At the end of the day, the teller counted

   the receipts slowly.

9. I followed.
   The ice cream truck was followed.
   I followed it with my eyes.
   I followed it wistfully.
   It was followed down the street.

   I followed the ice cream truck wistfully

   down the street with my eyes.

10. The librarian opened.
    The fines book was opened.
    It was opened to the last page.
    He opened it wearily.

    The librarian opened the fines book to the

    last page wearily.

Exercise E

Describe the action more precisely in each of the following sentences by adding an object complement and/or an adverb. (Some verbs are complete in themselves and do not take complements.) Then write a second version of the sentence with a slightly different meaning by changing the verb form and making any other changes needed to go along with the new verb's meaning.

EXAMPLE:

My sister screamed.
A. *My sister screamed for help.*
B. *My sister would never scream for help.*

1. The motor will start.

   A. _— — — after turning the key._

   B. _— — — wouldn't — — if there's not gas in the tank_

2. Maureen painted.

   A. _— — — — her room_

   B. _— — must paint — — —_

3. Dr. Hegge moved.

   A. _— — — — to the shelf_

   B. _— — — — had to move — — — —_

4. The reporter called.

   A. _____ His boss. _____

   _____

   B. _____ will call _____ _____

   _____

5. Jay passed.

   A. _____ his class _____

   _____

   B. _____ must _____

   _____

6. The telephone rings.

   A. _____ continiously _____

   _____

   B. _____ will ring _____ _____ _____

   _____

7. You can lift.

   A. _____ The whole pile of books _____

   _____

   B. You must not _____ _____ _____

   _____

8. The girls wear.

   A. _____ _____ skirts. _____

   _____

B. _____ ─ ─ ─must ─ ─ ─ ─ ─ _____

_____

9. The director has signaled.

A. _____ ─ ─ ─ ─ to start the play _____

_____

B. _____ ─ Must signal ─ ─ ─ _____

_____

10. The mail carriers raced.

A. _____ ─ ─ ─ down the street _____

_____

B. ─ ─ ─ Should race ─ ─ ─ ─ _____

_____

Summary: Making the Verb Effective

1. Choose the verb form that shows most accurately the time and tone you intend.
2. Choose adverbs to show the exact conditions of time, place, manner, and degree of action that you intend.
3. Clarify the action of the verb by using an object complement to show its goal or result.

MAKING THE SUBJECT EFFECTIVE

Choosing the Subject

Look at the sentences combined below:

Mrs. Burton planted.
Zinnias were planted.   Mrs. Burton planted zinnias.

This combined version of the sentence makes *Mrs. Burton* the subject or center of attention. But suppose you wanted to focus your reader's attention on the kind of flowers she planted? Then you could choose to make *zinnias* the subject of the sentence.

Zinnias were planted by Mrs. Burton.

Most sentences have more than one idea that you could choose as the subject. For instance, what options do you have for combining these sentences into one sentence?

The lawyer presented.　　　　　　1. The lawyer presented her case.
　　　　　　　　　　　　　　　　　　　　　or
Her case was presented.　　　　　　2. Her case was presented by the lawyer.

By making *lawyer* the subject, the first version puts the emphasis on *who* did the presenting. By making *case* the subject, the second version gives more importance to *what* got presented. Which version you chose to write would depend on which idea was more important in a particular writing situation. You can exercise control over a sentence by deciding which idea you want your reader to focus on and making that idea the subject.

Exercise F

Practice controlling the focus of a sentence by combining each of the following pairs of sentences in two different ways, each version emphasizing a different idea.

EXAMPLE:

Margie finished.
The report was finished.
(focus on Margie)　　　A. *Margie finished the report.*
(focus on the report)　　B. *The report was finished by Margie.*

1. Every sentence presents.
   A subject is presented.

(focus on sentence)　　A. <u>Every sutence presnts a subject</u>

(focus on subject)　　B. <u>A subject is preseted by ── ──</u>

2. We ordered.
   Three cheeseburgers were ordered.

(focus on we)   A.   We ordered — — — —

(focus on cheeseburgers)   B.   3 cheese burgers — — — by us

3.   Jacob has studied.
     The Talmud has been studied.

(focus on Jacob)   A.   Jacob studied — — — —

(focus on Talmud)   B.   The Talmud — — — by Jacob

4.   Visitors pass.
     The old Cotton Exchange is passed.

(focus on visitors)   A.   Visitors — — — —

(focus on Cotton Exchange)   B.   The old Cotton — — — by Visitors.

5.   Wallie pitched.
     A no-hitter was pitched.

(focus on Wallie)   A.   Wallie pitched — — —

(focus on no-hitter)   B.   — — — — by Wallie

6.   Spanish moss had draped.
     The southern oaks had been draped.

(focus on moss)   A.   Spanish moss had draped the S. oaks.

(focus on oaks)   B.   The S. oakes — — — — by Spanish

7.   General Sherman spared.
     The city was spared.

(focus on Sherman)   A.   Gn. — — the city

(focus on the city)   B.   The city — — by Gn.

8.   The group played.
     Scott Joplin's music was played.

(focus on group)   A.   The group — — —

(focus on music)   B.   — — — by the group

9. Someone should call.
   The police should be called.

(focus on someone)   A. _Someone should_ — — ———

(focus on the police) B. = —— —— _by someone_ ——

10. The statistics show.
    A decline is shown.

(focus on statistics)   A. _Statistics_ — — ———

(focus on decline)   B. —— —— — _by statistics_ ——

When your sentences emphasize the *doer* of an action, like

Mrs. Burton planted zinnias.

you are writing ACTIVE sentences. Most sentences are active because most of the time you and your readers are most interested in the *doer*.
When your sentences emphasize the *receiver* of an action, like

Zinnias were planted by Mrs. Burton.

you are writing PASSIVE sentences.
Passive sentences use a special verb form. Do you see the difference between *planted* and *were planted?* On pages 355–57 of this book there is a discussion of the use of passive verbs. You may refer to that in deciding whether or not to write a passive sentence.

Describing the Subject I

Having chosen which idea you want to focus on as the subject of the sentence, you can then add descriptive detail which will help your reader understand more precisely the idea presented in the subject.
A sentence like

The tenor was lazy.

emphasizes one quality of the singer, his laziness.
A sentence like

That book is green.

emphasizes one quality of the book, its color.

Notice how the verb in these descriptive sentences relates the subject to one particular quality. *Tenor* is linked to *lazy*. *Book* is linked to *green*. The word being described is the subject of the sentence; the quality used to describe it is the complement.

These descriptive sentences use a special group of verbs, the LINKING VERBS:

> am
> is
> are
> was
> were
> has been
> have been
> had been
> will have been

} Linking Verbs

(In the last section, you may have noticed that the words above functioned as *part* of the verb in passive sentences. But when these words function as linking verbs they stand alone as the main verb.) The linking verbs work almost like an equals sign (=) between the subject and the complement, showing how one idea identifies the other.

I am busy.

Amelia was angry.

His coats were plaid.

A complement used with a linking verb is called a SUBJECT COMPLEMENT since it refers back to and describes the subject.

Exercise G

Which words in the following sentences complete the action of a verb? Which completing words refer back to and describe the subject? (Not all these sentences have complements.)

EXAMPLES:

S   OC
Prehistoric hunters used *caves.*

S   SC
Dixie was *sick.*

1. June ate the strawberry preserves.
2. The fire destroyed one wing of the museum.

3. Lillian is his aunt.
4. The books were collected in boxes.
5. The skiers set a new record.
6. Computers will be installed next week.
7. The *Delta Queen* still cruises the Mississippi.
8. Tuna fish is my favorite sandwich filling.
9. You should dust your hands with flour.
10. Nefertiti was the queen of Egypt.
11. The flea found a comfortable home on the Great Dane.
12. The woods are beautiful at this time of year.
13. Cowboys were the work force of the Old West.
14 Pete donated twenty dollars.
15. This *moo goo gai pan* is wonderful.
16. Vesuvius covered Pompeii with ashes.
17. Conrad caught the early train to Philadelphia.
18. The Festival of Booths is my favorite Jewish holiday.
19. Venice was once the dominant sea power in the West.
20. The telephone rang for six minutes.

Exercise H

Emphasize one quality of each subject below by adding a linking verb and a subject complement.

EXAMPLE:

The flowers

The flowers were fragrant.

1. Spiders

   are dangerous.

2. Mr. Smalley

   is very curious

3. My car

   isn't new.

4. The night

   was cold

5. The girls

_____were tall_____

6. Several copies

_____are ready._____

7. The box

_____is not mine_____

8. Your garden

_____is beautiful_____

9. His poster

_____was hung on the wall_____

10. Conchita

_____is a Mexican name_____

Linking verbs are presented in more detail on pages 400–401. Refer to that section of the book if you need more information or practice with this sentence pattern.

Describing the Subject II

The linking verb sentence is a useful tool if the main point of your sentence is to describe some quality of the subject. Most of the time, though, you are trying to show the subject involved in some action. Then, the qualities of the subject are important, but they are not the main point of the sentence.

For instance, suppose you had this base sentence:

> The tenor sang his part badly.

You might want to influence the reader's attitude toward the tenor by explaining something about him. Perhaps the tenor was nervous, in which case the reader might sympathize. Or perhaps he was lazy, in which case the reader might criticize.

You could add a linking verb sentence to describe the tenor.

> The tenor sang his part badly.
> The tenor was nervous.

Or you could combine the two sentences to produce

> The *nervous* tenor sang his part badly.

The first option puts more emphasis on the nervousness of the tenor, but it also delays establishing the connection between his being nervous and his singing badly.

Suppose you want to add some information about the kind of part the tenor had to sing.

> The tenor sang the part badly.　　The *nervous* tenor
> The tenor was nervous.　　　　　　sang the *difficult*
> The part was difficult.　　　　　　part badly.

Here, the combined version is much more efficient at conveying the necessary information.

When you use words or phrases to give more precise information about some person or thing in a sentence, you are using ADJECTIVES. *Nervous* and *difficult* in the sentence above are both adjectives.

Adjectives usually answer the questions *which one?* or *what kind?*

For example:

> He was wearing a *red* shirt.   (what kind of shirt?)
> The girl *with the blue eyes* smiled.   (which girl?)

Notice that the normal position for a single-word adjective is right in front of the word it describes. If the adjective is a group of words, a phrase, it comes right after the word it describes.

> The *youngest* tenor *in the company* sang the part of *the hero's friend.*
>
> The girl *near the door* flirted with the *young* tenor.

Exercise I

In the following sentences, show some specific identifying detail about the subject or another noun by adding an adjective.

1. Boxes stood by the door.   (what kind of boxes?)

   Small

2. I read a book.   (what kind of book?)

   Science fiction

3. Several customers have complained about the clerk.   (which clerk?)

   in the office

4. Hats are coming back in style this year.   (what kind of hats?)

   Black

5. With a shout, Millie crossed the line.   (what kind of shout?)

   Sharp

6. The room was filled with the scent.   (which room?   what kind of scent?)

   My room   _of her perfume_

7. The steps creaked under my feet.   (what kind of steps?)

   wooden

8. The nights frightened me.   (what kind of nights?)

   Windy

9. We should never have voted for such a governor.   (what kind of governor?)

lazy

_____

10. The effort will fail.   (which effort?)

to obtain results
_____

Exercise J

Combine each of the following sets of sentences so that description and action are shown in one sentence.

EXAMPLE:

The waves rolled toward the beach.
They were lazy.
The beach was deserted.

The lazy waves rolled toward the deserted beach.

1. The gardener leaned on the rake.
   The gardener was tired.
   His rake was sturdy.

   The tired gardener leaned on the sturdy rake

   _____

   _____

2. My brother cleaned the kitchen.
   He cleaned it after dinner.
   The dinner was elaborate.
   The kitchen was littered.

   My brother cleaned the littered kitchen after the

   elaborate dinner

   _____

3. The bottles hung in the corner.
   There were three bottles.

The bottles were straw-wrapped.
The corner was in the wine cellar.

The three straw-wrapped bottles hung in the corner of the wine cellar.

4. We gathered pine cones in baskets.
The cones were from the trees.
The trees were in our aunt's yard.
The baskets were old-fashioned.

We gathered pine cones from trees in our aunt's yard and gathered them in old-fashioned baskets

5. The waiter took our order.
The waiter was smiling.
We ordered four lemonades.

The smiling waiter took our order of 4 lemonades.

6. The pilot flew the plane.
The plane was an experimental one.
The plane was solar-powered.*
The pilot was excited.

The excited pilot flew the experimental, solar-powered plane.

* Use a comma between two adjectives describing the same noun.

7. The baby frowned.
   The baby was adorable.
   Her frown was disarming.*

   The adorable baby frowned disarmingly

8. The breeze flipped the pages.
   The breeze was from the ocean.
   The pages were in a book.
   The book was on the table.

   The breeze from the ocean flipped the pages
   of the book ⌃which was on the table

9. A doctor can break news.
   The doctor is experienced.
   The news is tragic.
   The doctor uses a voice.
   The voice is reassuring.

   An experienced doctor can break tragic
   news with a reassuring voice

10. The students clustered around the desk.
    The students were anxious.
    The desk belonged to the teacher.
    The teacher was unsmiling.

    Anxious students clustered around the desk of
    the unsmiling teacher

---

*Turn this into an adverb telling how the baby frowned. Remember the *-ly* signal for adverbs.

11.   A salesgirl chipped my vase on the counter.
      The girl was careless.
      The vase was expensive.
      The counter was not protected.

      A careless salesgirl chipped my expensive vase on the counter which was not protected.

12.   The painting hung crookedly.
      The painting was by da Vinci.
      The painting had been forgotten.
      It hung on the wall.
      The wall was crumbling.
      The wall was in an apartment.
      The apartment was in Florence.

      The forgotten painting of da Vinci hung crookedly on the crumbling wall in an apartment in Florence.

13.   The team practiced the play.
      The team was for frisbee.
      The team belonged to the University of Iowa.
      The play was complicated.
      This practice was before the game.

      Before the game, the frisbee team of U. of Iowa practiced the complicated play.

14.   The driver eased the car.
      The driver worked for a general.

The car went on to the freeway.
The freeway was crowded.

The driver working for a Careal eased the
car to the crowded freeway.

___

15. The supervisor watched the crew.
The supervisor was stern.
The supervisor was suspicious.
The crew was doing construction work.
The crew was from the prison.

The stern and suspicious supervisor watched the
crew from the prison doing construction work

___

The forms and uses of adjectives are presented in more detail on pages 344–47. If you want to polish your skill with adjectives, refer to that section of the book.

Describing the Subject III

Another way of giving your reader more precise information about the subject is to follow it with a noun (the name of a person, place, or thing) which explains it.

For example, these two sentences:

> Her husband is a stamp collector.
> He has nearly 3,000 first-day covers.

could be combined like this, using one noun to explain the other:

> Her husband, a stamp collector, has nearly 3,000 first-day covers.
>
> *or*
>
> A stamp collector, her husband has nearly 3,000 first-day covers.

The noun *a stamp collector* is used to explain something about the noun *husband.* Notice that this explaining noun is set off by commas.

Here are a few more examples of nouns used to explain or define a subject:

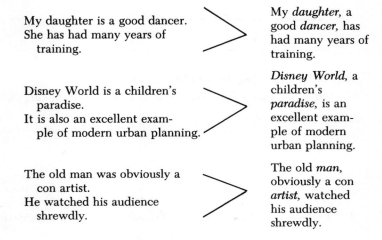

My daughter is a good dancer.
She has had many years of
    training.

My *daughter,* a
good *dancer,* has
had many years of
training.

Disney World is a children's
    paradise.
It is also an excellent exam-
    ple of modern urban planning.

Disney World, a
children's
paradise, is an
excellent exam-
ple of modern
urban planning.

The old man was obviously a
    con artist.
He watched his audience
    shrewdly.

The old *man,*
obviously a con
artist, watched
his audience
shrewdly.

Exercise K

Combine each pair of sentences below by explaining or describing the subject with another noun. Remember to put commas around the explaining noun.

1.   This apple is a winesap.
    It is my grandfather's favorite.

    This apple, a winesap, is my grandfather's
    favorite.

2.   That outlandishly costumed man is a famous rock star,
    He is mobbed by screaming young fans.

3. The shoe clerk was not a patient man.
   He spoke sarcastically to his irritating customer.

   _____

   _____

   _____

4. The woman was apparently the child's mother.
   She looked with exasperation at the small form fleeing down the sidewalk.

   _____

   _____

   _____

5. The mechanic was a grease-stained woman in her twenties.
   She raised the hood of the smoking car.

   _____

   _____

   _____

6. Thomas More was a scholar as well as a statesman.
   He served as Chancellor of England under Henry VIII.

   _____

   _____

   _____

7. Billie Jean King is the queen of tennis.
   In 1979 she held more Wimbleton titles than any other woman.

   _____

   _____

   _____

8. Richard Conway, is the director of the program,
    Next year he will become a vice-president.

_____

_____

_____

Exercise L

Make the sentences below more precise by adding an adjective or an explaining noun to one or more of the nouns. Give two versions. Remember to punctuate when necessary.

EXAMPLE:

The dog ran into the alley.

A. The *lame* dog ran into the alley *behind the garage.*

B. The dog, *John's constant companion,* ran into the *deserted* alley.

1. Margaret kissed her father's cheek.

    A. _____ after taking her gift

    _____

    B. On her birthday _____

    _____

2. The boys carried the trashbags to the street.

    A. _____ to empty them

    _____

    B. As they were full _____

    _____

3. Juanita made copies of the memo.

    A. _____ which is very useful

    To remember important things _____

B.   (Arkado)

_____

4.   The monster opened its mouth.

A.   _____ to eat his prey _____

B.   The angry monster _____

_____

5.   The prisoners filed by the warden.

A.   _____

_____

B.   _____

_____

6.   The governor held her press conference.

A.   _____ in the city hall _____

_____

B.   For the first time, a gov. - - - _____

_____

7.   The pillows sat on the sofa.

A.   _____ which was covered with blood ____

_____

B.   The yellow — _____

_____

8. His hand could not reach the shelf.

    A. _____ as he was only 4' tall __

    _____

    B. _____

    _____

9. He put his knitting on the table.

    A. _____ and forgot it there __

    _____

    B. After putting — _____

    _____

10. Charlene is the winner.

    A. _____ of this race _____

    _____

    B. 17 years' old — _____

    _____

***Summary:* Making the Subject Effective**

1. Choose as the subject the idea you want your reader to focus on.
2. Use a linking verb sentence to emphasize some quality of the subject.
3. Choose adjectives to describe the subject precisely.
4. Choose explaining nouns to clarify the subject.

ARRANGING THE SENTENCE

Basic Sentence Patterns

As you have seen in this chapter, most sentences are built around some basic arrangement of the subject–verb unit.

Here are the most common patterns:

1. Someone
   Something } ———> acted.

          S – V
   The truck stopped.

2. Someone
   Something } ———> acted on something.

          S – V – OC
   The truck hit the wall.

3. Someone
   Something } ———> was acted on

          S –V   (passive)
   The wall was hit.

4. Someone
   Something } is { someone
                      some quality

          S –   LV –   SC
   That driver   is   a daredevil.
   His truck   was   expensive.

Exercise M

Review the basic sentence patterns by composing three sentences for each one.

1. S – V.

   A. _James Pulled_____

   B. _____

   C. _____

2.   S – V – OC

A.   _The man was looking at how_

B.   _____

C.   _____

3.   S – V (passive).

A.   _She was noticed by the landlord_

B.   _____

C.   _____

4.   S – LV – SC.

A.   _Jane's voice was beautiful_

B.   _____

C.   _____

Varying the Basic Patterns

While these basic patterns are efficient in conveying information, they can get boring because the basic patterns are very similar. You can increase your flexibility in using sentences by mastering a few variations of the basic patterns. These variations can help you call attention to some particularly important aspect of the sentence.

Variation I: The Question   A simple statement can be turned into a question in order to suggest uncertainty rather than certainty.

> The truck stopped.
> *Has* the truck *stopped?*
> The truck hit the wall.
> *Did* the truck hit the wall?
> The wall was hit.
> *Was* the wall hit?
> His truck was expensive.
> *Was* his truck expensive?

Notice that the question is formed by using a helping verb in front of the subject.

Variation II: Reversing Word Order   You can call special attention to some part of a sentence by putting it out of its normal position. For instance,

> The wind was wild.

could become

> Wild was the wind.

In this second version, the descriptive word, *wild*, gets extra emphasis because it isn't where the reader would expect to find it.

Another example,

> An ugly beast was watching from the window.

could become

> Watching from the window was an ugly beast.

In this variation, the subject, *beast*, gets special emphasis. Again, the additional impact comes from the word's being out of its normal position.

Variation III: Introducing or Interrupting the Base Sentence   You can call special attention to an adjective or adverb by using it to introduce or interrupt the pattern of the base sentence.

For instance,

> The lawyer presented her case skillfully.

can become

> Skillfully, the lawyer presented her case.

The second version calls more attention to *how* the lawyer presented her case, *skillfully*, by opening the sentence with the adverb.

> The untrained tenor sang badly.

can become

> The tenor, untrained, sang badly.

In the second version, the reader is forced to pause over the adjective *untrained*, and so it gets more emphasis.

Notice that any construction which introduces or interrupts the base sentence is set off with commas.

The important thing to remember in using any variation of the basic sentence pattern is:

NEVER WRITE A SENTENCE THAT WILL CONFUSE YOUR READER.

Exercise N

Write one variation for each basic sentence below.

EXAMPLE:

Oil company profits have risen by 200 percent.
Have oil company profits risen by 200 percent?

1. Guttenberg's printing press was invented in the fifteenth century.

    In the 15th C., — —

2. That morning was beautiful.

    Beautiful was that morning.

3. His delicate photography captured the peace of the scene.

    The peace of scene was capt. by — —

4. Arnold's Bakery is famous for its pastry.

    Is Arnold — — — — ?

5. Thirty thousand acres of wilderness have been preserved by the efforts of the Sierra Club.

    Have — — — — — — ?

6. A fast strawberry picker can earn $30 in one day.

    Can a — — — — — ?

7. Some very ancient myths form the basis of many modern television shows.

    Many modern T.V. shows. are based — —

8. Community college students want career education by and large.

    Do — — — — ?

9. Good laws make good government.

    Good govt are made by — — —

10. The fire raced through the house hungrily.

    Hungrily, the fire — — —

> ## REVIEW
>
> *Basic Sentence Patterns*
>
> S-V   Evalina frowned.
> S-V-OC   The manager was observing her.
> S-V (passive)   She was observed by the manager.
> S-LV-SC   Evalina's anger was deep.
>
> *Variations*
>
> Question   Was Evalina's anger deep?
> Reversal   Observing her was the manager.
> Introduction/   Deeply angry, Evalina frowned.
> Interruption   Evalina, deeply angry, frowned.

Problems in Arrangement

Placement of Modifiers   When you use modifiers, that is, adjectives, adverbs, or explaining nouns, you have to be careful to place them so that it is absolutely clear what they are describing or explaining. Misplaced modifiers can confuse your reader.

For instance, if you wrote this note to a friend, your friend might not be able to figure out your meaning:

The teacher said on Thursday there would be a test.

Did the teacher make the announcement on Thursday, or is the test going to be on Thursday? It could make a big difference in your friend's plans for the weekend.

If you meant that the teacher made the announcement on Thursday, you should have said:

On Thursday, the teacher said there would be a test.

If you meant that the test would be on Thursday, you should have said:

The teacher said there would be a test on Thursday.

In general, a modifier should be as close as possible to the word it describes.

Exercise O

Rewrite each of the following sentences to include the modifier given in parentheses. Be sure that the modifier is placed where it will be clearly understood. Be prepared to explain which word the modifier describes.

EXAMPLE:

The man petted the monkey.
(in the red sweater)

The man *in the red sweater* petted the monkey.

The man petted the monkey *in the red sweater*.

1. Frank baked an apple pie.
    (seven years old)

    7 years old Frank — — —

2. Barb promised she would study with me.
    (that afternoon)

    that aftn.

3. Mickey saved discarded gum wrappers to trade for a baseball.
    (carefully)

4. The accused blackmailer told a different version of the story to the lawyer.
    (a person of questionable reputation)

5. Mr. Gonzales said that he never smoked.
    (during an interview with the doctor)

6. Professor McDonald assigned a term paper.
   (only)

   _____

7. The tour guide sold pieces of wood as souvenirs.
   (strange and twisted)

   _____

8. The missing ship was found.
   (with new sonar equipment)

   _____

9. The Cloverdale Cardinals won every game this season.
   (almost)

   _____

10. People came to hear his sermons.
    (from several states)

    _____

11. The newscaster announced a cease-fire.
    (on television)

    _____

12. Ms. Henderson asked the clerk to check the order.
    (at once)

    _____

13. My uncle has said he would write a novel.
    (for ten years)

    _____

14. A movie will be shown on how to repair engines.
    (in the Laudner Auditorium)

    _____

15. Several of my friends bought food processors.
    (without safety switches)

    _____

16. A stallion raced across the fields.
    (dark as night)

    _____

17. The queen gave Snow White a poisoned apple.
    (beautiful but evil)

    _____

18. It takes six months for the grant application to be processed.
    (nearly)

    _____

19. General Benjamin rode in the lead car.
    (in full World War I uniform)

    _____

20. I saw hundreds of starving children.
    (without the energy even to cry)

    _____

Adding Too Much   While you don't want all your sentences to be bare skeletons like "The man ran," you also don't want to write sentences that are too overloaded with detail:

> The man in the brown silk shirt with a red, rumpled handkerchief
> in the left breast pocket ran wildly out of the burning bank on the corner
> looking frantically in all directions for someone, friend, or even enemy,
> to help him.

A sentence like the one above has so much added to the basic sentence that a reader is likely to lose the underlying meaning and become confused. In writing sentences, you have to be careful to choose just the right amount of detail, enough to make sure your reader understands your idea clearly, but not so much that he or she gets lost.

Look again at the overloaded sentence above. Could some of the details be left out? If it's important to distinguish this man from some other man in the scene, then you would want the detail about what the man was wearing.

But it's unlikely that there are two men with brown silk shirts, so you probably don't need to give the extra detail about the handkerchief and which pocket it was in. In fact, if you are trying to create an atmosphere of panic, so much detail about the man's clothes may even distract the reader from that central idea.

It might even be effective to break this long sentence into two sentences, both of which emphasize the man's panic:

> The man in the brown silk shirt ran wildly out of the burning bank. He looked frantically for someone, even an enemy, to help him.

(*In all directions* could be eliminated since *frantically* suggests that anyway.)

Exercise P

In each of the following sets of sentences, you are given more detail than will work well in one sentence. Try to come up with two different versions in which you either select only enough detail for one good sentence or divide the details into two sentences that will work well together. Be prepared to explain why you chose certain details.

EXAMPLE:

The girl loaded her grocery cart.
The girl was pudgy.
The girl had blonde hair.
The girl wore green shorts.
The shorts were tight.
She loaded the cart dreamily.
She loaded it with treats.
She loaded it with cakes and pies.
She loaded it with bags of chips and pretzels.
She loaded the cart with cans of diet soda.
The soda was passion-fruit-flavored.
The cart was chrome.
The chrome gleamed.

A.   *The pudgy girl in tight green shorts dreamily loaded her cart with treats. The gleaming chrome was filled with cakes, pies, bags of pretzels and chips, and cans of passion-fruit-flavored diet soda.*

B.   *Dreamily, the pudgy blonde loaded her cart with treats: bags of chips and pretzels, cakes, pies, and cans of passion-fruit-flavored diet soda.*

1.   Mike struggled to start the truck.
     Mike is our neighbor.
     He is 80 years old.
     He is cranky.
     His struggle was unsuccessful.
     He struggled determinedly.
     The struggle lasted for an hour.
     He struggled in his back yard.
     The truck was red.
     It was rusted.
     It was a Ford.
     It was built in 1940.

A.   _____

     _____

     _____

     _____

B.   _____

     _____

     _____

     _____

2.   The counselor blew her whistle.
     She blew it after the game.
     The game was played by the boys.
     She blew it for attention.
     She blew it loudly.
     The counselor was tanned.
     The counselor was athletic-looking.
     The counselor was 5' 11".
     The whistle was plastic.

It was yellow.
It was chipped.
It was the symbol of her power.

A. _____

_____

_____

_____

B. _____

_____

_____

_____

3. The boys turned the pages.
   The boys were twins.
   They were 10 years old.
   They were curious.
   The pages were in a copy of *Playboy*.
   The copy was old.
   The copy was torn.
   The pages were turned slowly.
   The pages were turned with many giggles.
   The giggles were stifled.
   The pages were turned with cautious glances.
   The glances were toward the door.

A. _____

_____

_____

_____

B. _____

_____

_____

_____

4. The kitten chased the ball.
   The kitten was gray.
   The kitten was no bigger than Bob's hand.
   The kitten's name was Emily.
   She chased the ball all over the room.
   The room was sunny.
   She chased the ball ferociously.
   She chased it like a panther.
   She chased it for most of the morning.
   The ball was huge.
   It was black and white.
   It had a slow leak.

A. _____

_____

_____

B. _____

_____

_____

5. The bus pulled into the station.
   It did this with a jerk.
   It was exactly four hours late.
   The bus was dust-covered.

The bus was filled with band members.
The bus was filled with instruments.
The band belonged to Garfield High School.
The station was in Pittsburgh.
The station was dark.
The station was empty.
The band members were tired.
The band members were hungry.

A. _____

_____

_____

_____

B. _____

_____

_____

_____

Exercise Q

Combine each set of sentences below into one sentence which describes the subject and the action precisely. In constructing your sentences, remember the techniques of emphasis that have been presented in this chapter: choice of subject, time or tone of verb, arrangement of sentence parts. Write two versions of each sentence, each one emphasizing a different aspect of the idea being presented. Feel free to change the verb form to suit your emphasis. Be prepared to discuss the difference in emphasis.

1. Canada is our neighbor.
   It is to the north.
   It is a land mass.
   The land mass is vast.
   It is over 3,000 miles wide.

A. _____

_____

B. _____

_____

2. Use will ruin.
   The use is of gas.
   The gas is leaded.
   Valves and plugs will be ruined.
   The use is continued.
   The ruin will be in many cars.
   The cars are modern.
   The ruin will be soon.

A. _____

_____

B. _____

_____

3. A name has been associated.
   The association is with a type.
   The type is of learning.
   The name is Ivan Pavlov.
   The learning is conditioning.
   The conditioning is classical.
   The association is a long one.

A. _____

_____

B. _____

_____

4. China flourished.
   This took place during the T'ang dynasty.
   The T'ang dynasty lasted from A.D. 618 to 907.
   China was a state.

The state was the richest and most powerful.
The state was on the globe.

A. _____

_____

B. _____

_____

5. Man experiences himself.
Man is modern.
The experience is as a part.
The part is of nature.
According to E. F. Schumacher, this statement is not true.

A. _____

_____

B. _____

_____

6. Every order will be processed.
The orders are for this album.
The album contains disco hits.
The processing will be immediate.
The processing will be by our staff.

A. _____

_____

B. _____

_____

7. Accounts are obsolete.
The accounts are for passbook savings.
These accounts are like buggy whips.

The buggy whips are of the modern age.

This is according to Jane Bryant Quinn.

She is an economics writer.

She writes for *Newsweek*.

A. _____

_____

B. _____

_____

8. There are pyramids at El Mirador.

El Mirador means "the lookout."

El Mirador is in Guatemala.

The pyramids are 3,000 feet around their bases.

A. _____

_____

B. _____

_____

9. Growth is linked to developments.

The developments are varied.

The developments are such as ragtime, dress designs, and Ziegfeld's Follies.

The growth is of dance.

The dance is modern.

A. _____

_____

B. _____

_____

10. Alvar Aalto was a master.

His mastery was of the "international style."

The style was of architecture.

He believed.
His belief was in a living environment.
His belief was in a natural environment.
His belief was passionate.

A. _____

_____

B. _____

_____

11. The aroma filled the air.
The aroma was tantalizing.
The aroma was of pizza.
The pizza was cheese-topped.
The filling was quick.
The air was around the kitchen.

A. _____

_____

B. _____

_____

Exercise R

Make each of the following basic sentences more effective by adding COMPLEMENTS, ADVERBS, ADJECTIVES, or EXPLAINING NOUNS. Change the form of the verb if necessary to suit the purpose of your sentence.

1. The story recreates an age.

_____

_____

2. Mark closed.

_____

_____

3. The tree fell.

_____

_____

4. The car seems.

_____

_____

5. The party lasted.

_____

_____

6. Colleges are expensive.

_____

_____

7. The fly landed.

_____

_____

8. Barbara opened the card.

_____

_____

9. The leader strode.

_____

_____

10. The pig escaped.

_____

_____

11. The sun is fading.

_____

_____

12. Sales should increase.

_____

_____

13. The boat moved.

_____

_____

14. The instructor shouted.

_____

_____

15. Their trip began.

_____

_____

WRITING PRACTICE

Write five or six sentences describing a person or a place with which you are very familiar, such as your room or your best friend. Make your reader see that person or place exactly as you see it by using adjectives, adverbs, explaining nouns, and complements to make your sentences effective.

Try to make all the sentences work together to create in your reader's mind one central impression of the subject.

Here are some opening sentences that suggest one main idea for a description.

My room is always messy.

My friend Charlie always looks sharp.

Coordination

3

So far you have concentrated on presenting one idea completely and precisely. However, you can make a sentence do even more than this. You can use the form of a sentence to show the relationship between two or more ideas. One of the basic relationships that you can set up between ideas is COORDINATION.

When you *co*ordinate ideas, you say that one idea is just as important as, or has equal rank with, another idea. (*Co-* means *with, on the same level; co-*captains of a team, for instance, have *equal* importance.) The seven words in the box below can be used to show a coordinate relationship between ideas.

Coordination Signals

Remembering the two words BOY FANS may help you remember what the seven coordinating words are.

But
Or
Yet
For
And
Nor
So

COORDINATING SUBJECTS WITH *AND*

The subject of the sentence, as you remember from Chapter 1, tells a reader who or what is the focus of attention in the sentence. If you want your sentence to focus on two subjects equally, you would coordinate them:

Better supervision will be necessary to improve this office.

Broad reorganization will be necessary to improve this office.

Better supervision *and* broad reorganization will be necessary to improve this office.

In the sentence above, you want to emphasize that both things must be done before the office will improve.

Exercise A

Combine the following sentences to produce a sentence giving two subjects equal weight.

1. Soap operas ~~show a lot about our problem~~s. *and*
   Situation comedies show a lot about our problems.

   _____

   _____

2. ~~Renee took the bus down from Newark.~~
   Renee & Towanda took the bus down from Newark.

   _____

   _____

3. Revving his motor ~~gave Chuck a thrill.~~ *and*
   Making his tires smoke gave Chuck a thrill.

   _____

   _____

4. ~~Katharine Hepburn became one of the great movie stars of American films.~~

K.H & ⟶ Spencer Tracy became ~~one~~ ^{two} of the great^{est} movie stars of American films.

_____

_____

5. Koala bears ^{and} ~~live only in Australi~~a.
   Wombats live only in Australia.

_____

_____

Look at another example:

George doesn't like New York.

Sheila doesn't like New York.

} George *and* Sheila don't like New York.

    This sentence emphasizes that both of the people dislike New York, but notice how the verb changes from *doesn't* to *don't* when you add to the subject. When you coordinate two subjects with *and,* you have to use a plural verb form. Most of the time this is no problem since most plural verbs look just the same as singular verbs. The only exceptions are the verbs which describe action taking place in the present time. When these verbs have a subject that is a *he,* a *she,* or an *it,* they end in -*s.* When their subject is a *they,* these verbs don't end in -*s.* For example:

> George *does.* (He *does.*)
>
> George and Sheila *do.* (They *do.*)
>
> Better supervision *is* necessary. (It *is.*)
>
> Better supervision and broad reorganization *are* necessary. (They *are.*)
>
> Hazel *misses* her father. (She *misses.*)
>
> Hazel and her brother *miss* their father. (They *miss.*)

(There is a more detailed discussion of verb forms on pages 378–80. Refer to that section if you need more explanation or examples.)

Exercise B

Combine the sentences below to produce one sentence with two subjects coordinated by *and*. Be sure to use the appropriate verb form.

1. An elm ~~would look nice in the back yard~~. *and*

    A birch would look nice in the back yard.

    _____

    _____

2. Fishing ~~is John's favorite sport~~. *and*

    Swimming ~~is~~ John's favorite sport*s*. *are*

    _____

    _____

3. Cats ~~are people's best friends~~. *and*

    Dogs are people's best friends.

    _____

    _____

4. Napoleon ~~could not capture Russia~~. *and*

    All his troops could not capture Russia.

    _____

    _____

5. *Both* Newton ~~discovered the calculus~~. *and*

    Leibnitz discovered the calculus. (Both)

    _____

    _____

6. *Both* France ~~will lead Europe in the twenty-first century~~. *and*

    Germany will lead Europe in the twenty-first century.

    _____

    _____

7. Mark ~~runs~~ five miles a day. _[handwritten: Both ... and]_
   Les runs five miles a day.

   _____

   _____

8. The winner ~~looks exhausted~~. _[handwritten: Both ... and]_
   The loser looks exhausted.

   _____

   _____

9. The china ~~sparkles.~~ _[handwritten: Both ... and]_
   The silverware sparkles.

   _____

   _____

10. The new refrigerator ~~has been installed~~. _[handwritten: Both ... and]_
    The new stove has been installed. _[handwritten: had (or have?)]_

    _____

    _____

COORDINATING SUBJECTS WITH *OR*

Another way of coordinating subjects is to use *or*. When you use *or* (or *nor*), you are asking your reader to consider each subject separately. *Or* is used to suggest a choice between two alternatives, each of which deserves the same attention from your reader. For example:

Better supervision is necessary.

Broad reorganization is necessary.

} Better supervision *or* broad reorganization is necessary.

In this sentence, only one of the two requirements must be met, not both. Notice how this differs from a sentence which joins the subjects by *and*. In this sentence the verb stays singular because each subject is considered separately.

Exercise C

Combine the following sentences to produce one sentence whose subjects are coordinated by *or*.

1. A kitten ~~or~~ ~~makes a great gift for a child.~~
   A puppy makes a great gift for a child.

   _____

   _____

2. Barney ~~or~~ ~~will be able to prepare the report.~~
   Lynn will be able to prepare the report.

   _____

   _____

3. Overeating ~~or~~ ~~causes weight gain.~~
   Lack of exercise causes weight gain.

   _____

   _____

4. The Orioles ~~or~~ ~~will be leading the league in September.~~
   The Yankees will be leading the league in September.

   _____

   _____

5. Jogging ~~or~~ ~~will help keep you in shape.~~
   Swimming will help keep you in shape.

   _____

   _____

| The first grade class is not allowed to go. The second grade classes are not allowed to go. | Neither the first grade class *nor* the second grade classes are allowed to go. Neither the second grade classes *nor* the first grade class is allowed to go. |

In these examples, although there are two subjects, each subject is considered separately. Notice how this separation affects the verb form. In the sample on page 65, you had two singular subjects and you used a singular verb—*is.* In the sample above, however, one subject is singular and one subject is plural. How do you decide whether the verb should be singular or plural? You solve this problem by making the verb agree with the subject closer to it.

Thus, if you say "neither the first grade class nor the second grade classes," you use the plural verb *are* because *classes* is plural. If you say "neither the second grade classes nor the first grade class," you use the singular verb *is* because class is singular. Putting the plural subject closer to the verb usually makes a sentence sound more natural.

Exercise D

Combine each of the following sentences two different ways. The first time use *and* to coordinate the subjects. The second time use *or* or *nor.* (When using *or,* you may use *either* with it. When using *nor,* you may use *neither* with it.) Be sure to select the appropriate verb form for each combination. Be prepared to discuss the difference in meaning.

EXAMPLE:

Uncle Bob is Liz's favorite relative.

Aunt Helen is Liz's favorite relative.

A.   *Uncle Bob and Aunt Helen are Liz's favorite relatives.*

B.   *Neither Uncle Bob nor Aunt Helen is Liz's favorite relative.*

Sample Analysis: The statements are complete opposites. The use of *nor* in the second makes the statement forceful.

1.   New York ~~is~~ *and* ~~America's most exciting city.~~

     Los Angeles ~~is~~ *are* America's most exciting ~~city.~~ *cities*

A.   _____

     _____

B.   Neither N.Y. nor L.A. *is* __ __ __ __ __ __

     _____

2.   The canary ~~wants to be fed all the time.~~ *and*

     The parrots want to be fed all the time.

A. _____

_____

B. _Neither the canary, nor the parrot want_ - - ──

_____

3. English is ~~often a child's worst subject in elementary~~ school. _and_

Arithmetic ~~is~~ often a child's worst subjects in elementary school. _are_

A. _____

_____

B. _Neither English nor Arithmetic are a child's_ ─ ── -   _is_

_____

4. Batman ~~will rescue the trapped~~ miners. _and_

Superman will rescue the trapped miners.

A. _____

_____

B. _Neither Batman nor Superman will_ . - ──

_____

5. A light-rail system ~~solves that transportation~~ problem. _and_

Express buses solve that transportation problem.

A. _____

_____

B. _Neither a light-rail system nor_ ─ ── ── ──

_____

6. Forty cases of frozen food ~~are delivered every~~ week. _and_

A truckload of canned goods ~~is~~ delivered every week. _are_

A. _____

_____

B. *Neither 10 cases of frozen food nor — — —*

_____

            and
7. The workers ~~have not backed down on the contract.~~
   Management h~~a~~s not backed down on the contract.
        have

A. _____

_____

B. *Neither workers nor management have backed — —*

_____

           and
8. North Dakota ~~suffers extremely cold~~ winters.
   Montana suffers extremely cold winters.

A. _____

_____

B. *Neither N.D. nor Montana suffers*

_____

           and
9. Sometimes a teacher ~~gives a wrong answer.~~
   Sometimes a student gives a wrong answer.

A. _____

_____

B. *Either a teacher or a student — —*

_____

       and
10. Adam ~~dislikes soap operas.~~
    His best friend dislikes soap operas.

A. _____

_____

B. *Neither Adam nor his best friend.* ⟶ _____

_____

COORDINATING VERBS

Coordination also allows you to involve the subject of the sentence in several actions, each of which gets equal emphasis. You can do this by joining two verbs in a sentence with a coordinating word. For instance:

A. I will cook the dinner.
    I will wash the dishes.

    I will either cook the dinner or wash the dishes.

B. Every summer, Hope goes to Barbados.
    Every summer, Hope gains ten pounds.

    Every summer, Hope goes to Barbados and gains ten pounds.

In case there are more than two verbs to be coordinated, commas should be used to separate each verb from the others.

The little ones laughed, shouted, and jumped for joy.
Parker struck a match, lit the two fuses, and ran for cover.

Another consideration when there is a series of actions to be coordinated is the order in which they should be presented in the sentence. Be sure to choose the most logical sequence for the events. Move in a time order from first to last, or from least important action to most important action. The model in the exercise below shows the actions arranged in a logical time sequence.

Exercise E

Combine the following sentences to show the same subject performing several actions.

EXAMPLE:

Everyone on the tour gets up early.
Everyone on the tour boats down the Nile.

Everyone on the tour picnics in the shadow of the Pyramids.
 (*and*)

*Everyone on the tour gets up early, boats down the Nile, and
 picnics in the shadow of the Pyramids.*

1. Every morning, someone honks a horn,
    ~~Every morning, someone~~ slams a door. or
    ~~Every morning, someone~~ yells. (*or*)

    _____

    _____

2. Worker bees attend the queen,
    ~~Worker bees~~ gather honey. and
    ~~Worker bees~~ feed the newborn. (*and*)

    _____

    _____

3. Jefferson wrote the Declaration of Independence,
    ~~Jefferson~~ founded the University of Virginia. and
    ~~Jefferson~~ served as President. (*and*)

    _____

    _____

4. The pilot took off clumsily. and
    ~~The pilot~~ banked too steeply. (*and*)

    _____

Neither ———— took

5. The hurricane ~~did not take~~ any lives. nor
    ~~The hurricane did not~~ damage any property. (*nor*)

    _____

    _____

6. The children can come with me. or
   ~~The children can~~ go with their grandmother. (*or*)

   _____

   _____

7. Carmine bought a new car,
   ~~Carmine~~ had a sun-roof put in. and
   ~~Carmine~~ lowered the front end. (*and*)

   _____

   _____

8. Russ lunged across the rocks,
   ~~Russ~~ saw Mary's foot slip. but
   ~~Russ~~ did not catch her. (*but*)

   _____

   _____

9. Shirley drank a glass of lemonade,
   ~~Shirley~~ guzzled down a gallon of water. and
   ~~Shirley~~ finished off a pitcher of beer. (*and*)

   _____

   _____

10. Roger would beg from strangers. or
    ~~He would~~ borrow from friends. (*or*) but
    ~~He~~ would not steal from anyone. (*but*)

    _____

    _____

COORDINATING COMPLEMENTS

Sometimes an action may have several effects, or an idea may be completed in several ways. Coordination lets you give equal emphasis to each of the ways in which an action or idea may be completed. Remember to arrange the complements in some sensible order and use the punctuation needed to help the reader see the series. For example:

> The Angels won the game, the series, and the pennant. (order of importance)
>
> This tour visits Universal Studios, Disneyland, and Sea World. (time order)

Exercise F

Combine the following sets of sentences so that you produce one sentence showing several aspects of the subject or completions of the action.

EXAMPLE:

Franklin D. Roosevelt was Assistant Secretary of the Navy.
Franklin D. Roosevelt was President of the United States.
Franklin D. Roosevelt was Governor of New York.

Franklin D. Roosevelt was Governor of New York, Assistant Secretary of the Navy, and President of the United States.

1. Mike has been a roofer,
   Mike has been a carpenter. *and*
   Mike has been a cab driver. (*and*)

   _____

   _____

2. Paulo filed three folders of correspondence. *and*
   Paulo filed the minutes of the board meeting. (*and*)

   _____

   _____

3. The Great Plains are flat,
   The Great Plains are arid. *and*

The ~~Great Plains are~~ empty under a big sky. (*and*)

_____

_____

4. I enjoy loafing,
   ~~I enjoy~~ lying back. and
   ~~I enjoy~~ taking things easy. (*and*)

_____

_____

5. In English, Charlie wrote three essays.
   ~~In English, Charlie wrote~~ two exams. and
   ~~In English, Charlie wrote~~ a term paper. (*and*)

_____

_____

6. The coach did not want offensive players. but rather
   ~~The coach wanted~~ defensive players. (*but*)

_____

_____

7. Debbie can run the meetings. or
   ~~Debbie can run~~ the fund raiser. (*or*)

_____

_____

8. The plant (does not have) aphids. nor   neither
   ~~The plant does not have~~ spider mites. (*nor*)

_____

_____

9. Admiral Ward was firm. but
    ~~She was~~ pleasant, ~~(but)~~
    ~~She was~~ strict. but
    ~~She was~~ reasonable. ~~(but)~~

    _____

    _____

10. Should we pay the rent?
    ~~Should we pay~~ the gas and electric? or
    Should we pay the oil bill? (*or*)

    _____

    _____

COORDINATING MODIFIERS

Sometimes, in order to communicate your idea clearly to the reader, you need more than one modifier. These modifiers can be arranged several ways.

Adjectives: Before Noun

You remember from Chapter 2 that most adjectives are placed right before the word they describe, as in:

Our *new* sales manager clinched a *big* deal today.

Adjectives: After Noun

Sometimes it is more effective, especially with coordinated modifiers, to put them *after* the word being described, as in:

The redwoods, *tall and majestic*, reach toward the sky.

This kind of placement puts even more emphasis on the coordinated adjectives. (Remember, if you use this placement, you should set off the modifiers with commas.)

Adverbs

Adverbs, or words which describe the action of the verb, can be placed in any of several positions in the sentence.

For instance, these two sentences:

> The nurse assessed the patient's progress sympathetically.
>
> The nurse assessed the patient's progress professionally.

could become:

> *Professionally but sympathetically,* the nurse assessed the patient's progress.
>
> *or*
>
> The nurse *professionally but sympathetically* assessed the patient's progress.
>
> *or*
>
> The nurse assessed the patient's progress *professionally but sympathetically.*

The placement depends on the amount of emphasis you want to give to the coordinated adverbs and on your sense of the rhythm of the sentence.

Sometimes no coordinating word is used between two modifiers, producing sentences like these:

> *Professionally, sympathetically,* the nurse assessed the patient's progress.
>
> *or*
>
> The *fiery, listing* ship was finally abandoned.

Notice that in these examples a comma takes the place of a coordinating word.

Modifiers should always be chosen very carefully to point out to your reader something especially vivid or unusual; when you decide to coordinate your modifiers, you should choose with even greater care.

Exercise G

Combine each of the following sets of sentences to produce one sentence that presents an idea more clearly by using several modifiers. Don't just string together vague or colorless words. As in the exercises above, remember to punctuate with commas in a series of more than two items.

EXAMPLE:

Joey chinned himself with great concentration.

Joey chinned himself slowly.

Joey chinned himself efficiently.

Joey chinned himself slowly, efficiently, and with great concentration.

or

With great concentration, Joey chinned himself slowly and efficiently.

1. The soldiers were eager.

    The soldiers were reluctant. (*or*)

    All the soldiers were marched into battle. were eager or reluctant

    _____ e or r _____

    _____

2. ~~Her face was~~ wrinkled. but

    ~~Her face was~~ cheerful. (*but*)

    The old woman's face reflected a lifetime of hard work.

    wrinkle but cheerfull

    _____

3. Neither

    The porridge ~~was not~~ too hot. nor

    ~~The porridge was not~~ too cold. (*neither . . . nor*)

    The porridge tasted just right to Goldilocks.

    _____

    _____

4. The police attempted to break up the demonstration.

    The attempt was quick.*

    The attempt was without success.

    Quickly , but unseceesfully,

    _____

    _____

* Turn this into an adverb.

restored & gleaming

5. Sheila's Trans-Am stood in the driveway.
    The Trans-Am was gleaming.
    The Trans-Am was restored. *(and)*

    _____

    _____

    and high

6. Jane went in fast for the dunk shot.
    ~~Jane went in high for the dunk shot.~~ *(and)*   (*Jane's eyes were red*)

    _____

    _____

7. A watch was expensive.
    A watch was symbolic. *(and)*

    A symbolic & expensive ~~A~~ watch was once a gift reserved for very special occasions.

    _____

    _____

    Suddenly neither

8. ~~Suddenly the bear was not~~ cute. *nor*
    ~~Suddenly the bear was not~~ comic, *(neither . . . nor)*
    The bear snarled at us.

    _____

    _____

Coolly & deliberately,

9. The girl stole another piece of candy from the counter.
    ~~The stealing was cool.~~ °
    ~~The stealing was deliberate.~~ ° *(and)*

    _____

    _____

° Use adverb form.

10. The marriage service should be conducted joyously. *but reverently*

~~The marriage service should be conducted reverently. (*but*)~~

_____

_____

Exercise H

Expand and improve the following sentences by coordinating one of the parts: subject, verb, complement, or modifier. Give two different expansions for each sentence. Feel free to move any word to a different position in the sentence. Be prepared to explain the differences between the sentences you have made.

EXAMPLE:

The children waited impatiently for the show to begin.

A. *The children and their parents waited impatiently for the show to begin.*

B. *The children fidgeted and waited impatiently for the show to begin.*

1. The queen passed sedately through the crowd.

A. _____

_____

B. _____

_____

2. Versatile herbs are found in every part of the world.

A. _____

_____

B. _____

_____

3.   Louis Joliet bravely explored the uncharted Mississippi River.

A.   _____

_____

B.   _____

_____

4.   Ice cream is America's favorite food.

A.   _____

_____

B.   _____

_____

5.   The miserable baby wailed steadily.

A.   _____

_____

B.   _____

_____

6.   A used car should be inspected thoroughly.

A.   _____

_____

B.   _____

_____

7.   The Indian women made exquisite jewelry.

A.   _____

_____

B. _____

_____

8. The narrow road wound its way through the jungle.

A. _____

_____

B. _____

_____

9. The menu this week will feature eggs.

A. _____

_____

B. _____

_____

10. The grant proposals will be evaluated on the basis of their practicality.

A. _____

_____

B. _____

_____

COORDINATING SENTENCES

Comma, Coordination Signal

In Chapter 1 you saw that most sentences begin with a capital letter and end with a period so that a reader will be able to tell where one idea ends and the next one begins. Sometimes, though, two sentences are so closely related that you want your reader to consider them together, as part of the same idea. In that case, you can choose to coordinate those two sentences by replacing the period and the capital letter with a coordination signal. For example:

> Harry wanted a pizza.
>
> Everyone else wanted Mexican food.

To show the link between these two sentences more clearly, you might write them like this:

> Harry wanted a pizza, but everyone else wanted Mexican food.

Here you have used one of the coordination signals that you are already familiar with to join two sentences. Writing the sentence this way gives equal emphasis to each idea. Notice that a comma must be used with the coordination signal between two sentences.

Here are some other possibilities for coordinating those two ideas:

> Harry wanted a pizza, and everyone else wanted Mexican food.
>
> Harry wanted a pizza, so everyone else wanted Mexican food.
>
> Harry wanted a pizza, for everyone else wanted Mexican food.

The different coordination words suggest different relationships between the two ideas. *But* emphasizes the contrast between Harry's wishes and everyone else's. *And* just presents the fact that there were two alternatives. *So* suggests that everyone else chose Mexican food simply to be different from Harry. *For* implies that Harry just wanted to be different from everyone else.

All of the coordinating words put equal emphasis on each idea, but each coordinating word suggests a slightly different relationship between the two ideas.

Exercise I

Show the connection between each of the following pairs of sentences by using a comma and one of the seven coordinating words (**but, or, yet, for, and, nor, so**). Try two different combinations for each pair, and be prepared to explain any difference in meaning between the two versions.

> EXAMPLES:
>
> Alex didn't have the money to take Kate out.
>
> He told her he was busy.
>
> A.   *Alex didn't have the money to take Kate out, but he told her he was busy.*
>
> B.   *Alex didn't have the money to take Kate out, so he told her he was busy.*
>
> *Discussion:* In the first sentence, the *but* emphasizes the *contrast* between the truth and Alex's version of reality. In the second, the *so* emphasizes that the lie was an *effect* of Alex's lack of money.

Greece has little good farm land.

The ancient Greeks developed a brilliant civilization.

A.   *Greece has little good farm land, <u>yet</u> the ancient Greeks developed a brilliant civilization.*

B.   *Greece has little good farm land<u>, but</u> the ancient Greeks developed a brilliant civilization.*

Discussion: There is no important difference between the sentences; both point to the *contrast* between the poor land and the brilliant civilization.

1.   Gary grew up in a beach town.

He swims like a fish. (*and, so*)

A.   _____

_____

B.   _____

_____

2.   Clarissa could buy herself a new motorcycle.

She could afford a weekend in Philadelphia. (*and, or*)

A.   _____

_____

B.   _____

_____

3.   Mark Antony could not keep power in Rome.

Cleopatra remained his mistress. (*for, yet*)

A.   _____

_____

B.   _____

_____

4. Cats are independent and intelligent.
   Some people prefer dogs. (*yet, so*)

A. _____

   _____

B. _____

   _____

5. Harry grew up watching "I Love Lucy."
   Now he is addicted to reruns of "Laverne and Shirley." (*so, **but***)

A. _____

   _____

B. _____

6. We can hire an attorney to sue them. and, so
   We can demonstrate in front of their headquarters.

A. _____

   _____

B. _____

   _____

7. Grandpa disapproved of the marriage. but, yet
   Grandma approved of it.

A. _____

   _____

B. _____

   _____

8. Ruth Hill produced a remarkable novel about the Plains Indians. but, and
   She spent 14 years studying their way of life.

A. _____

_____

B. _____

_____

9. Donna always seems to look fashionable. *but, while*
   She spends little money on clothes.

A. _____

_____

B. _____

_____

10. Bart did not break the American record. *?*
    He did not *even* come close to the world record. *?*

A. _____

_____

B. _____

_____

Semicolon, Linking Adverb

In coordinating sentences you have another option besides a comma and one of the coordination signals. You can also use a semicolon (;), as in the sentence below:

> Agatha Christie specializes in the very British murder story; Ross Macdonald gives murder a contemporary American setting.

A semicolon emphasizes the closeness between the two ideas but does not specify the kind of relationship. Therefore, you may want to use a special kind of linking adverb with the semicolon which will show your reader the specific relationship you intend between the two ideas.

For instance:

> Peter insulted his great uncle; as a result, Peter lost his inheritance.

(Notice that you should use a comma after the linking adverb to emphasize the relationship you are signaling.) Some of the most frequently used linking adverbs are:

as a result	moreover
consequently	nevertheless
furthermore	on the other hand
however	therefore
in addition	thus

Exercise J

Use a semicolon to combine the sentences below and indicate the closeness between them. Then use a linking adverb to bring out the *specific* relationship you want the reader to see. Be prepared to discuss any difference in meaning between the two versions.

EXAMPLES:

Alex didn't have the money to take Kate out.

He told her he was busy.

A. *Alex didn't have the money to take Kate out; he told her he was busy.*

B. *Alex didn't have the money to take Kate out; therefore, he told her he was busy.*

Discussion: In both combined sentences, the second idea shows the *result* of Alex's lack of money, but in the first combination the reader has to guess at the connection. In the second, it is spelled out. The *extra help* given the reader is the difference.

Greece has little good farm land.

The ancient Greeks developed a brilliant culture. (; – *in spite of this*)

A. *Greece has little good farm land; the ancient Greeks developed a brilliant culture.*

B. *Greece has little good farm land; in spite of this, the ancient Greeks developed a brilliant culture.*

Discussion: In the first combination, the reason the writer joined the sentences may not be clear to the reader; therefore, the semicolon alone would not be a very effective way to do the combining. In the second combination, the writer's *contrasting* of the poor land with the brilliant culture is made obvious to the reader by adding *in spite of.* The *increased clarity* is the difference.

1. Gordon has always rooted for the Colts.
   His best friend, Smitty, is a long-time fan of the Steelers. (; – *on the other hand*)

   A. _____

   _____

   B. _____

   _____

2. Ant society is often compared to the human.
   The similarities are very slight. (; – *however*)

   A. _____

   _____

   B. _____

   _____

3. France once controlled the entire Mississippi Valley.
   Many cities along the river have French names. (; – *as a result*)

   A. _____

   _____

   B. _____

   _____

4. Maria got a promotion.
   She moved into a bigger apartment. (; – *therefore*)

   A. _____

   _____

B. _____

_____

5. Paulette used to own her own beauty shop. ⟵ _____

She soon found out she didn't like the extra responsibility. (; – *however*)

A. _____

_____

B. _____

_____

6. Japan borrowed its writing system from China. (; – in addition)

It added characters of its own.

A. _____

_____

B. _____

_____

7. The water supply in the American West is limited (; – however)

People keep moving there and planting lawns.

A. _____

_____

B. _____

_____

8. Trees cool and clean the air. (; – therefore)

Many cities are using them for urban renewal.

A. _____

_____

B. _____

_____

9. Frank works for General Motors. (; – however)
    He drives a Subaru.

A. _____

_____

B. _____

_____

10. That waiter was rude and sarcastic. (; – furthermore)
    He was incompetent.

A. _____

_____

B. _____

_____

Exercise K

Add a sentence to each of the following. Try to use different combining patterns rather then relying on just one. Be sure to choose the coordination signal or linking adverb that most clearly expresses the relationship you want to show between the two ideas. Remember the punctuation that goes with each pattern.

EXAMPLES:

Mt. Etna erupts about every twenty years.

Mt. Etna erupts about every twenty years, yet people still live on the slopes.

No one knows what to do with nuclear waste.

No one knows what to do with nuclear waste; nevertheless, the government is going ahead with reactor development.

1. The Senate hearing dragged on.

    _____

    _____

2. I did not receive a reward.

    _____

    _____

3. Kevin's apartment has a fine view of Central Park.

    _____

    _____

4. Pledges to the building fund came in very quickly.

    _____

    _____

5. More than 2,000 children a year die of cancer.

    _____

    _____

6. We do not think this is the best route for the new Interstate Highway.

    _____

    _____

7. All the children wanted to meet Big Bird.

    _____

    _____

8. A professional woman's clothes should make her look efficient.

    _____

    _____

9. Soccer is less violent than football.

_____

_____

10. One does not usually look for a fine restaurant in an airport.

_____

_____

EDITING PRACTICE

Read the following paragraphs carefully, checking for errors in using the writing techniques presented thus far. Make sure there are no sentence fragments. Make sure that singular subjects have singular verbs. Make sure that items in a series are separated by commas when necessary. Make sure there is correct punctuation between coordinate clauses.

Underline any errors you find and then copy the paragraph, correcting those errors.

1. Some famous diamonds have altered the course of history. The "Shah of Persia" was once owned by a Shah, however, it was given to the Soviets as part of the payoff for the murder of a Russian ambassador. The "Orloff" is now in the Russian scepter, but it came to Russia as a love gift to Empress Catherine. France and England has also owned some legendary gems. The "Regent," once a French possession, was pledged to Holland for war funds, Redeemed by Napoleon I and mounted in the hilt of his state sword. The "Koohinoor"* ancient and heroic, was discovered in India; however, it finally made its way to England. There it was recut and it is now the central stone in the Queen's state crown. No wonder neither rubies nor pearls is considered as romantic as the diamond.
                        are

2. Home computers may soon take over many routine household chores. A week's menus, complete with recipes and a shopping list. Can be punched out in a few seconds. The checkbook balance and the savings account balance is available at the touch of a button. Budgeting often tiresome and frustrating is much simpler. When the computer can supply a complete analysis of spending patterns. The temperature inside the house can be controlled by computer and the thermostat can be automatically reset every night and every morning. The Christmas card list a calendar of family appointments or a roster of emergency phone numbers are easily maintained by computer. At present, few homes have computers however in a few years they will be as common as calculators and much more useful.

* pronounced _KOH-i-nor_

WRITING PRACTICE

Write five or six sentences in which you show the advantages and the disadvantages of some action. Give equal emphasis to the good points and the bad points by using the techniques of coordination. Some possible topics might be:

1. Going to college right after high school
2. Mothers working outside the home
3. Renting an apartment
4. Having children
5. Watching television
6. Living in the city
7. Working for a small company

Sample opening sentence:

> *Having children can keep your imagination active, but it can make your body tired.*

Subordination

4

Through coordination, you make one idea in a sentence just as important as another. With SUBORDINATION, you can show a logical relationship between two ideas, but you keep the reader's attention focused on one of the ideas. All the sentences which you do not want to be the focus of attention are reduced to SUBORDINATE WORD GROUPS, arranged so they define or describe parts of the BASE SENTENCE.

SUB. WORD GROUP   BASE SENTENCE
When winter comes, the sun is lower in the sky.

BASE SENTENCE   SUB. WORD GROUP
I'll probably win the title *because I'm in the best condition.*

In both sample sentences, the subordinate word group makes the idea in the base sentence more precise, but the reader's attention remains focused on the base sentence.

When you subordinate an idea, you put it in some form that is less than a complete sentence. To be considered a sentence, a group of words must express a complete idea: it must present a subject and a verb that shows time, and they must not be introduced by a subordination signal. If any one of these requirements is missing, you do not have a sentence, but a SUBORDINATE WORD GROUP.

> You can make a sentence into a subordinate word group by:
>
> 1.   using a subordination signal
> 2.   removing the subject
> 3.   removing the verb

Throughout this chapter, you will discover ways to keep your reader's attention focused on the central idea of your sentence and to make your ideas more precise by showing the relationships among them.

USING SUBORDINATION SIGNALS

Subordination signals turn sentences into subordinate word groups telling when, where, how, or why the action occurs. Such word groups clarify the action in the base sentence.

These word groups can be introduced by any of the subordination signals in the box below.

Subordination Signals

Time	Space	Comparison	Cause and Effect
After	Where	Although	Because
As soon as	(there?)	As	If
Before		As if	In case that
Once		As though	In order that
Until		Even though	Inasmuch as
When		Less than	Provided that
Whenever		More than	Since
While		So long as	So that
		Than	Unless
		Though	Whereas

Notice that the use of different subordination signals can suggest quite different relationships between ideas.

> Marie likes dumplings.
>
> Her mother makes them every Saturday.
>
> A. Because Marie likes dumplings, her mother makes them every Saturday.
>
> B. As if Marie likes dumplings, her mother makes them every Saturday.
>
> C. Although Marie likes dumplings, her mother makes them every Saturday.

When you begin a sentence with this kind of subordinate word group, you should avoid any chance that your reader might not see when the base sentence begins by marking the end of the introductory word group with a comma.

> INTRODUCTORY
>
> *Because he had been trained in Paris,* the new chef demanded a high salary.

In addition, since it is always important to help your reader see the base sentence, you should surround with commas any subordinate word group which interrupts the base sentence.

> INTERRUPTING
>
> The new chef, *because he had been trained in Paris,* demanded a high salary.

If you choose to put the subordinate word group on the end of the base sentence, the subordination signal itself serves to tell the reader that the base sentence is over, so usually no punctuation is needed.

> The new chef demanded a high salary *because he had been trained in Paris.*

Exercise A

Combine the following sentences using the signals given in parentheses. You should have two different combinations for each pair of sentences. Remember to punctuate correctly for the placement of the subordinate word group. Explain the relationship between the ideas in each sentence: either time, space, comparison/contrast, or cause and effect. Also explain which idea is the focus in each sentence.

EXAMPLE:

Cory danced by the edge of the sea. (*while*)
She could hear music from under the waves. (*because*)

A. While Cory danced by the edge of the sea, *she could hear music from under the waves.*

B. *Cory danced by the edge of the sea* because she could hear music from under the waves.

Sample explanation: In the first sentence, she hears the music at the same time she is dancing. In the second, the music causes her dancing.

EXAMPLE:

Ellie is very lovely. (*even though, because*)
Ellie has few good friends.

A. Even though she is very lovely, *Ellie has few good friends.*

B. Because she is very lovely, *Ellie has few good friends.*

Sample explanation: In the first, the expectation that physical attractiveness brings popularity contrasts with the reality of Ellie's lack of friends. In the second, the writer says physical attractiveness causes a lack of good friends.

1. Spring begins. (*as soon as*)
   The dogwood unfurls its simple flowers. (*when*)

A. _____

B. _____

Explanation _____

_____

2. The serpent slithered across the quilt. (*as*)
   Sherlock Holmes struck at it with his stick. (*when*)

A. _____

B. _____

Explanation _____

_____

3. John likes intelligent women. (*even though, because*)
   John detests Valerie.
   he

A. _____

B. _____

Explanation _____

_____

4. Misery loves company. (*even though*)
   Being miserable is usually lonely. (*because*)

A. _____

B. _____

Explanation _____

_____

5. The sap starts to rise. (*after*)
   It is time to start tapping the trees. (*when*)

A. _____

B. _____

Explanation _____

_____

SIGNALING WITH PRONOUNS

The subordination signals *who, that, which,* and *whose* can be used to change a
sentence into a subordinate word group. For example, look at this combination:

> Lynn writes sensitive poetry.
> Lynn has just published her second book.
>
> A. Lynn, *who writes sensitive poetry,* has just published her
>   second book.

B. Lynn, *who has just published her second book,* writes sensitive poetry.

Sentence (a) emphasizes the book publication by keeping it in the base sentence. Sentence (b) emphasizes the kind of poetry Lynn writes by putting that
in the base sentence.

Here is another example:

Everyone calls the lion the King of Beasts.

The lion is an impressive creature.

The lion, *which everyone calls the King of Beasts,* is an impressive creature.

Which idea gets more emphasis in the sentence above, the fact that the lion is
the King of Beasts or the fact that he is impressive?

When you use this subordination technique, there are several points to
keep in mind.

1. These subordinate groups are always placed right after the words
they are referring to so the reader will have no difficulty seeing the connection.
In the sentences above, for instance, *who,* comes immediately after *Lynn* because *who* really stands for *Lynn; which* comes immediately after *lion* because
which stands for *lion.*

2. *Who is used for people.* Sometimes, sentiment may make a writer
use *who* when referring to a pet or some object he or she thinks of as having a
personality (ships, the earth, the sea, countries, and so on), but normally *that*
and *which* are used for animals and objects.

3. *Whose* is a special case. Here is an example of its use:

Helen's beauty caused a war.

The Greeks believed Helen was a god's daughter.

The Greeks believed Helen, *whose beauty caused a war,* was a
god's daughter.

The common point in both sentences is Helen, but in one sentence she pos-
sesses something. In this situation, the common point can be replaced by
whose.

Gary's car was stolen Tuesday.

Gary broke his leg by running for the bus Wednesday.

Gary, *whose car was stolen Tuesday,* broke his leg running for
the bus Wednesday.

4. If the *who, which, that,* or *whose* group interrupts the flow of the
sentence to give the reader some extra information, then it is placed between

commas, as in the examples. (Cases where commas are not needed will be discussed later in this chapter.)

Exercise B

Combine each of the following sets of sentences using *who, which, that,* and *whose*. In some cases, you may be asked to give two different versions of the sentence, each emphasizing a different idea. Don't forget to put commas around the interrupting word groups to focus attention on the base sentence.

EXAMPLE:

Henry James wrote about Americans in Europe.

Henry James lived most of his life in England.

A. (subordinate where he lived)

Henry James, *who lived most of his life in England,* wrote about Americans in Europe.

B. (subordinate what he wrote about)

Henry James, *who wrote about Americans in Europe,* lived most of his life in England.

1. Lydia who was heavily tattooed.

Lydia became the subject of a famous song.
     who

A. (Subordinate her being tattooed.)

_____

_____

B. (Subordinate her becoming the subject of a song.)

_____

_____

2. Harold's parents who don't approve of gambling.

Harold has taken a job in Atlantic City's biggest casino.

_____

_____

3. Oslo which is the capital of Norway. is

Oslo used to be called Christiana.

A.   (Subordinate its former name.)

_Christrana, which _ _ _ ('Oslo)_

_____

B.   (Subordinate its being the capital.)

_Oslo which is the capital _ _ _ _

_____

4.   The moon's surface *which* is covered with craters.
      ~~The moon~~ is too small ever to have had a protective atmosphere.

_____

_____

5.   The Himalayas *which* were pushed up when India collided with Asia.
      The Himalayas include some of the highest mountains on earth.
      which

A.   (Subordinate how the Himalayas were formed.)

_____

_____

B.   (Subordinate what the Himalayas include.)

_____

_____

6.   The Dog-Star *which* rises with the sun in August.
      ~~The ancients~~ thought ~~the Dog-Star was~~ the cause of the scorching heat.
      was   *by ancients to be*

_____

_____

7.   Old Fez *which* has changed little since feudal times.
      Old Fez is in Northern Morocco.
      which

A. (Subordinate the location of Old Fez.)

_____

_____

B. (Subordinate the lack of change.)

_____

_____

8. I knew Helen, ~~in Algeria.~~ who was
    ~~Helen was~~ an Englishwoman. whose
    ~~Helen's~~ husband worked for the national oil company.

_____

_____

9. Anne of France ‸who ruled while her brother was too young.
    ~~Anne of France~~ later retired to a castle near Gien. whose
    ~~The castle's~~ elegance still tells much about its mistress's taste.

_____

_____

10. Leslie ‸who wanted to be a star is now doing commercials for a company. which its (whose)
    ~~Leslie wanted to be a star~~.
    ~~The company's~~ product can't be shown on TV.

_____

_____

PUNCTUATING SUBORDINATE WORD GROUPS

As you saw in earlier exercises, you can use punctuation to keep the reader's attention focused on the base sentence. Thus, you put commas around any subordinate word group that interrupts the flow of the sentence. Some subordinate word groups, however, do not interrupt; they are, in fact, necessary parts of the base sentence. They narrow or make particular the meaning of some part of the base sentence they modify, as in this sentence:

Citizens *who don't vote* are still responsible for the outcome of elections.

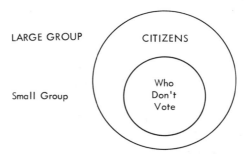

The subordinate word group *who don't vote* narrows down the meaning of citizens from a broad group to a smaller group. It is not an interruption, but an important, necessary part of the sentence. Without it, the sentence does not mean the same thing.

Subordinate word groups which narrow rather than interrupt *do not* get set off by commas.

Interrupting and *narrowing* word groups are not always easy to distinguish. You must look closely at the purpose of their use. Compare these two sentences:

Alcatraz, which is in San Francisco Bay, was a famous federal prison.

A team that loses three games in a row needs more practice.

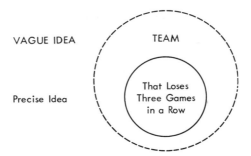

In the first, the word modified, *Alcatraz,* doesn't need narrowing down to be identified correctly: there is only one Alcatraz; no confusion is possible. The subordinate word group, therefore, is extra information *interrupting* the sentence. (Read it out loud; you will hear the interruption.)

In the second sentence, the word modified, *team,* is vague. You have to make it clearer what kind of team you are talking about, so you *narrow* down to a particular kind of team: one that has lost three games in a row. This word group is not an interruption but a meaningful part of the flow of the sentence. (Read this one without the subordinate word group. Is the meaning the same as before?)

Try another example.

> Penguins which live in Antarctica are relatively large.
>
> Penguins, which are flightless birds, have unusual nesting habits.

In the first sentence, you have taken the general group of penguins and narrowed it down to the smaller group of penguins that live in Antarctica (as opposed to Tierra del Fuego, New Zealand, or the Falklands—other penguin habitats). Only penguins in this group are large. Penguins living elsewhere may be small. In the second sentence, you are not narrowing down: *all* penguins, the whole group, are flightless birds. You are simply choosing to get in the information about flightlessness by interrupting the sentence.

To summarize, when the subordinate word group is used to narrow a vague word or a general group down to a specific case, you are *not* interrupting the sentence and *no* commas can be used.

Exercise C

Identify the subordinate word groups in the following sentences by writing *I* (Interrupting) or *N* (Narrowing) in the blank. Insert commas in the sentences which are interrupted.

1. __N__ People who have violent tempers shouldn't marry.

2. __N__ Paintings that are done on walls are called murals.

3. __I__ My cousin Arthur, who lives in Dubuque, flies jumbo jets.

4. __N__ Only shells that are unbroken fetch high prices.

5. __N__ The letter that his girlfriend wrote contained bad news.

6. __I__ *The Wizard of Oz,* which was made in 1939, is a classic musical.

7. __I__ Our team, which has a winning record, may go to a bowl game.

8. __N__ People who live in glass houses shouldn't throw stones.

9.   __N__   Trees that lose their leaves in winter are deciduous.

10.   __N__   A beginning jogger who is over 35 should get a checkup.

Exercise D

In Exercise B, all the subordinate word groups were interrupting. In the following combining exercise, you are given both kinds of groups. You must decide what kind you are dealing with. One new note: when a narrowing word group has its complement replaced by *who, that,* or *which,* the pronoun is usually dropped.

The message (that) you were waiting for never came.
The boots (that) she bought yesterday cost plenty.

Not only should you drop these pronouns when no confusion results, but the dropping is a good test to see if you really have a narrowing word group. Combine the following sentences and punctuate appropriately.

1.   Portia disguised herself as a judge.

Portia's lover was on trial for murder.

Portia, whose lover was on trial for murder, - - —

2.   The radio has been stolen.
You left the radio on the back seat.

The radio, which you left on the back seat, - - - -

3.   That song is driving me crazy.
You whistle that song morning, noon, and night.

That song, which you whistle - - - - - -,

4.   ~~Utah prairie dogs~~ are an endangered species.
Utah prairie dogs are small, burrow-building rodents, *which*

5. Elmer Fudd *who* always got the worst of the deal,
~~Elmer Fudd~~ tried endlessly to capture the "wabbit."

_____

_____

6. ~~2 People~~ love to visit the park.
1 The people *who* live in Baltimore.
3 ~~The park looks~~ *looking* over the Inner Harbor.

_____

_____

7. Mozart was an infant prodigy.
who ~~Mozart~~ wrote *Don Giovanni.*
which ~~Don Giovanni~~ is about a nobleman. *who*
~~The nobleman~~ is damned for betraying his responsibilities.

_____

_____

8. The book ~~is full of pictures.~~
You gave me ~~the book~~ for Christmas. *is full of pictures which*
~~The pictures~~ remind me of my childhood dreams.

_____

_____

9. In the TV series, ~~Bronowski traces the progress.~~
That Bronowski made ~~the series~~ before he died,
traces the progress Humanity has made ~~the progress~~ in science and culture.
(The ascent of man)

_____

_____

10. Nineveh *which* is now dust and ruins,

~~Nineveh~~ was once the center of a great empire. *wh●*

~~The empire~~ ruled the Near East when Rome was a village.

_____

_____

REMOVING THE SUBJECT

Another way of subordinating an idea is to remove the subject and use one of the three verb forms which don't show time. These verb forms are called VERBALS.

Every verb has three verbal forms, that is, forms which don't indicate the time of an action:

to + verb	To speak
verb + -ing	Speaking
past participle	~~have~~ Spoken

Any of these forms may be used to make a subordinate word group.

Look at these examples:

1. My friend Sara ran to catch the bus.
   She met Jeff.

   Running to catch the bus, my friend Sara met Jeff.
   My friend Sara, *running to catch the bus*, met Jeff.

2. Pete Thorpe was gunned down in cold blood.
   He was buried at Boot Hill.

   Gunned down in cold blood, Pete Thorpe was buried at Boot Hill.
   Pete Thorpe, *gunned down in cold blood*, was buried at Boot Hill.

3. Mark got downtown.
   He took a cab.

   To get downtown, Mark took a cab.

First, notice the forms of the verbals. In each case, the subject is eliminated and the verb is changed. In the first example, the verb changes from *ran*, which tells the time of the action (in the past), to *running*, which does not. The verb in the second example, *gunned,* takes the form used with the helping verb *have,* called the past participle. (For example, in the verbs *have shown* and *have gone, shown* and *gone* are past participles.) Used alone, the past participle does not show when the action happened. Finally, in the last example, the verb is put in the form used with *to* (to get), which does not indicate any time relationship.

Second, notice the relationships. The sentence, "Gunned down in cold blood, Pete Thorpe was buried at Boot Hill," emphasizes where Thorpe was buried by putting that idea in the base sentence. The sentence, "Buried at Boot Hill, Pete Thorpe was gunned down in cold blood," emphasizes how Thorpe died by putting that idea in the base sentence.

Finally, notice the punctuation. Commas are required when the subordinate word group opens or interrupts the sentence.

Exercise E

Combine the following sentences by changing one sentence to a subordinate word group. Be prepared to explain which idea gets the main emphasis in your new sentence.

EXAMPLES:

A. Marcia felt like death warmed over.   (*-ing*)
    Marcia dragged herself to work.

Feeling like death warmed over, Marcia dragged herself to work.

B. *The Odyssey* was composed when Greece was young. (*composed*)
    The Odyssey is still as fresh as dawn.

The Odyssey, composed when Greece was young, is still as fresh as dawn.

C. Tom developed his physique.   (*to —*)
    Tom took hormones.

To develop his physique, Tom took hormones.

1. The town sweltered in the heat.   (*-ing*)
    The town lay open to the sun.

    _____

    _____

2. Melvin had been lost since the Blizzard of '78.   (*lost*)
   Melvin wandered home yesterday.

   _____

   _____

3. Sheila will be a surgeon. (*to —*)
   Sheila will have to go to school for years.

   _____

   _____

4. The rock had been worn by the ocean for centuries.   (*worn*)
   The rock was smooth and shaped to the hand.

   _____

   _____

5. Lester sang to himself.   (*-ing*)
   Lester jogged through the autumn leaves.

   _____

   _____

6. You make a great martini.   (*to —*)
   Add a very small amount of quality vermouth.

   _____

   _____

7. The Fertile Crescent runs from Iraq to Egypt.   (*-ing*)
   The Fertile Crescent nourished the first agricultural states.

   _____

   _____

8. The University of Virginia was designed by Thomas Jefferson. (*designed*)
   The University of Virginia is a model of classical architecture.

   _____

   _____

9. Bentley inherited Lady Emmilina's fortune. (*to —*)
   Bentley slipped cyanide in Lady Emmilina's tea.

   _____

   _____

10. Vinnie was summoned to appear in court. (*summoned*)
    Vinnie got himself a good lawyer.

    _____

    _____

11. The textile workers negotiated a union contract. (*to —*)
    The textile workers have to win recognition.

    _____

    _____

12. Tivoli was built as an adult amusement park. (*built*)
    Tivoli stands in the center of Copenhagen.

    _____

    _____

13. Monet captured the essence of light. (*to —*)
    Monet painted with contrasting, isolated spots of color.

    _____

    _____

14. Palmer had pitched a perfect game for seven innings.   (*-ing*)
    Palmer had to be replaced in the eighth.

    _____

    _____

15. Radio telescopes sweep the skies in precise patterns.   (*-ing*)
    Radio telescopes listen for messages from other civilizations.

    _____

    _____

Look again at the pair of sentences you just combined. Following the instructions for number 15, you probably produced

> Sweeping the skies in precise patterns, radio telescopes listen for messages from other civilizations.

However, you could also have combined these sentences using the *which* signal.

> Radio telescopes, which sweep the skies in precise patterns, listen for messages from other civilizations.

In many cases you can choose either of these two methods of subordination.

Exercise F

Combine each of the following sets of sentences in two ways. First use a *who, which,* or *that* signal to subordinate one or more ideas. Then use a verbal to subordinate.

> EXAMPLE:
>
> Summer session begins July 2.
> Summer session lasts six weeks.
> Summer session requires a lot of work.
>
> A. Summer session, *which begins July 2 and lasts for six weeks,* requires a lot of work.
> B. *Beginning July 2 and lasting six weeks,* summer session requires a lot of work.

1. Divorce breaks up one out of every three marriages.
    Divorce has become a familiar part of American family life.

    A. _____

        _____

    B. _____

        _____

2. Walter intends to climb the face of El Capitan.
    Walter practices every weekend.

    A. _____

        _____

    B. _____

        _____

3. Superman was orphaned by the destruction of Krypton.
    Superman was sent to Earth to make it a better place.

    A. _____

        _____

    B. _____

        _____

4. We want to boast about humanity to possible audiences in space.
    We could transmit the music of Bach.

    A. _____

        _____

    B. _____

        _____

5. Godzilla has grown to full size.
   Godzilla can devour whole parking lots.

   A. _____

   _____

   B. _____

   _____

6. Alma loves mystery stories.
   Alma is suspicious of everybody.
   The mystery stories involve deep intrigue.

   A. _____

   _____

   B. _____

   _____

7. Falling Water is preserved by the state of Pennsylvania.
   Falling Water was built by Frank Lloyd Wright.
   Falling Water was once a beautiful private residence.

   A. _____

   _____

   B. _____

   _____

8. The *New English Bible* is written in a clear, elegant style.
   The *New English Bible* is the work of scholars.
   The scholars were assembled from around the world.

   A. _____

   _____

   B. _____

   _____

9. Claire worked day and night.
    Claire finished her new movie.
    The new movie shows the funny side of growing up.

A. _____

    _____

B. _____

    _____

10. Salmon swim upstream.
    Salmon want to find their birthplace.
    Salmon spawn and die.

A. _____

    _____

B. _____

    _____

ARRANGING WORD GROUPS WITH VERBALS

Subordinate word groups with verbals define or describe parts of the base sentence. Since their subjects have been removed, you must be particularly careful in arranging them. Place them as close as possible to the part of the base sentence they describe. If you don't, the reader may have difficulty seeing precisely what they are describing or defining, as in the following sentences:

> Growing in the front yard, we saw a rose bush. (What was growing?)
>
> Running down the street, the English book fell in the gutter. (Who was running?)

In the first case, all that is needed is some rearranging. Put the subordinate word group next to rose bush, and the sentence becomes clear.

> We saw a rose bush growing in the front yard.

The second is harder. No part of the base sentence did the action. You must change either the subordinate word group or the base sentence:

> As I was running down the street, the English book fell in the gutter.
>
> Running down the street, I dropped my English book in the gutter.

Exercise G

Expand each of the following word groups either by completing the idea with a base sentence or making the idea more precise with an appropriate subordinate word group. Be very careful that every subordinate word group can attach itself logically to some part of the base sentence. Place the subordinate word group next to the part it modifies.

EXAMPLES:

A. Filling two notebooks . . .

Filling two notebooks, Dr. McFarland's journal explained his theory in detail.

B. The animals died in a matter of moments.

Exposed to the dangerous drug, the animals died in a matter of moments.

1. To explore space, _U.S. spend millions of dollars_ .

2. Preparing lasagne, _?_ .

3. _After deciding doing so_ , they moved the furniture into the den.

4. Signed by the governor, _all papers carried the state seal_ .

5. _In respect to his performance_, Meredith was named Most Valuable Player.

6. To find the treasure, _first find the treasure map_ .

7. Swinging on the gate, _she soon fell out of the garden_ .

8. Created by Walt Disney, _Mickey Mouse became internationally famous._ .

9. _Wearing their armors_ , the knights prepared for the battle.

10. To double his investment, _he gave $1000 more and at the end he lost all of it._ .

11.   Loaded with 150 pounds of groceries, _he could hardly walk_ .

12.   _Slamming the door behind him_ , he waited for silence in the room.

13.   Repairing my bike, _I broke my screwdriver_ .

14.   Founded in 1927, _The society was bankrupt in 1928,_ .

15.   _____ , her father shouted encouragement.

16.   To save money, _don't spend it !_ .

17.   Gliding lazily over the city, _the plane cashed down, instead of landing !_

18.   _____ , several companies bid on the job.

19.   Leaping over the net, _____ .

20.   _____ , the hairdresser gasped in dismay.

REMOVING THE VERB

Explaining Nouns

Explaining nouns are formed when the sentence is stripped of its verb. The resulting subordinate word group is used to explain a noun in the base sentence. For example,

> Sloane decided to change his life.
>
> Sloane is the man in the gray flannel suit.
>
> Sloane, *the man in the gray flannel suit,* decided to change his life.

Here, the noun *man* and its modifiers are used to explain the noun *Sloane. The man in the gray flannel suit* is a subordinate word group, which means it gets less emphasis than the base sentence, "Sloane decided to change his life."
  Look at another example:

> Rome has been important for over 2,000 years.
>
> Rome is called the Eternal City.
>
> Rome, *the Eternal City,* has been important for over 2,000 years.

Which idea is more important in this sentence, the fact that Rome has been important for 2,000 years or the fact that Rome is called the Eternal City? Whatever is in the base sentence gets more emphasis. Whatever is in a subordinate word group gets less emphasis.

Exercise H

Combine the following sentences by making one sentence into an explaining noun. Be prepared to explain which idea in your new sentence is getting more emphasis:

1. Benedict Arnold tried to sell West Point to the British.
    Benedict Arnold was the most famous traitor in American history.

    _____

    _____

2. Mr. Jefferson has been our accountant for thirty years.
    Mr. Jefferson is a loyal, trusted employee.

    _____

    _____

3. The Cheat is a river in West Virginia.
    The Cheat is an excellent site for whitewater rafting.

    _____

    _____

4. Bessie Smith was one of the greatest blues singers of all time.
    Bessie Smith was a victim of segregated hospitals.

    _____

    _____

5. The pyramids are one of the Seven Wonders of the Ancient World.
    The pyramids were the work of generations of Egyptians.

    _____

    _____

Prepositional Phrases

Another kind of subordinate word group without a verb is the prepositional (adjective or adverb) phrase. Most prepositions, as you can see from the list below, relate ideas or objects by their positions in time or in space.

Space	Time	Possession or Other Relationships
above	about	because of
across	after	for
against	at	in spite of
around	before	of
at	during	with
behind	since	without
below	throughout	
beneath	until	
beside		
by		
down		
from		
in		
into		
near		
next to		
on		
over		
through		
to		
under		
up		
upon		

A prepositional phrase used as an adjective to give the sentence greater precision is usually placed immediately after the person or thing being described.

> The rain puts me to sleep.
> The rain is on the roof.
> The rain *on the roof* puts me to sleep.

Where a prepositional phrase is used as an adverb telling when, where, why, or how the action occurs, it can be placed in several positions. If it begins the sentence, it is usually set off by a comma. If it breaks into the sentence, you may use commas to set it off if you want to emphasize the interruption. If it comes at the end, you don't need punctuation.

Helen won the election.

Helen won by a large margin.

By a large margin, Helen won the election.

Helen, *by a large margin*, won the election.

Helen won the election *by a large margin*.

Notice, though, that all of these sentences subordinate the size of Helen's victory and emphasize that fact that she won.

Exercise I

Combine the following groups of sentences using prepositional phrases. Be sure to use commas where they are needed. Be prepared to explain which idea in the sentence is getting the most emphasis.

1. The rain fell.

    ~~It fell~~ on the leaves.

    ~~It fell~~ during the night.

    ~~It fell~~ with a soft hissing.

    _____

    _____

2. Meg's marriage was a disaster.

    The failure was during its first year.

    Her marriage was to Floyd.

    The failure was in spite of her efforts.

    In spite of her efforts, Meg's marriage to Floyd was a disaster during its first year

3. The file has disappeared.

    The file is on our current accounts.

    The disappearance was from Miller's desk.

    The disappearance happened since last Friday.

    Last Friday, the file on our current accounts has disappeared from Miller's desk.

4. The river runs.
    It comes from the High Sierras.
    It comes across the farmland.
    The farmland belongs to northern California.
    It runs into San Francisco Bay.

    The river coming from the High Sierras across the farmland
    of northern Cal. runs to SF bay.

5. A mysterious boom echoed.
    ~~It occurred~~ during the night.
    ~~The echo was~~ throughout the city.

    _____

    _____

Exercise J

In the following groups you are given the same kind of sentences you had above, but this time the prepositions have been left out. Combine the sentences and fill in the blanks with appropriate prepositions.

1. The snow fell.
    ~~It fell~~ _by_ the dawn.
    ~~It fell~~ _without_ a sound.
    ~~It fell~~ all _over_ the farm.

    _____

    _____

2. Winnie lives.
    ~~She lives~~ _in_ the city.
    ~~She lives~~ _near_ the cathedral.
    ~~She lives~~ _with_ her uncle Charlie.

    _____

    _____

3. Claire hardly ever talks.
    ~~She hardly ever talks~~ _at_ work.
    ~~She hardly ever talks~~ _to_ her boss.

    _____

    _____

4. The river rose rapidly.
    It rose _____ the melting snow.
    It rose _____ the evening.
    It rose _to_ a record level.

    _____

    _____

5. The beach sweltered.
    It sweltered _____ the July sun.
    It was _____ noon.
    The beach was _____ Piney Island.

    _____

    _____

Exercise K

Now you are on your own. Choose any method of subordination: subordination signals, verbals, explaining nouns, or prepositional phrases. Subordinate any of the sentences you choose. Arrange the word groups in any order you choose. Be prepared to explain the exact meaning of your new sentence.

1. Anne has a husband and two children. _so she_
    _____ ~~Anne~~ gets an enormous amount of work done.

    _____

    _____

    When
2. The island of Thera exploded,
    The shock wave destroyed Cretan civilization.

3. Poor people have many experiences in common.
   Their ethnic inheritance determines their outlook.

Wha the

4. Orion rises,
   The summer heat becomes intolerable.

Wha

5. The Santa Ana wind blows in from the desert,
   The Angelenos do strange things.

6. Many people were shocked.
   ~~Benny~~ was always so healthy.
   when He got seriously ill.,   _because he_

7. Juana left home at an early age. _and_
   ~~She~~ went to work. _because_
   She wanted independence.

8.   Timbuktu became a great trading center.

Lying ~~It lies~~ on the caravan route to North Africa.

Begin → → - - As Its surrounding territory was united under one ruler,

_____

_____

9.   Gold has been valued for centuries.

because It doesn't rust.

Although It has little practical use.

_____

_____

Although it

10.   ~~Television~~ has great potential,

Television has remained disappointing.

because it ~~Television~~ puts commercial success first.

_____

_____

11.   Wine grapes rot in the fall.

Wine grapes produce extra sugar at this time.

Grapes picked late make rich, sweet wine.

Rotting in fall, wine grapes picked late make rich, sweet

wine because they produce extra sugar at this time

Although

12.   Harold was never late for work. *and*

He always did as he was told.

His boss fired him.

~~The boss~~ didn't like fat people.

Because he

Although

13. Joyce has trouble reading.
    She passed English.
because   She worked hard. *and*
    She showed the teacher she cared.

_____

_____

14. The fireflies lit up in the grass.
    A gentle wind ruffled the water.
    We walked along the river path.
    We reached the old graveyard.

_____

_____

15. Seasonal rains fall in Central Africa. *causing to*
    ~~They~~ raise the level of the Nile. *which*
    ~~It~~ overflows its banks. *and*
    It enriches the soil.

_____

_____

Exercise L

Combine the following sentences using any technique that you think is appropriate. Be prepared to explain which idea in your new sentence is getting the main emphasis.

1. Pete finished dinner early.
   He washed the dishes.

Ways to Subordinate Ideas

1. Attach a subordination signal to the front of a sentence:

   The defendant lost the case.
   ↓
   because the defendant lost the case
   ↓
   Because the defendant lost the case, he was ruined.

2. Replace one word in the sentence with *who, whose, which,* or *that:*

   The defendant lost the case
   ↓
   who lost the case
   The defendant, who lost the case, was ruined.

3. Remove the subject and change the verb to a verbal:

   The defendant lost the case
   ↓
   losing the case
   Losing the case, the defendant was ruined.

4. Remove the verb from the sentence:

   The defendant lost the case
   ↓
   The defendant
   ↓
   Ellery, the defendant, was ruined.

The dishes were dirty.
He found the tv schedule.
He sat down for an evening.

He sat down in front of the set.
The evening was one of quiet enjoyment.

_____

_____

_____

2. Sacramento was the center of the Gold Rush.
    The Gold Rush was in 1849.
    Sacramento is the capital of California.
    California was then a province of Mexico.

_____

_____

_____

3. The Pioneer spacecraft sent back pictures.
    The pictures were marvelous.
    The pictures were of Jupiter.
    Jupiter hangs like a huge ball.
    The ball is orange.
    The hanging is in the sky.
    The sky is black.

_____

_____

_____

4. Santa Catalina lies off the California coast.
    Santa Catalina is 26 miles from the coast.

Santa Catalina was once a desert island.
Santa Catalina is now covered with ranches.

_____

_____

_____

5.   Larry makes his spaghetti sauce.
     He makes it from scratch.
     He cuts up whole tomatoes.
     He dices garlic.
     He simmers onions.
     The sauce gets thick.
     The thickening is slow.

_____

_____

_____

6.   Cichlids* are a type of tropical fish.
     They are hard to breed.
     They require prepared conditions.
     The preparation must be careful.
     With preparation, they can raise their young.

_____

_____

_____

7.   Skunk cabbages sprout early.
     Snow is still on the ground.
     The cabbage produces its own heat.

* Pronounced SICK-lids.

It melts the snow.
The melting occurs all around the plants.

_____

_____

_____

8. Maude likes backpacking.
It invigorates her.
Maude is 72 years old.
She hikes the Muir Trail every summer.

_____

_____

_____

9. Moslem armies swept out of Arabia.
They were motivated by faith.
They reached southern France.
They were beaten by Charles Martel.

_____

_____

_____

10. The rains ended.
The flowers shook off the water.
The rabbits watched the rainbow.
They watched through the web.
The web belongs to the spider.

_____

_____

_____

Exercise M

Expand the following sentences by adding a second sentence to each. First coordinate the two ideas. Then subordinate the sentence you added.

EXAMPLE:

Toni was an ideal candidate.

Coordinate: Toni was an ideal candidate, but Martin's views were too radical.

Subordinate: Although Martin's views were too radical, Toni was an ideal candidate.

1.   The Senate hearings dragged on.

CO _____

 _____

SUB _____

 _____

2.   I did not receive a reward.

CO _____

 _____

SUB _____

 _____

3.   Sue wrote the report on the marina.

CO _____

 _____

SUB _____

 _____

4.   The shoes were expensive.

CO _____

 _____

SUB _____

_____

5. We saw that movie four times last year.

CO _____

_____

SUB _____

_____

6. All the children wanted to meet Big Bird.

CO _____

_____

SUB _____

_____

7. It took a month to unpack the books.

CO _____

_____

SUB _____

_____

8. The accident victim's heart stopped.

CO _____

_____

SUB _____

_____

9.   In 1978, the parts division showed a 15% increase in profits.

CO   _____

_____

SUB   _____

_____

10.   The Norwegian skiers placed third in the cross-country race.

CO   _____

_____

SUB   _____

_____

EDITING PRACTICE

1.   In the following paragraph, you will find errors in the punctuation of subordinate word groups, making it difficult for the reader to identify the base sentences: narrowing groups are set off with commas, introductory groups are not followed by a comma, interrupting groups are without commas. Correct these errors.

Concerned about the crises in public education the school board, that our community elected last month, has decided to hold hearings with parents. The board hopes to involve parents in planning curriculum. Sally Lunn who is the new board president says, "Parents, who care about their children's education, must participate in planning that education." Lunn who is herself a parent intends to hold these hearings in every elementary school in the district.

2.   In the paragraph below, you will find examples of most of the major sentence construction problems you have encountered up to now: nonagreement of subject and verb, incorrect use of commas, missing punctuation, sentence fragments. Rewrite this paragraph correcting any such errors.

Max who is trying to win the Mr. Teenage New Jersey title go to the gym every day. After changing into his workout clothes his routine for the day begins. Mondays Wednesdays and Fridays, he works his calves thighs back and arms, Tuesdays Thursdays and Saturdays he concentrates on his stomach. Which is his weakest feature and his chest. The exercises, that he does for his stomach definition, involves repeated twisting. With a bar across his shoulders. Either his arms or his chest take an award in contests he enters if he can just improve his stomach he will have a good chance at the title, he covets.

WRITING PRACTICE

Write five or six sentences showing the advantages and disadvantages of some action. Emphasize the advantages and subordinate the disadvantages. Some possible topics might be:

1.   Going to college right after high school
2.   Mothers working outside the home
3.   Renting an apartment
4.   Having children
5.   Watching television
6.   Living in the city
7.   Working for a small company

Sample opening sentence:

> *Although much of children's television is boring and unimaginative, television does offer some entertaining and educational programs for children.*

Practice
in Sentence
Combining

5

In the preceding chapters, you practiced various ways of constructing sentences to express thoughts more precisely and to make the relationships between ideas clearer to your reader. You have practiced modifying the different elements in a sentence (subject, verb, complement); you have coordinated sentences and parts of sentences; you have tried out different kinds of subordination.

This chapter contains more exercises in writing sentences. The first sections provide a review of the techniques you have studied. Since you are already familiar with these various kinds of combining, the models provided in these sections are *not* intended to show you all the techniques reviewed in the exercises, but rather to remind you of some of them.

If you run into a type of sentence combination not shown in the model and you are unsure of the options you have, turn back to the chapter where the related techniques were introduced and review the models and exercises to discover the choices you can make. Compare your choices with those of your classmates.

ADDING TO THE BASIC SENTENCE

Exercise A

MODELS:

A. ADJECTIVES

John sent a message.
The sending was to his neighbor.

The message was threatening.

The neighbor lives next door.

John sent a threatening message to his next-door neighbor.

B. ADVERBS

Salome danced.

Her dancing was provocative.

Her dancing was before Herod.

Salome danced provocatively before Herod.

C. EXPLAINING NOUNS

The silver gleamed.

The silver was a gift.

The gift was from my aunt.

The silver, a gift from my aunt, gleamed.

1. A *black hole* is an object.

The object has density.

The object is mysterious.

Its density is almost unbelievable.

The object is in space.

2. Neon gives streets a look.

The streets are in the city.

The look is flashy.

The look is unreal.

The giving is at night.

3. American cars grew.

They grew faster.

They grew longer.

They grew gaudier.

All this happened during the Fifties.

4. The archeologist said he saw things.

The things were wonderful.

He saw them through a hole.

The hole was in the door.

5. Autumn turns the woods to colors.

The colors are bright.

The colors are reds.

The colors are golds.

       The colors are yellows.

       This happens in one week.

       The week is magic.

6. Hans Christian Andersen wrote stories.

       Andersen was a Dane.

       The stories are famous.

       The stories are for children.

7. Greece gave ideas to civilization.

       Greece was ancient.

       The civilization was Western.

       The ideas were important.

       The ideas were many.

8. Class was boring.

       The class was about physics.

       The boring was extreme.

       The class met today.

9. Marie loved that dog.

       The love was real.

       The dog was black and white.

       The dog was little.

       The dog was a present.

       The present was from her boyfriend.

10. The beach stretches.

       The beach is below Assateague.

       The stretching goes for miles and miles.

       The beach is white.

       The beach is clean.

       The stretching is under a sky.

       The sky is cloudless.

MORE PRACTICE IN COORDINATION

Exercise B

MODEL:

A. It was only January.

       Winter seemed eternal. *(and – but)*

It was only January, and winter seemed eternal.

It was only January, but winter seemed eternal.

Analysis: Both sentences are making a comparison between the *actual* time (only January) and the length of time that it *seems* (eternal). *But* emphasizes the contrast between real time and felt time.

B.   Harold's aunt is very rich.

Harold does what she says.   (; – *so*)

Harold)'s aunt is very rich; Harold does what she says.

Harold's aunt is very rich, so Harold does what she says.

Analysis: Both sentences express a cause and effect. The semicolon only implies the relationship. The *so* makes it explicit.

1.   Winter teaches us about hope.

Spring gives us satisfaction.   (; – *so*)

2.   Money talks.

Hunger is quiet.   (*but* – *so*)

3.   Cats are enchanting.

Dogs are devoted.   (*and* – *however*)

4.   My sister always said I should marry a Gemini.

Geminis are so tolerant.   (; – *for*)

5.   Morning rush hour is awful.

Evening rush hour is just as bad.   (; – *but*)

6.   The Declaration says, "All men are created equal."

The Constitution originally allowed slavery.

7.   Biology is the science of life.

Physics is the science of matter.

8.   Evolution is a long, painstaking process.

Revolution is quicker and sharper.

9.   Africa is old.

It is divided.

It is changing.

10.   San Francisco is every traveler's favorite city.

Los Angeles is bigger, sassier, and uglier.

MORE PRACTICE IN SUBORDINATION

Exercise C

MODELS:

A.   George drove for 48 hours straight.   (*after, while–ing*)
     George fell sound asleep.

After George drove for 48 hours straight, he fell sound asleep.
While driving for 48 hours straight, George fell sound asleep.

Analysis: Both sentences deal with cause and effect. In the first, George may have made it to the rest stop *before* dozing off. In the second, he is in serious trouble: he is sleeping *while* driving.

B.   John likes Margo.   (*because*)
     Margo likes John.   (*because*)

Because John likes Margo, she likes him.
John likes Margo because she likes him.

Analysis: Both sentences deal with cause and effect. In the first, Margo is the one responding to John's affection; in the second, John is the one responding to affection.

1.   My cat adores me.   (*because*)
     I feed her specially prepared meals.   (*because*)

2.   He spent his lifetime working in a bank.   (*since, although*)
     He never made much money.

3.   Joe selects his ingredients carefully.   (*who*)
     Joe knows his stew is worth the trouble.   (*-ing*)

4.   Rome spread its rule over the Mediterranean.   (*-ing*)
     Rome brought peace.   (*-ing*)

5.   Nellie liked nice things.   (*even though, -ing*)
     Nellie married Stanley.

6.   Ulysses wandered for ten years.   (*-ing*)
     Ulysses searched for his home island of Ithaca.   (*-ing*)

7.   Some TV stars shine too brightly.   (*because, -ing*)
     Some TV stars fade quickly when canceled.

8.   Joan always sides with the underdog.
     Joan does not like her cousin much.

9.   Winston has lived in Italy for thirty years.
     Winston loves spaghetti.

10. Middle Eastern cities controlled the caravan routes to Asia.
    Middle Eastern cities were ruined by the discovery of new sea routes.

11. Sharp cold freezes the sugar in the leaves.
    The leaves change from green to the colors of fall.

12. Helen prefers mysteries.
    Harold prefers golf.

13. Galileo perfected the telescope.
    Galileo made many important discoveries about the planets.

14. Romantic heroines are always beautiful and helpless.
    Romantic heroines are popular with romantic heroes.

15. Mr. Harrison owns several apartments in the city.
    Mr. Harrison is fairly wealthy.

16. Thelma fell lifeless beside the corpse.
    Thelma saw the serpent.
    The serpent had bitten Brent.

17. Leonard rose to the occasion.
    Leonard refused to pay the man.
    The man had "fixed" Leonard's roof.

COORDINATION/SUBORDINATION

Exercise D

Now put it all together.

MODEL:

The Nile waters the Valley of Egypt.

    The Nile flows out of the heart of Africa. (*-ing*) (*;*)

The river's flooding deposits soil along the banks.

    The depositing makes agriculture possible.   (*-ing*)

Flowing out of the heart of Africa, the Nile waters the Valley of Egypt; the river's flooding deposits soil along the banks, making agriculture possible.

Note: The signal for coordinating the sentences is given after the first set of sentences. Thus, in the model, the *;* appears to the right of the sentence "The Nile flows out of the heart of Africa" and appears *after* the whole first sentence, joining it to the second.

1. Evelyn lives in a big house.

    The house is near the woods.   (*so*)

   Evelyn is able to keep a kennel.

2. The swordsmith strikes the steel.

    He keeps time with a gong.   (*-ing*) (*;*)

    A priest sounds the gong.

    He chants to set his rhythm. (*-ing*)

3. Some small, feathered dinosaurs survived.

    The big dinosaurs died.   (*when*) (*;*)

    Scientists think these creatures were the ancestors of birds.

4. Brandon left Marilyn.

    Brandon was aware of her cheating.   (*because*) (*but*)

    Brandon went to Barbara.

    Barbara was worse than Marilyn was.   (who)

5. Linda wanted a clone.

    The clone resembles her completely.   (*-ing*) (*however*)

    Many thought one Linda was enough.

6. Hector writes his English papers.

    Everyone has gone to sleep.   (*after*) (*so*)

    Hector uses a typewriter.

    The typewriter has a silencer.

7. The Sahara was once a great savanna.

    The savanna was filled with antelope and ostriches.

    The Sahara stretches from the Red Sea to the Atlantic.
    (*-ing*) (*but*)

    The Sahara dried out slowly.

    The drying out trapped many animals.   (*-ing*)

8. Mr. Mikulski runs a bakery.

    The bakery is on Lombard Street.

    Mr. Mikulski has served his neighborhood.

    He has done this for forty years.

    His neighborhood is Polish and Lithuanian.

9. Harper stared along the barrel of his gun.

    Harper sighted Dandridge.

    Dandridge tried to scramble up the hillside.

    Harper fired.

    The shot hit home.

    The shot started a small avalanche.

10.   The Snow Queen put a splinter of ice in Hans's eye.
        The Queen wanted to keep him.
        The splinter made Hans completely unemotional.
Hans left home.
        Hans forgot his family and friends.

11.   Atlanta has become the finance capital of the South.
        Atlanta has grown rapidly since the Depression.
Atlanta's first big money came from Coca-Cola.
        Coca-Cola is the world's most popular drink.

12.   Big cities have special problems.
        These problems come from economic changes.
Few real solutions can be found.
        City planners are ingenious.
        The money just isn't there.

13.   *Hamlet* is one of the world's most popular plays.
        It is long.
        It is difficult to stage.
Certain theatergoers like Shakespeare's drama.
        These theatergoers enjoy a challenge.

14.   The Appalachians are among the oldest mountains on Earth.
        They run from New England to Alabama.
They are low, rounded, and tree-covered.
        They have been eroded by wind and water.

15.   The panda has an unusual thumb.
        The thumb has evolved from a bone in the wrist.
It is used to strip leaves from bamboo shoots.
        Bamboo is the panda's main food.

FREE EXERCISES

Exercise E

Use these sets of sentences to practice different ways of showing relation-ships among ideas. Be prepared to explain why you made the choices you did.

1.   The National Road runs from Maryland to Ohio.
      It helped open the Old Northwest to Americans.

This happened after the Revolution.

The Road goes through the Cumberland Gap.

2. Brainstorming is like "shaking out."

   Athletes "shake out" before competing.

   Writers brainstorm.

   They write down phrases about a topic.

3. The Red Shift is a natural phenomenon.

   It measures the speed of some stars.

   These stars are moving away from Earth.

4. Dr. Gould writes for *Natural History*.

   He is a professor at Harvard.

   He writes on biology.

   His writing is elegant.

5. Francis Scott Key wrote the National Anthem.

   He was imprisoned in Fort McHenry.

   The King's troops were shelling the fort.

   They wanted to capture Baltimore.

6. Immigrants came to this country.

   They came from every part of the world.

   They came to escape famine and unemployment.

   American farmlands and industry offered them hope.

7. There was no spring for centuries.

   This happened in Europe and much of Asia.

   This happened during the Ice Ages.

   No buds opened.

8. Dante wrote the *Divine Comedy*.

   He was in exile in Ravenna.

   He describes a journey through Hell to Heaven.

   The *Comedy* is the greatest poem of the Middle Ages.

9. Tides are caused by the moon's gravity.

   The gravity tugs at the oceans.

   The gravity makes a huge bulge of water.

10. *The Twentieth Century* was a train.

    It ran from New York to Los Angeles.

    It brought stars to Hollywood.

Many stars made their names on Broadway.

This happened back in the Thirties.

11. It is still possible to get lost in Toledo.

Toledo is the ancient capital of Spain.

It is one of the most romantic cities in the world.

Its streets are narrow.

Its streets are winding.

12. The first British colony in America was in Virginia.

It was on the James River.

It was named after King James.

It was destroyed by bad planning.

Sickness helped destroy it.

Indians helped destroy it.

13. An early civilization was built on the Indus River.

We know little about it.

It had an advanced plumbing system.

It employed a network of dams and canals.

14. Many science fiction writers lack political imagination.

They put monarchies in the future.

The monarchies are full of dukes, earls, and ladies.

The writers never explain how this situation could be.

15. The mustang ran swiftly.

He led the herd.

They galloped in terror.

The hunters pursued them.

Their hoofbeats echoed off the canyon walls.

16. The Museum is next to the Brandywine.

It is in an old mill.

It has paintings by the Wyeths.

17. Alice told Bill about Carol.

Carol had left George.

George was Bill's best friend.

Carol took all George's record albums.

18. Twenty inches of snow fell.

It fell in eight hours.

It blocked the city streets.

It brought all traffic to a halt.

19. Somewhere a dog was barking.

    A shadow crept along the wall.

    A shot rang out.

    A woman's voice screamed.

20. The evil sisters laughed at Cinderella.

    She was dressed in rags.

    She was miserable.

    They were going to a ball.

21. Venice is sinking.

    It is sliding into the lagoon.

    The lagoon once protected it from enemies.

    Venice is built on islands in a marsh.

22. The tumbleweed rolled.

    It ran into the steps of the old church.

    The church's windows had been shot out.

23. They were giant ants.

    Nuclear radiation made them monsters.

    They got into the drains under Los Angeles.

24. The woman played the guitar.

    She sang.

    Her mother beat on a bucket turned over her knee.

    They won the talent show.

25. The rain splattered on the window.

    The cat purred.

    The fire glowed.

    The writer ran a pencil down the paper.

    A poem appeared.

26. The figure walked in the rain.

    The car headlights lit the figure.

    The figure turned.

    The figure was Dracula.

27. Michael paints pictures.

    His pictures depict storybook characters.

He is 30 years old.

He lives near San Francisco.

28. Taos is a small town.

It is in the New Mexico mountains.

It is north of Santa Fe.

It is an artists' colony.

29. The Greeks thought salamanders were magical.

Salamanders are lizard-like reptiles.

The Greeks thought they lived in fire.

30. Paris stole Helen.

She was the wife of the king of Sparta.

The king followed them to Troy.

Troy was destroyed.

31. The pendulum swung closer.

It cut the air.

It whistled.

The victim listened.

The pendulum had a knife-edge.

The victim was terrified.

32. Money talks.

Talent demurs.

Genius just listens.

33. Danny owns a diner.

He serves cheeseburgers.

He serves soda.

He can't boil water.

34. Cows are sacred in India.

Cows provide labor.

Cows provide milk.

Families sometimes eat cows.

This happens in famines.

Afterwards, these families are poorer.

35. The basement is flooding.

The snow is melting.

Rain is falling.

The water is rising.

36. Christopher was an orphan.

He was nasty.

A snake ate him.

Everybody was relieved.

37. Julie loves Dennis.

She cooks for him.

She keeps house.

She works full-time.

Dennis never considers Julie's feelings.

Julie is leaving Dennis.

38. China has a 4,000-year history.

Historians study China's history.

They find that every year a disaster occurred.

The disasters were famines.

The disasters were plagues.

39. The batter swung hard.

He twisted his body hard.

He let go of the bat.

The bat almost hit the umpire.

The umpire called, "Strike three!"

40. Crocuses bloom.

They thrust above the snow.

They are yellow and blue.

The snow is half-melted.

This all happens in the spring.

PATTERN IMITATION

Exercise F

In the following exercise, you will create your own sentences, on any subject of your choosing, imitating the sentences given.

EXAMPLE:

When winter comes, the bears hibernating in their warm caves
sleep like contented children.

Imitation: When night comes, the taxis cruising the city streets scatter like frightened birds.

1. In the middle of this family party lay a cat with its paws tucked under its chest and its eyes closed in complete relaxation.
2. Spencer was a big spender, but when he died the funeral was cheap.
3. During the night there fell a fine snow, which covered the clearings and stretched out on the branches of the pines.
4. Immediately, the call went out over the radio, covering all channels, and sirens began to wail.
5. We valued our days for their activity and our nights for their freedom.
6. From time to time, she closes herself in her room, types furiously, and creates a children's story.
7. Vic wanted to get away from home not because he disliked his family, but because he longed for experience.
8. Jazz is loose and it is unplanned, but it is not shapeless and it is not senseless.
9. Children aren't easily impressed; special effort is required to catch their imaginations.
10. I hum a bit and croon some, but when I go for a high note, my voice cracks.
11. The great wars and tyrants get all the press coverage, but it is the millions of quiet lives that shape history.
12. Blanche was dreaming about a ferris wheel when the alarm went off, waking her.

PROFESSIONALS' SENTENCES

Exercise G

The following sentences are taken from the writings of professionals. The originals have been broken down so you can try reassembling them. Compare your results with the professionals' solutions found at the end of the chapter. What are the differences? Can you account for the choices you made and those the professionals made? If your solutions differ from those of the professionals, yours are not necessarily *wrong*. The professionals are responding to particular situations, and their choices are offered as possibilities, not *answers*.

1. A man sat.

    His hands were clenched.

    His hands rested on his knees.

His eyes were bent.

The bending was on the ground.

The sitting was amidst a scene.

The scene was sordid.

2. Sage brush is a very fair fuel.

Sage brush is a distinguished failure.

Its failure is as a vegetable.

3. There stood a geranium.

It stood on the window seat.

It was diseased with yellow blotches.

The blotches had overspread its leaves.

4. The songs told a tale.

The tale was of woe.

The tale was then altogether beyond comprehension.

The comprehension was mine.

The comprehension was feeble.

They were tones.

The tones were loud.

The tones were long.

The tones were deep.

They breathed the prayer of souls.

They breathed the complaint of souls.

The souls were boiling over with anguish.

The anguish was the bitterest.

5. Significant events are measured in years or less.

These events are in our personal lives.

Our lifetimes are measured in decades.

Our family genealogies are measured in centuries.

All of recorded history is measured in millenia.

6. A line of gray cars crawls along a track.

The track is invisible.

The line gives out a creak.

The creak is ghastly.

The line comes to rest.

All this happens occasionally.

7. I went to Walden.

My purpose was not to live cheaply there.

My purpose was not to live dearly there.

My purpose was to transact some business.

The business was private.

I wanted the fewest obstacles.

8. A city is stones.

   A city is people.

   It is not a heap of stones.

   It is not just a jostle of people.

9. The mass will never have any zeal.

   The mass is of mankind.

   The zeal is ardent.

   The zeal is for seeing.

   The seeing is of things.

   The things are as they are.

   Ideas will satisfy them.

   The ideas are very inadequate.

   This is always true.

10. I celebrate myself.

    I sing myself.

    You shall assume something.

    I assume something.

    These assumptions will be the same.

    Every atom belongs to me.   (for)

    It as good as belongs to you.

11. The summer soldier will shrink.

    The sunshine patriot will shrink.

    The shrinking will be from service.

    The service is of their country.

    This will happen in this crisis.

    He stands it *now*.   (but)

    He deserves love.

    He deserves thanks.

    These are of man.

    These are of woman.

12. Elizabeth was sitting by herself.

She was writing to Jane.

This happened the next morning.

Mrs. Collins was gone on business.

Maria was gone on business.

They were in the village.

Elizabeth was startled.

Her start was by a ring.

The ring was at the door.

The ring was a sign.

The sign was certain.

The sign was of a visitor.

Professionals' Choices

1. Amidst this sordid scene sat a man with his clenched hands resting on his knees, and his eyes bent on the ground.

   —Charlotte Bronte, *Jane Eyre*

2. Sage brush is a very fair fuel, but as a vegetable it is a distinguished failure.

   —Mark Twain, *Roughing It*

3. On the window seat there stood a geranium diseased with yellow blotches, which had overspread its leaves.

   —Nathaniel Hawthorne, "The Birthmark"

4. The songs told a tale of woe which was then altogether beyond my feeble comprehension; they were tones loud, long, and deep; they breathed the prayer and complaint of souls boiling over with the bitterest anguish.

   —Frederick Douglass, *Narrative of the Life of Frederick Douglass, an American Slave, Written by Himself*

5. Significant events in our personal lives are measured in years or less; our lifetimes in decades; our family genealogies in centuries; and all of recorded history in millenia.

   —Carl Sagan, *The Dragons of Eden*
   Copyright © 1977 by Carl Sagan. Reprinted by permission of Random House, Inc.

6. Occasionally a line of gray cars crawls along an invisible track, gives out a ghastly creak, and comes to rest.

   —F. Scott Fitzgerald, *The Great Gatsby*
   Charles Scribner's Sons, 1953.

7. My purpose in going to Walden Pond was not to live cheaply nor to live dearly there, but to transact some private business with the fewest obstacles.

    —Henry David Thoreau, *Walden*

8. A city is stones and a city is people; but it is not a heap of stones, and it is not just a jostle of people.

    —Jacob Bronowski, *The Ascent of Man*
    Little, Brown and Company, 1973.

9. The mass of mankind will never have any ardent zeal for seeing things as they are; very inadequate ideas will always satisfy them.

    —Matthew Arnold, *The Function of Criticism*

10. I celebrate myself, and sing myself,
    And what I assume you shall assume,
    For every atom belonging to me as good as belongs to you.

    —Walt Whitman, "Song of Myself"

11. The summer soldier and the sunshine patriot will, in this crisis, shrink from the service of their country, but he that stands it *now* deserves the love and thanks of man and woman.

    —Thomas Paine, *The American Crisis*

12. Elizabeth was sitting by herself the next morning and writing to Jane, while Mrs. Collins and Maria were gone on business into the village, when she was startled by a ring at the door, the certain sign of a visitor.

    —Jane Austen, *Pride and Prejudice*

Sentences
in the Context
of Paragraphs

6

So far, you have looked at various ways of putting ideas into a single sentence. However, most writing situations require more than one sentence. Therefore you should be aware of some of the special problems of writing a series of sentences on the same subject.

PRONOUNS

As soon as you write more than one sentence on the same subject, you will probably use pronouns. Instead of *"Pete Ross* is the best coach the Thunderbolts have ever had. *Pete Ross* demands a lot of hard work from *Pete Ross's* players," you would probably write: *"Pete Ross* is the best coach the Thunderbolts have ever had. *He* demands a lot of hard work from *his* players."

The pronoun *he* can substitute for the noun *Pete Ross.* The possessive pronoun *his* can substitute for the possessive *Pete Ross's.* A pronoun, in other words, is a word that can substitute for a noun.

As you may have noticed, pronouns can take more than one form depending on how they function in a sentence. The box below shows pronouns grouped according to sentence use.

Subject/ Subject Complement	Object Complement/ Object of Preposition	Possessive Modifier	Possessive Complement
I	me	my	mine
you	you	your	yours
he	him	his	his
she	her	her	hers
it	it	its	its
we	us	our	ours
they	them	their	theirs

When you replace a subject or a subject complement, you must use a subject pronoun; when you replace an object complement or the object of a preposition, you must use the object form; when you replace a possessive complement, you must use the possessive complement form. For example:

S   OC   OP
Henry gave the best years of his life to Sylvia.

S   OC OP
He gave   them to her.

S   OC
The Danish invaders settled the Danelaw in the ninth century.

S   OC
They   settled it in the ninth century.

S   SC
The champion was Stella.

S   SC
It was she.

S   PC
Those gloves are Bruce's.

S   PC
They are his.

Exercise A

Change the subjects, complements, and objects of prepositions in the following sentences to the appropriate pronouns.

EXAMPLE:

George sprained his ankle running for the bus.
He sprained it running for the bus.

1. Great-aunt Constanza left her entire estate to Lucille. *(she)*
2. The first president was George Farrara. *(him)*
3. So grown up were Alice and Peter that John and I hardly recognized Alice and Peter. *(He) (they) (them)*
4. Don cooked a wonderful ragout of wild rabbit and onions for Joanne. *(he)*
5. Bill made a pottery necklace for Colette. *(He) (her)*
6. The winner was Alma. *(her)*
7. Prince Charming kissed Sleeping Beauty. *(her)*
8. Swimming develops long, smooth muscles. *(It)*
9. The company gave a gold watch to George on his retirement. *(him)*
10. Students usually dislike snap quizzes. *(They) (them)*

Exercise B

Replace the possessives in the following sentences with appropriate possessive pronouns.

1. Debbie found Debbie's sweater, but Bill couldn't find Bill's. *(her) (his)*
2. We lowered your and Albert's boat carefully into the water. *(his)*
3. Members must pay members' dues by the 15th. *(their)*
4. Sue's daughters gave Sue's daughters' approval. *(her)*
5. I can't believe that the money is belonging to me. *(it?)*

When you are writing a series of sentences and you use pronouns, there are two special problems to look out for.

1. A pronoun must refer clearly and specifically to one noun.
2. A pronoun must agree with the noun that it refers to.

Pronoun Reference

Look at these sentences:

> My father and my brother visited my grandparents. *He* told *them* about *his* trip to Canada.

In the second sentence, it is not clear who *he* is or who *they* are. A pronoun doesn't convey any meaning unless your reader knows what the pronoun stands for. The second sentence above would have to be rewritten to make the pronouns clear:

> *Dad* told *them* about *his* trip to Canada.
> *or*
> *Jerry* told *them* about *his* trip to Canada.
> *or*
> *Grandpa* told *Dad and Jerry* about *his* trip to Canada.

Note the use of pronouns in these sentences:

> Sheila wants to be a doctor. She thinks *it* is a very lucrative pro-fession.

The pronoun *it* has no noun that it can refer back to. To correct this fault, you have two options: put in a noun that *it* will stand for (Sheila wants to enter the medical profession. She thinks *it* is very lucrative.) or eliminate the pronoun (Sheila wants to be a doctor. She thinks medicine is a very lucrative pro-fession.)

Exercise C

Rewrite the following pairs of sentences so that any pronouns refer clearly to one noun.

1. Monica wrapped the gifts for her sister. She had an eye for artistic ef-fects.

   _____

   _____

2. Both the boxer and the baseball player must train their muscles. It is im-portant to their success as athletes.

   _____

   _____

3. I have known Jessica much longer than I have known Mark. We met at a New Year's Eve party.

   _____

   _____

4. After the rain, the whole forest looked fresh. They spread their leaves to make a cool shade.

   _____

   _____

5. The nursing home looked bleak. They had not painted the halls in years.

_____

_____

6. Frances drove with Mary to the airport. She was going to Duluth.

_____

_____

7. Miguel sings beautifully. They seem to be a way of expressing his own private emotions.

_____

_____

8. Fred spoke to his dad. He told him he really needed a new suit.

_____

_____

9. Walt, for instance, missed seventeen questions. It was just too hard for most of them.

_____

_____

10. Looking at the ruined house, Karen and Doris began to cry. Finally, she patted her friend on the back and began to pick through the rubble for anything worth saving.

_____

_____

Pronoun Agreement

The second problem in using pronouns correctly involves choosing the right pronoun to match the noun being referred to. For instance, a feminine noun like *the girl,* as a subject, would require the feminine pronoun *she.* A plural noun like *the cars* would require the plural pronoun *they.*

When a noun does not have an obvious sex, like *student* or *driver* or *doctor,* writers have traditionally used the pronouns *he, him,* or *his.* Recently, however, some people have pointed out that using masculine pronouns gives writing a masculine bias. One solution is to use *his or her,* but this can become rather clumsy if it is overused. The National Council of Teachers of English recommends that when you are using singular nouns of indefinite sex, you alternate the pronoun sex to avoid the impression that every person is a *he.*

Here are some examples of sentences that have nouns of indefinite gender.

Each member of our club owes the balance of *his or her* dues by Monday.

When a criminal seeks rehabilitation, *she* should get it.

Every child must be allowed to grow into *his* own person.

Another way of handling the masculine/feminine pronoun problem is to make the noun plural and use a plural pronoun. For instance,

When criminals seek rehabilitation, *they* should get it.

Exercise D

Fill in each blank in the following sentences with an appropriate pronoun. Draw an arrow back to the noun that each pronoun agrees with.

EXAMPLE:

James and Kim wrote the script. ___*They*___ worked every weekend to finish ___*it.*___

1. The customer bought the shoes. However, ___*He*___ thought ___*they*___ were too expensive.

2. The ship waited three miles offshore. ___*Its*___ crew was afraid to enter the port.

3. The papers piled up for weeks. Chris was just too busy to read ___*them*___ .

4. The fox prowled around the chicken coop. ___*It*___ thought there might be a free meal there.

5. The recipe calls for six eggs. _____It_____ was handed down to me by _____my_____ grandmother.

6. The operator broke in on my conversation with Bob. _____I_____ complained to _____her_____ supervisor.

7. When the march was finished, the soldiers were exhausted. Because _____they_____ had covered an incredible 100 miles in just one day, the general commended _____them_____.

8. The patients continued to stare straight ahead as the doctor spoke to them. _____He_____ finally gave up _____his_____ efforts and noted in _____the_____ report that _____they_____ were unreachable.

9. The rules were written out clearly: You must turn in all _____the_____ money to the director. _____You_____ must wear _____a_____ uniform at all times while _____you_____ are on duty.

10. Her brothers and I packed the trunk yesterday. _____They_____ had trouble fitting all her clothes into one small box.

11. The rocker was delicately carved. _____It_____ had roses across the back, and _____its_____ arms were decorated with swans.

12. Phyllis is superb at word games. _____She_____ combines a photographic memory and keen intellect to put together _____her_____ winning performance.

13. You and Marcia have tied for the championship. _____You_____ will both be awarded medals for _____your_____ efforts.

14. The clerk was bent nearly double by the sack of mail. _____It_____ must have weighed more than _____he_____ did.

15.   Rabbi Stanley is a great favorite with the children. _____He_____ is a gentle

man and ___his___ pockets always seem to have an extra piece of

candy in ___them___ .

Exercise E

After each of the following sentences, add two more sentences which use the pronouns you have been practicing. Be sure that the pronouns refer clearly to one noun and that they agree with the nouns they refer to. Circle the pronouns you use.

1.   The *Enterprise* shot out into space with the incredible power of warp drive.

It was its last mission. After this mission it

would be destroyed

2.   We left two poinsettia plants in each ward of the hospital.

Both of them grew up quickly. At the end of the

month they almost looked like trees.

3.   Cars of the 1980's are much more efficient than the cars of the 1970's.

Because they are built with the high tech. of the 80's.

Plus they are more fuel efficient than the cars made in the

70's.

4.   Working at the candy counter turned out to be a boring job.

Plus it is not satisfying in financial terms. I

like candies but not to sell them, to eat them.

5. Sharon took only half an hour to hang the new light fixture.

(It) was a difficult job for her. Furthermore
it was the first time she tried to do (it.)

6. The baby cried when I couldn't find his yellow blanket.

When I found (it) he was already asleep. After I
put (it) on him, he began to cry again.

7. Running wildly away from the house, North suddenly tripped over a
body sprawled across the driveway.

(He) was scared a little bit but he tried not to show it.
It was the first time something like (that) happened to him.

8. Mr. Falston and I have been in charge of the paint department for 20
years.

(We)'re very good friends (We) spent almost every day
together.

9. Your grocer is having a special this month on avocados.

He says that (they) are delicious. If I were you,
I wouldn't believe (him)

10. Louise and Tom had everyone in the family planting tulip bulbs so the yard would look nice for the reception.

(They) worked for hours to finish planting. But wha (they) began to grow, they were very happy of the result.

CONSISTENCY

When you begin to write a series of sentences, you have to be careful to be consistent from one sentence to the next in verb tense and in point of view.

Consistency in Verb Tense

If you were telling a story about something that happened to you in the past, you would confuse your reader if you jumped around in time like this:

I have never forgotten my first plane ride. I (was) four years old, and I (am) terrified of the noise of the engines. My mother (drags) me down the aisle and (strapped) me into my seat. Even the stewardess's offer of a piece of gum (does) not calm me down. I (was) convinced that the monster (will eat) me.

Written this way, the story moves from the past to the present to the future without any logical reason. All these actions happened in the same time period, but the verb tenses don't show that. It would be correct to tell this story in the past tense since it happened in the past, but you could also tell it in the present tense as if you were reliving the events as you were describing them. You have to be sure, though, that you tell the story consistently in the present or the past tense. Both of the versions shown below use verb tenses consistently.

a. *Present Tense*

I (am) four years old, and I (am) terrified of the noise of the engines. My mother (drags) me down the aisle and (straps) me into my seat. Even the stewardess's offer of a piece of gum (does) not calm me down. I (am) convinced that the monster (is) going to eat me.

b. *Past Tense*

I (was) four years old, and I (was) terrified of the noise of the engines. My mother (dragged) me down the aisle and (strapped) me into my seat. Even the stewardess's offer of a piece of gum (did) not calm me down. I (was) convinced that the monster (was) going to eat me.

Generally, if you start a series of sentences using one verb tense, you should stay with that verb tense through the whole series. The only time it's all right to change tenses is when the time reference really changes. For instance:

New Year's Eve ⬚is⬚ traditionally a big party night. Tonight ⬚will be⬚ no exception. Nearly every club in the city ⬚has planned⬚ some special entertainment for New Year's revelers.

The first sentence uses the present tense to show that New Year's Eve is always "a big party night." The second sentence refers to time that has not yet arrived—tonight. The third sentence uses verb tense to show that the planning began in the past and continues into the present.

If the article above went on to list the plans of the various clubs, it would use the future tense since all the action would be happening at some later time. For example:

At the Cross Street Club, the music of the Freemen ⬚will be featured⬚. The party here ⬚will last⬚ from 9 P.M. to 5 A.M. The Sandlot, on Western Avenue, ⬚will provide⬚ jazz by the Ravens. The $15 cover charge ⬚will entitle⬚ patrons to a cold buffet. All drinks ⬚will be⬚ $1.50 at the cash bar.

Exercise F

Rewrite the following sentences to make the time shown in the verbs consistent.

1. By the time Willa Cather becomes editor of *McClure's Magazine* in New York City, she had lived in Virginia, Nebraska, and Pennsylvania. She will be strongly influenced by her years in Pittsburgh.

_____

_____

_____

2. Many teachers say that there are four kinds of writing. One kind was narration; another will be description; a third type is exposition, and last there was argument.

_____

_____

_____

3. I get lonely when I am tired, when I have spent too much time with strangers, or when my emotions were churned up.
    are

    _____

    _____

    _____

4. One hundred and fifty years ago, a man sometimes kills a buffalo and used *killed* only a small part of it, throwing the rest away. Today, when not many buffalo are left, people will be horrified at such wasteful behavior.

    _____

    _____

    _____

5. At first, the princess refused to marry the handsome prince because he *was wearing* wears polka-dot ties. Later, however, she realizes that his clothes didn't matter as long as he was a kind person.

    _____

    _____

    _____

Exercise G

Show the time connections in the following sentences by a consistent use of verbs. If you use more than one tense, make sure there is a logical reason for doing so.

1. Holography, a form of photography, ___*is a*___ photographic film

    and laser light to create three-dimensional images. It ___*was*___ de-veloped in the 1960's by two scientists from the University of Michigan.

2. Embassy guards ___*are*___ an elite branch of the Marine Corps. The

    guards, ___*trained*___ at a special school in Virginia where they

    ___*learn*___ everything from the social graces to the latest alarm sys-tems.

3. Racing across the Russian tundra, hunters ___look___ for wolf tracks
in the snow. When they ___found___ their prey, they ___?___ in
for the kill. Sometimes they ___use___ helicopters which
___?___ down on the pack.

4. In her Nobel Prize acceptance speech, Mother Teresa ___talk ?___ on
poverty. In the Western world, she ___said___, there ___was___ a
hunger for love which ___was___ far greater than the hunger for rice.

5. Scripture scholars ___say___ that each Gospel writer ___gives___
us a slightly different portrait of Christ. Each evangelist ___have use ?___ a
somewhat different purpose in writing.

6. Rodgers' and Hammerstein's *Oklahoma* ___is___ the American musical. The 1943 show ___had ?___ plot, music, and dance to produce a
hardy new breed, a musical with well-rounded characters and some
tough social problems. *Oklahoma* ___was___ the beginning of the
truly *American* musical theater.

7. College athletic programs ___are___ very vulnerable to corruption.
High school transcripts ___are___ altered to qualify promising athletes for college. Some players ___receive___ credit for courses they
___don't take___. Other athletes ___receive___ money or cars to stay at
certain schools and play football or basketball.

8. They ___wear___ black robes and lace scarves. They ___earn___
$66,500 tax-free, every year. They ___are___ the ideal of peace
through world law. They ___are___ the fifteen judges of the International Court of Justice.

9. Poinsettias ___were brought___ to America by Joel Poinsett, James Madison's
confidential agent to Mexico. When Poinsett ___saw___ Mexican

gardens filled with the wonderful plant, he ___took___ cuttings home for his garden in Charleston, South Carolina.

10. By the year 2080, if computer technology ___develops___ at its present

pace, a single computer ___will have___ a memory equal to 16,000 human

memories. In the next hundred years or so, computers ___play with___ our

children, ___repair___ our transit systems, and ___control___ our health.

Consistency in Point of View

In writing a series of sentences, you have to be consistent about the point of view you use. There are three points of view—the first person, the second person, and the third person.

With the first-person point of view, you focus the reader's attention on yourself, the speaker, by using the first person pronouns: *I, me, mine, my, we, us, ours, our.* The paragraph below, for example, is written from a *first-person point of view.*

> *My* garden gives *me* many hours of enjoyment, even before *I* set foot in it. Early in the winter, *I* gather together *my* new seed catalogs and read about this year's developments in vegetables and flowers. Then *I* list the varieties *I* think *I'd* like to plant, usually two or three new ones each year plus a lot of *my* old favorites. *I* really enjoy planning *my* garden every winter.

With the second-person point of view, you focus attention on the audience, the person or persons being spoken to, by using the pronouns *you, your,* and *yours.* This paragraph, for example, is written from the *second-person point of view.*

> *You* can begin to enjoy *your* garden even before *you* start to plant it. Gather up *your* seed catalogs early in the winter and read about the new vegetables and flowers developed this year. Then pick out a few that *you'd* like to try along with *your* old favorites. *You* can then begin to anticipate *your* delicious rewards while snow is still on the ground.

With the third-person point of view, you focus attention on the subject you are discussing by using nouns that refer to the subject, as well as the third-person pronouns: *he, she, it, him, her, his, hers, its, they, them, their, theirs.* The paragraph below, for example, is written from a *third-person point of view.*

> An enthusiastic *gardener* enjoys *his* garden even before the planting season begins. *He* or *she* gathers up seed catalogs early in the winter to read about the latest in vegetables and flowers. Experienced *gardeners*

usually try one or two new varieties each year along with *their* old favorites. For many *gardeners,* planning is as much fun as planting.

Which point of view you choose depends largely on the kind of relationship you want to have with your audience. The important thing is that you have to stick with a point of view once you have chosen it. Otherwise, your audience will become uncomfortable with your shifting perspective.

Exercise H

Rewrite the following paragraphs so that each one maintains a consistent point of view.

1.   By following a few simple suggestions, almost anyone can improve his or her photography. First of all, know what your camera is capable of. Shoot a few practice rolls before you try to capture a vacation or a sister's wedding on film. I would also recommend taking more close-up pictures. I always come as close as I can to my subject without eliminating any important part of the background. Finally, a good photographer tries to compose each picture so that there is a natural frame. He also tries for unposed shots of people doing things rather than stilted, formal poses. These ideas can make the difference between an "Oh!" and an "Uhh . . ." when you show off your pictures.

2.   The alligator, Florida's leading reptilian citizen and the animal you are probably most interested in seeing, is not the same as the crocodile. You can find the alligator all along the Atlantic coastal plain, whereas the crocodile is found only in a limited section of southern Florida. Each species generally prefers a different territory: 'gators inland in fresh water and crocs along the coast or just offshore. Even their physical characteristics mark the two animals as different. Alligators are blackish with broad, shovel-shaped snouts as opposed to the greenish crocodile with its narrow, tapering snout. Now, I don't think you should have any trouble telling the difference between an alligator and a crocodile.

SENTENCE PATTERNS

In earlier chapters, you saw that most sentences are built around a few basic patterns:

s — v
Turner won.

s — v (passive)
The contest is finished.

s — v — oc
They awarded the prize.

s — lv — sc
Turner was excited.

You have also practiced a number of ways of varying these basic patterns through coordination and subordination techniques.

When you begin to write a series of sentences, you need to think about the patterns of the sentences you are using so that you can vary a pattern or repeat a certain pattern in order to make your writing more interesting or to call attention to some point.

Variation

Look at the patterns of sentences in this paragraph:

>   s   v   oc   s
> West Point owes its distinctive character to Sylvanus Thayer. He
>   v   oc   s   v
> transformed the school. The new military academy started as a shaky
>   s   v   oc   s
> enterprise. Thayer made it supreme in science and engineering. Thayer
>   v   oc   s   lv   sc
> studied French military schools. Thayer became the superintendent of
>   s   v   oc
> West Point in 1817. Thayer imbued West Point with the best of the military tradition.

Every sentence here begins with the subject. Every sentence is short. Every sentence uses the same pattern: s–v–c. But there doesn't seem to be any particular reason for so much repetition of one pattern. What the paragraph on Thayer needs is more variation in its sentence structure.

Here is one way the paragraph could be written so that the sentence patterns are more interesting.

>   s   v   oc
> West Point owes its distinctive character to Sylvanus Thayer.
>   INTRODUCTION   s   v   oc
> *After studying French military schools,* Thayer transformed, the academy.
>   s   INTERRUPTION   v
> Thayer, *who became superintendent in 1817,* made the shaky new
>   oc
> military enterprise supreme in the fields of science and engineering.
> INTRODUCTION s   v   oc
> Overall, Thayer imbued West Point with the best of the military tradition.

Here the sentence patterns are varied by introductory and interrupting word groups. There is also a greater variety in the lengths of the sentences.

Besides making your writing generally more interesting, variation can also be used to call attention to one point. When there are several sentences in a row that use the same pattern, one different sentence will stand out to the reader. For example, a short sentence following several long sentences will get more emphasis in a reader's mind.

Look at the way this paragraph uses sentence patterns:

> The average cadet has scored better on the S.A.T. than the average American college freshman. (15) More significantly, most cadets have been "A" students in high school, with one out of ten having been class valedictorian or salutatorian. (22) In one recent year, over 200 of the plebes had been Eagle Scouts. (13) Cadets are, in short, over-achievers. (5)

The last sentence in this paragraph should get the reader's full attention because its pattern is significantly different from the sentences that came before it.

Repetition

It is also possible to use pattern repetition to emphasize a point, if the point is that two ideas are quite similar or quite different. For instance, look at the way repetition is used here:

> My two uncles are completely different in temperament. *While Bob is* thoughtful and slow to show emotion, *Randy tends* to speak his feelings before he has thought about them. *While Bob is* home-loving and has never been farther than 50 miles from home, *Randy* is a wanderer who has visited 40 states and six foreign countries. Most telling of all, *while Bob has* few friends and keeps mainly to himself, *Randy is* always accompanied by half a dozen of the friends he has acquired in his travels. How can twin brothers be so different?

(Notice how variation is used in the last sentence. A question stands out from all the direct statements.)

Exercise I

Combine each of the following sets of sentences to produce a more effective paragraph. Use pronouns where necessary, but be sure they are used correctly. Make sure the verb tenses and points of view stay consistent. Use repetition and variation of sentence patterns.

1. **The Cyclone State**

Kansas has long been known as the "Cyclone State."
This distinction is sometimes credited to the Irving tornado.
I believe this.
This tornado was exceptionally violent.
This tornado occurred nearly a century ago.
Others credit the distinction to authorities.
The authorities were authorities on tornadoes.
These authorities were the early ones.

The authorities lived in Kansas.
The authorities worked in Kansas.
Or this name is given because of Dorothy.
Dorothy's flight to Oz began in Kansas.
You remember Dorothy.
Or this name is given because twisters are photogenic.
The photogenic quality is exceptional.
The twisters are in Kansas.
Kansas has an open sweep of prairie.

2.   **Honeymoons**

The industry began in 1945.
The industry is for honeymoons.
The industry is mighty.
The industry is in the Poconos.

Rudolf van Hoevenberg opened a resort.
The resort was specifically for honeymooners.
The hideaway was called The Farm on the Hill.

You had to submit a statement.
The statement was informal.
The statement was about yourself.
The statement included a description.
The description was of the future plans.
The plans were of the couple.

The couple was evaluated.
You were found easy to get along with.
The couple would get a small cottage.
Each couple was surrounded.
The surrounding was by other couples.
The other couples shared the anxiety.
The anxiety was of the honeymooners.

The resort reduced the possibility for surprise.
The resort reduced the possibility for error.
The possibilities are on the wedding trip.

The honeymooners craved this security.
A new industry was born.

3.   **Marjoram**

Marjoram came from western Asia.
Marjoram came from the Mediterranean.
The scent of marjoram has always been highly prized.
In some countries marjoram is the symbol of honor.

Marjoram is the symbol of happiness.
I have discovered this.
The Greeks used marjoram.
The Romans used marjoram.
Marjoram was used to create crowns.
The crowns were worn by couples.
The couples were young.
The couples were happy.
Marjoram was planted on graves.
The planting was to delight the souls.
The souls belonged to your loved ones.
In England marjoram was a charm.
In Germany marjoram was a charm.
You used the charm against witchcraft.
The people believed.
The belief was that witches could not endure the fragrance.
The fragrance belonged to the happy herb.
Marjoram is my favorite herb.

4.   **Clean-Up**

Our troop had a service project.
Eighteen scouts took part.
The project was the first one of the year.
The project is a clean-up.
The clean-up was at Emerson Park.
We arrived at 9 A.M. on Saturday.
We brought rakes, shovels, and wheelbarrows.
We picked up trash.
There were 23 bags of trash.
We raked the grass.
We weeded the flower beds.
We swept the paths.
We painted the benches.
You really get tired after a few hours of cleaning.
We will relax with a cookout.
The cookout comes after the morning's work.
Our troop received an award.
The award is from the mayor.
The award was for this clean-up project.

EDITING PRACTICE

Rewrite the following paragraphs to correct any sentence fragments, agreement problems, mistakes in punctuation, or inconsistencies in point of view or verb tense, which may distract the reader.

1.   You as parents can help your child develop a sense of responsibility. First of all let your child make mistakes. If your son spends his whole allowance on a poorly designed toy that breaks the first time he play with it. He learned to think more carefully about his purchases. You should also let children see the direct consequences of her actions. A daughter who can't bring her dirty jeans shirts socks and underwear to the laundry can do without clean clothes. Finally I encourage volunteer activities. Community involvement such as Trick or Treat for UNICEF or reading to patients at a nursing home show young people how your actions affect others. Your children needs your loving help to take control of their own actions and by helping them toward responsibility we help them find themselves.

2.   Football is a descendant of soccer. In 1823 at Rugby, England, one of the students who was taking part in a soccer match becomes disgusted with his lack of success in kicking the ball. So he decided to pick it up and run with them. At that time it was a violation of the rules. However, the advantages of carrying the ball led to approval of this kind of play at Rugby in 1841. This new approach gain wider acceptance. And resulted in two types of football. The kind that does not permit the use of the hands——soccer——and the type where you can use your hands——Rugby football. Today's popular autumn contest are thus descended from the "hands-on" version of soccer.

WRITING PRACTICE

Choose the thing you think you do best and explain to someone else how to do it. Choose something limited enough to be explained in ten sentences or so. Be sure you don't leave out any important steps. Some possible topics are:

1.   The best way to lay sod
2.   The best way to pitch a baseball
3.   The best way to begin a stamp collection
4.   The best way to balance a checkbook
5.   The best way to entertain children on a rainy day
6.   The best way to plan a party
7.   The best way to choose a car

When you have finished writing, check your sentences for any errors in sentence construction or punctuation that might prevent your reader from understanding your ideas.

COMPOSING
PARAGRAPHS

A sentence, clear and well-constructed, can be a very useful tool for communicating ideas. Through the use of modification (adjectives, adverbs, and explaining nouns), coordination, and subordination, all of which are presented in the first part of this book, you can express some fairly complicated ideas and also show a precise relationship between one idea and another within the same sentence.

However, sentences do have limits. If you try to push too much information into one sentence, you can easily confuse or distract your readers. If you try to relate too many ideas in one sentence, your readers may not be able to figure out which idea you really want them to pay the most attention to. So the paragraph, a series of sentences carefully developing one idea, can be even more useful than a single sentence for sharing your idea with someone else.

This section of the book will present a basic model for paragraphing and then show you some methods for generating and organizing the ideas that go into paragraphs. You will also be able to practice shaping paragraphs from series of sentences.

Basic Structure
of a Paragraph

7

One way of thinking about a paragraph is as an extension of the sentence. In a sentence, there is one subject–verb unit which serves as the focus, and all the other ideas are arranged around it. In a paragraph, one sentence gives the focus, and all the other sentences are arranged to explain, expand, and generally clarify that idea.

Although there are many possible forms for a paragraph, in this book you will concentrate on one basic pattern for paragraph construction: a *topic sentence*, which focuses the main idea; *support*, an arrangement of subordinate ideas; and a *conclusion*, which coordinates with the topic sentence by restating the focus.

Here is a typical paragraph that uses the pattern of a topic sentence, followed by supporting detail, followed by a concluding sentence.

Topic Sentence (main idea)
According to our study, then, the change from 24-hour to 8-hour shifts for firefighters would not benefit the city.

Support (subordinate details)
At the least, three shifts each day instead of one are more difficult to schedule for overtime salaries. In addition, to keep all stations fully staffed under the new system, the city would have to hire and train an additional 200 men and women, at a cost which would be prohibitive. Equally undesirable alternatives for implementing the change would be the closing of some stations, staffing stations below minimum standards, or floating crews from station to station, any of which would make the city's fire protection service less efficient.

Conclusion
(coordi-
nates
with T.S.)

In the light of these drawbacks, therefore, the Commission on Fire Protection recommends that the city retain the present system of 24-hour shifts for firefighters.

In this paragraph, which is being used to summarize a longer report, the focus idea is stated in the topic sentence. Then three reasons, which are subordinate to the topic sentence, are given to show why the focus idea is valid. Finally, the conclusion, coordinating with the topic sentence, restates the main point in slightly different words.

When you have mastered this form, you may wish to develop other paragraph structures, as many professional writers do. In the meantime, though, this basic three-part paragraph can be used for many different kinds of writing, from letters to term papers to professional reports.

TOPIC SENTENCE

The topic sentence in a paragraph has two main purposes: to identify the subject of the paragraph and to show the focus you are going to use in discussing that subject. Look at the topic sentence in the sample paragraph above. What is the subject of the paragraph, according to the topic sentence? *The change from 24-hour to 8-hour shifts for firefighters.* That subject could be written about from a number of different angles: costs, advantages, comparison to other cities. But, in a paragraph, you really can't do justice to more than one of these. You have to choose one aspect to focus on. What focus does this sentence give for the subject? *Would not benefit the city.* In other words, the topic sentence tells the reader right away what to expect from this paragraph. It will present the ways in which a particular change would not be beneficial.

> SUBJECT + FOCUS =
>
> TOPIC SENTENCE

Exercise A

Here are some additional examples of topic sentences. Pick out the subject and the focus of each one.

1. Compared to nuclear energy research, solar energy research is underfunded.

2. Sacajawea, the guide for Lewis and Clark's expedition, led a dramatic life.

3. The consequences of the Six Day War in 1967 were largely unexpected.

4. Although many people play some bridge, it is one of the most difficult card games to master.

5. Living on a farm can be just as stressful as living in a large city.

6. According to recent research, loneliness may cause us to die sooner from cancer, heart attacks, and other diseases.

7. Fictional detectives are frequently presented as smarter than ordinary human beings.

8. The use of coupons can save shoppers 40 percent of their weekly food bills.

9. If it is done on a regular schedule, home maintenance is simple.

10. In a marketing-oriented company, customer needs determine company policy.

11. Today's amateur athletes tend to be talented in more than one sport.

12. Because it is frequently used for movie settings, San Francisco has a number of different images as a city, depending on the film one views.

You should have observed some characteristics of topic sentences as you were doing this exercise.

a. A topic sentence must be a complete sentence, not a fragment.

b. A topic sentence is usually a direct statement, not a question.

c. The subject of the topic sentence is usually the subject idea of the paragraph.

d. The verb and complement of the topic sentence usually show the focus of the paragraph.

e. The focus part of the topic sentence usually presents a judgment or attitude about the subject.

f. A subordinate word group is sometimes used in the topic sentence to define the focus still further.

Exercise B

Keeping these characteristics in mind, try combining the following sets of sentences into good topic sentences. Identify the subject and the focus of each sentence. (If you have trouble doing this combining, you might want to review Chapter 4 on subordination.) Compare your topic sentences to those of your classmates and discuss any differences in wording or arrangement that you and your teacher notice. Does one version of the sentence seem better to you than another? Can you explain why?

EXAMPLE:

Dentists go into debt.

The dentists are opening new practices.

The going into debt almost always happens.

SUBJECT   FOCUS
Dentists who open new practices almost always *go into debt.*

or

SUBJECT   SUBJECT
Opening a new practice almost always causes a *dentist* to go

FOCUS
into debt.

or

SHARPER FOCUS   SUBJECT
When she opens a new practice, a dentist almost always *goes*

FOCUS
into debt.

1. Teaching is a job.

   The teaching is in kindergarten.

   The job demands great patience.

   Teaching in a kindergarten is a job which demands great patience

2. A bride should begin.

   Planning should be begun.

   The bride wants a perfect wedding.

   The planning should be in advance.

   The advance should be at least six months.

   A bride wanting a perfect wedding, must begin to plan it at least six months in advance.

3. Arson is a crime.

   It is detected.

The detection is difficult.
The difficulty occurs often.

> Arson is a crime which difficulty often occurs in
> _f_
> its detection.
>   s

4. The desire flows.
   The desire is to explore.
   The exploration is of the stars.
   The flowing is out of a need.
   The need is to evolve.
   The need is felt by man.

> The desire flies to explore the stars flows
> out of a man need to evolve

5. Insects may be our source.
   The source is for protein.
   This may happen in the future.

> In the future, the insects may be our source
>   s   f
> for protein

6. The attempt is not new.
   The attempt is to identify the elements.
   The elements are of an education.
   The education is a good one.

> The attempt to identify the elements of a good
>   s
> education is not new.
>   f

7. I stood before the audience.
   The audience was hostile.
   I was overwhelmed.
   The overwhelming was by feelings.
   The feelings were of despair.

> I stood before the hostile audience and was overwhelmed
>   s
> by the feelings of despair.
>   f

8. A college wants support.

   The support is continuing.

   A college must maintain relations.

   The relations are with its alumni.

   The relations are good.

   A college must maintain good relations with its alumni
   and need continuous support.

9. Gasoline is expensive.

   Cars sell.

   The cars are small.

   The selling is brisk.

   As gasoline is expensive, sale of small cars is
   brisk.

10. Any reconstruction must begin with a survey.

    The reconstruction is of a site.

    The site is historical.

    The survey is archeological.

    The reconstruction is to be accurate.

    Any accurate reconstruction of a historical site, must
    begin with an archeological survey.

11. Teachers strive.

    They are effective.

    They make themselves unnecessary.

    Teachers are effective in making themselves
    unnecessary

12. Schools help students.

    The schools are open-space.

    The teachers are trained.

The training is appropriate.

The teachers are in such schools.

_____

_____

Limiting the Subject and Focus

Each of the topic sentences below contains some sort of a subject and a focus, but one of each pair presents these two basic parts more clearly than the other. Which one in each pair gives the reader a clearer idea of what to expect in the paragraph that will follow?

1. A. I like music.
    B. A folk song called "Simple Things" saved my job for me one summer when I was sixteen.
2. A. My hometown is nice.
    B. Frenchman's Point is the ideal place for a young family.
3. A. My hometown was nice.
    B. Twenty years ago, Frenchman's Point was an inexpensive place to live.
4. A. That book is interesting.
    B. Richard Lattimore's translation of the Gospels is easier to read than the Knox version.
5. A. Democrats are better than Republicans.
    B. The Democrats on the County Council this year have shown more interest in the elderly than the Republicans on the Council.

In each case, you should have noticed that the second topic sentence gives the reader a more precise statement of the subject and the focus than the first topic sentence. Words like _nice, interesting,_ and _better_ don't work very well to focus an idea because they suggest so many different meanings that a reader isn't really sure what to focus on. Similarly, a broad subject like _music_ or _Democrats_ doesn't help your reader understand which particular aspect of that topic you want to tell her about.

Exercise C

Rewrite the word groups below so that each one is a topic sentence with a clearly limited subject and a well-defined focus.

1. Changing a tire.

   _____

   _____

2. He is a nice man.

   _____

   _____

3. Boys are better than girls.

   _____

   _____

4. A time when I was embarrassed.

   _____

   _____

5. The room is beautiful.

   _____

   _____

6. Why should you vote for Jackson Brown?

   _____

   _____

7. Baseball is great.

   _____

   _____

8. Science is very interesting.

   _____

   _____

9. College is different from high school.

     _____

     _____

10. She looks good.

     _____

     _____

11. I don't like sports.

     _____

     _____

12. The show was pretty good.

     _____

     _____

13. That class was terrible.

     _____

     _____

14. The best way to meet people.

     _____

     _____

15. Do you have a future with the Army?

     _____

     _____

SUPPORT

The second important part of a paragraph is the support. You write a paragraph so that someone else can understand and perhaps accept your idea. Therefore, you have to do more than just present a general statement of your idea. You have to move to a more specific level of reasons, explanations, or examples that will clarify the idea for your reader.

For example, the paragraph on firefighting shown earlier in the chapter doesn't just keep making coordinate statements:

> This change would not benefit the city.
> This change would not be good for the city.
> This change has many disadvantages.

Instead, it moves from a general statement that a change in shifts would not be beneficial to specific, subordinate details of scheduling, costs, and efficiency.

Just as subordinate parts of a sentence help to clarify and define the base sentence, so does the support part of a paragraph help to clarify and explain the topic.

Look at the paragraphs below. Which one more effectively supports the topic sentence?

Topic Sentence: Although many people think of dinosaurs as cold-blooded swamp creatures, they were really, according to some scientists, warm-blooded land animals.

A. Dinosaurs, these scientists explain, would not have successfully ruled the earth for 130 million years if they could not generate heat from within their own bodies. Unlike cold-blooded lizards, who can't function without the sun's heat, dinosaurs had to be able to defend themselves and kill their prey even if the sun weren't shining. Another thing that paleontologists (PÁY-LEE-ON-TÓL-OGISTS: people who study very old forms of life) point out is that dinosaurs did not have the kind of protection needed by cold-blooded animals.

B. For one thing, paleontologists say, it makes sense logically that they should be warm-blooded. They look like lizards, but they were not like lizards. Lizards wouldn't have been able to kill mammals because they get too cold. Finally, their size wouldn't help them. Being big isn't that much of an advantage. Dinosaurs did have to compete with other animals, and being big might slow them down. So they must have had some advantage. And since size was no good, it must have been their warm blood. Otherwise it would have been hard to compete.

While turtles, for example, have a protective shell, and snakes can hide in their holes, dinosaurs couldn't escape their enemies like that. Therefore, these scientists say, the dinosaurs must have had the speed and strength of being warm-blooded as their protection. Even giant size would not have enabled the dinosaurs to compete with the more efficient warm-blooded mammal unless the dinosaurs too were warm-blooded.

Conclusion: All in all, these paleontologists conclude, it is highly likely that dinosaurs were not just giant lizards, but were, instead, warm-blooded creatures capable of protecting themselves very effectively from mammal predators.

What differences do you see in the kind of support provided in the two paragraphs above?

1. Paragraph A provides more reasons than B. A makes three points; B makes only two, one of which is repeated several times.
2. Paragraph A gives more detailed information than B. For instance, A explains more clearly the difference between warm-blooded and cold-blooded creatures; A explains the meaning of "paleontologists"; A uses specific references to turtles and snakes to illustrate a point.

Paragraph A, then, shows two important qualities of support: there should be enough support, without padding, to make your point convincingly (the more difficult the point, the more support is needed), and it should be as specific and as factual as possible. A few vague generalizations will not make your ideas clear to an audience.

Topic sentences, as you have seen, tend to present attitudes or opinions, about which people may disagree. Support, on the other hand, tends to be more factual. The facts used for support may be details observable by your senses, such as what a person looks like or sounds like. Or you may use the events of your own life and those of your family and friends as facts to support some idea. Or you may use the written experiences of others as facts for support. (Historical fact and the attitudes of experts in various fields, for instance, are frequently presented in books and magazines, which are good sources of factual support.)

Exercise D

Decide which sentences in the following list would be appropriate statements of factual support. Be prepared to explain your choices.

1. The Nile begins at Lake Victoria in central Africa.
— 2. Great enterprises often have obscure beginnings.
3. Linda gets to work early every morning.
4. Linda is arriving at Penn Station at 8:04 Thursday evening.
5. More than one million people lined the streets of Paris for Victor Hugo's funeral.
6. Joe made only 74 on the grammar test.
— 7. You can fool some of the people all of the time.
— 8. Absolute power corrupts absolutely.
— 9. Fresh-water fishing is a relaxing recreation for many people.
10. Last summer in Quebec, I caught a rainbow trout 13 inches long.
11. This pair of designer jeans cost Wade $25.
12. The Baltimore–Washington area is the fourth largest marketing region in the United States.
— 13. Every day, I seem to make a serious mistake about money.
14. The record holder stayed ten days in a cage with 27 poisonous snakes.
15. Michelangelo's dome on St. Peter's is 132 meters high.

Exercise E

Combine each of the following sets of sentences into one sentence. Then decide whether that sentence would be better as a topic sentence for a paragraph or as a supporting sentence and circle your choice.

T.S.   1. Movements can convey.
Support   Attitudes can be conveyed.
               The movements are of the body.
               Expressions can convey.
               The expressions are facial.
               The attitudes are of a speaker.
               The attitudes are real.

_____

_____

T.S.   2. Personnel make the mistake.
Support   The personnel are professional.
               The personnel are in hospitals.

The mistake is of overspecializing.
This happens in too many cases.

_____

_____

T.S.   3.   Millions of butterflies are sold.
Support   The selling is to museums.
                 The selling is to scientists.
                 The selling is to collectors.
                 The collectors are private.
                 This takes place every year.

_____

_____

T.S.   4.   The movies implied something.
Support   Money was poison.
                 Only folks knew the way.
                 The folks were regular.
                 The way was to have fun.
                 This happened during the Depression.

_____

_____

T.S.   5.   The rodeo has emerged.
Support   The emergence is as a way of life.
                 The way is national.
                 The way is major.
                 This has happened in the last two decades.

_____

_____

T.S.   6.   Rodeos drew 16.5 million customers.
Support   The customers were paying.
                 Rodeos distributed $7.2 million.

This money was for prizes.

The distribution took place last year.

_____

_____

T.S.	7.	A mound covered.
Support		The mound was of magazines.

The magazine was Skateboarder.

The magazines were old.

The bunk was the top one.

The bunk was covered.

_____

_____

T.S.	8.	George is a hard worker.
Support		I think about George.

My thought is that he does not have ability.

The ability is administrative.

The ability is for the job.

The job is of the foreman.

_____

_____

T.S.	9.	This method should save.
Support		The method is for packaging.

The packaging is of candy.

The method is new.

The savings will be over $300,000.

The savings will be for the company.

The material is cheaper.

The material is for packaging.

_____

_____

T.S.	10.	Rockaway Candy Co. will make a profit.
Support		This will take place next year.

The packaging is successful.

The packaging is new.

_____

_____

Exercise F

For each topic sentence below, try to supply three factual details that could be used to support it.

EXAMPLE:

Science fiction seems to be making a comeback on TV.

A.   *Battlestar Galactica*

B.   *Space 1999*

C.   *The Incredible Hulk*

1.   Our state capital has many historic buildings.

A.   _____

B.   _____

C.   _____

2.   Gardening is a healthy activity.

A.   _____

B.   _____

C.   _____

3.   More and more college sports are opening up to women.

A.   _____

B.   _____

C.   _____

4. Three distinct types of students attend our college.

A. _____

B. _____

C. _____

5. My father is (not) a very organized person.

A. _____

B. _____

C. _____

6. Several U.S. Presidents have expanded the size of the country by adding land.

A. _____

B. _____

C. _____

7. My dog looks like a mixture of several breeds.

A. _____

B. _____

C. _____

8. To be effective with patients, doctors need three basic qualities.

A. _____

B. _____

C. _____

9. Owning a car is expensive.

A. _____

B. _____

C. _____

10. There are three important sources of factual support.

A. _____

B. _____

C. _____

CONCLUSION

The final part of paragraph structure is the concluding sentence. This sentence should bring the discussion of the main idea to a close by returning to the general level of the subject and the focus of the paragraph. For example, in the paragraph on firefighters presented earlier, the topic sentence states: ". . . the change from 24-hour to 8-hour shifts for firefighters would not benefit the city." The conclusion coordinates by restating that idea in slightly different language: ". . . the Commission on Fire Protection recommends that the city retain the present system of 24-hour shifts for firefighters."

The conclusion also brings the discussion to a close by means of the phrase "in the light of these drawbacks," which asks the reader to recall the arguments that have been made.

Notice the relationship between topic sentence and conclusion in the paragraph on dinosaurs found earlier in this chapter:

> *Topic Sentence:* Although many people think of *dinosaurs* as cold-blooded swamp creatures, they were really, according to some scientists, *warm-blooded land animals.*
>
> *Conclusion: All in all,* these paleontologists conclude, it is highly likely that *dinosaurs* were not just giant lizards, but were, instead, *warm-blooded creatures* capable of protecting themselves very effectively from mammal predators.

The conclusion repeats the key words of the topic sentence and uses the phrase "all in all" to indicate the summing up of the discussion.

Exercise G

Study the following paragraphs, particularly the topic sentences, and then try to write for each one a concluding sentence which coordinates with the topic sentence.

1.   Even nonmechanics can do some things to keep their cars running efficiently. For one thing, anyone can check the oil level. First, pull the dipstick out of the engine and wipe it off with a rag. Then put it back in the engine again. This time, when it is pulled out, see where the oil level is on the stick. If it is low, add however many quarts of oil it will take to make it full. Another thing anyone can check is the water level in the radiator. First, make sure the radiator is not hot when you take the cap off. As long as the water level is within one inch of the top of the radiator, it is fine. Finally, anyone can make sure the tires are properly inflated. At most gas stations there is an air pump. However many pounds of pressure it says on the tire, that is what the air pump should be set on. When the bell on the pump stops ringing, the tires are fully inflated.

_____

_____

2.   Our inspection team found incredibly unsanitary conditions at Fred's Restaurant. The counters and floors were littered with scraps of meat and vegetables, some of which were starting to rot. The garbage cans were uncovered and overflowing. Insects and rodent droppings were discovered in several boxes of flour and crackers. Milk and butter were left standing at room temperature because the refrigeration system was broken. The kitchen staff did not observe the hand-washing rule.

_____

_____

3.   As I looked out over the huge audience, I was overwhelmed with nervousness. First, my throat became clogged, and no amount of coughing could clear it. Then my hands began to shake. When I tried to steady myself against the podium, I just succeeded in scattering the pages of my speech across the stage. I thought my legs would collapse as I tried to collect them. Once I finally began to speak, my voice was so soft it could hardly be heard over the loud BA-BOOMP of my heart.

_____

_____

4.   Ocean Beach in October can still be a great vacation spot. You don't have to worry about not finding a room. All the major hotels stay open until December. And most of them offer big discounts for late fall visitors, sometimes as much as 50%. You an also find good prices on resort clothes in the fall. Your savings on next summer's wardrobe could finance another vacation next fall. During the fall, too, the cool weather is perfect for exhilarating walks along the ocean. And, per-

haps best of all, you won't have to share all these benefits with a crowd of other vacationers.

_____

_____

5.   If your child doesn't seem to respond to your questions, perhaps you need to raise the level of the conversation. First level conversations begin with a question that asks for a factual reply: "Do you have any homework, dear?" There's no real opportunity for give-and-take here. The second level of conversation asks for opinions: "Did you like that movie?" This kind of question can lead to a more interesting discussion since more thought is required to reply. However, the third level, abstraction, can lead to the most rewarding conversations because it requires the use of imagination. "What do you think it would be like to be a pilot?" Here is a chance for stimulating discussion both for your child and for you.

_____

_____

FROM PARAGRAPH TO ESSAY

One of the advantages of learning this form of paragraphing is that it is so easily adaptable to longer pieces of writing. Instead of relating sentences, you coordinate and subordinate whole paragraphs.

Here is an essay of several paragraphs that follows the pattern of introducing the subject, supporting it, and then summarizing the main idea.

Topic Statement (focuses main idea)

Being divorced has caused me problems financially, emotionally, and as a parent, that I did not face when I was married.

Support (presents subordinate details)

Since the divorce, my financial situation has certainly changed. Before, I could depend on my husband's $298 a week salary to pay the rent, buy groceries, and clothe the three of us. The extra $100 a week that I made as a part-time bookkeeper could be used for extras like a vacation or new dining room chairs. However, since Ben and I separated, my full-time salary of $200 a week is barely enough to rent a small apartment, buy groceries and gasoline, and pay for baby-sitting for my son, Mark.

The financial strain has not made my emotional adjustment to divorce any easier, either. The divorce raised all kinds of frightening questions for me about my value as a person. Instead of Ben telling me that I'm lovable, I have to convince myself that I am. The loneliness is hard, too. There's no one but my four-year-old to confide my problems in. I often feel depressed because I don't think I can handle all the responsibilities I have now.

Of course, my chief responsibility is raising Mark, and the divorce has made parenting more difficult. Ben was able to be firm with Mark, while I find discipline very hard to maintain. Since I'm working all day, I find I have less energy at night to play with Mark. In fact, sometimes I'm just plain irritable with him. I never realized before how much easier it is to be able to share the responsibility for child raising. A single parent doesn't get much time off from parenting.

Conclusion
(coordi-
nates
with T.S.)
All in all, the first few months after my divorce have caused great changes in my financial situation, in my emotional situation, and in my relationship to my son. But, as each day passes, I'm more and more sure that I'll make a good life for Mark and me.

In general, any comment made in this book about paragraphing applies equally to longer pieces of writing.

Before
Writing:
Exploring

8

Chapter 7 presented some general principles of paragraph structure. However, while it is useful and necessary to know these general concepts, they will not, by themselves, produce compelling writing. A paragraph that has a topic sentence, support, and a conclusion is not necessarily a good paragraph. It's what you put into that paragraph form that makes the difference between writing that is merely correct and writing that really reaches its audience and achieves its purpose.

To write paragraphs that are effective and not just correct, you have to explore the problems and possibilities of each individual writing situation and adapt what you know about writing in general to one particular piece of writing.

A good exploration of the writing situation will focus on three factors: the subject you are writing about, the audience you are writing for, and the purpose you hope to achieve.

Exploring the Writing Situation

1. What is significant about the subject?
2. Who am I writing for?
3. What is my purpose in writing?

These aspects of the writing situation can be explored in any order, and your thinking about one area may overlap into another. Your exploration of audience, for instance, may suggest something about the subject that you had overlooked before. Or your thinking about the subject may suggest the perfect audience for this subject. In short, the exploring part of the writing process is not really as neat and orderly as it may look on the pages of a textbook.

If you do a good job of prewriting exploration, you'll probably be jumping back and forth among considerations of subject, audience, and purpose, and you'll end up with several rather messy-looking sheets of paper. Don't let the mess worry you when exploring. Your mind will be churning up odd scraps of information and opinion, sometimes helping you clarify what you already know, sometimes showing you what you don't know, sometimes producing a startling new insight. So, when you are in the process of exploring, don't stop to be critical; just let your mind generate ideas freely. Later, you can work on organizing your ideas, filling in gaps in your thinking, or rejecting some ideas as not really relevant.

STARTING POINT: A GOOD QUESTION

In every writing situation, there is some question that a writer really wants to answer. Unfortunately, many writers start writing before they know what that question is. As a result, their writing may sound uninteresting or irrelevant to their readers and even to the writers themselves.

Finding the right question to guide your exploration of a writing situation is very important. A good starting question is one that captures your sense of what is curious, puzzling, or significant in a certain situation. While there is no magic formula that can guarantee you a good starting question, one way of framing your starting point is to look at your subject from two perspectives: inside yourself and outside yourself. Curiosity, puzzlement, or significance usually arises from some kind of delicate imbalance between the way a situation is and the way you expect it to be. A good starting question is one that will lead you to a restoration of balance.

For example, suppose that you've just moved into your first apartment and you want to write to your family about it. First, list some of your expectations about moving. This list can be as long as you like.

Expectations about moving   (Inside perspective)

> new city, no friends
> I'll be lonely
> less space than home
> will there be room for my books?
> chance for independence
> my own place

Then try a second list: how does the present situation differ from your expectations?

Situation as it exists   (Outside perspective)

> Too busy to be lonely
> many details - lease, phone, furniture,
> finding stores
> dependence on lots of others
> but my decision

Comparing the two lists, you might notice a certain imbalance between the degree of independence you expected and the independence you actually have. Thus, you might come up with a starting question like:

> How does my new apartment encourage me to be myself?

Here's another example of finding a starting question for writing. Suppose you are concerned about the lack of good health care in your community. First, you can look at your expectations about health care.

Expectations about health care   (Inside perspective)

> basic right to health
> people will take care of their bodies
> people will trust doctors

Then list the aspects of the present situation that differ from your expectations.

Situation as it exists   (Outside perspective)

people afraid of doctors
dont know how to take care
health care expensive
too busy to visit doctors

Looking at the two lists, you might come up with a starting question like:

How can people be encouraged to take care of their
health?

In the two writing situations described above, you as a writer started with an initial area of interest and then tried to formulate the exact question you wanted to explore in writing. In many situations, however, writing is done at someone else's initiation. Your client wants a written proposal. Your teacher wants a term paper. Your boss wants a report. In these writing situations, it is even more important to have a good starting question, to find the aspect of the subject that really seems significant to you. The writing has to seem interesting to you if it is going to seem interesting to anyone else.

If your political science teacher asks you to write a paper on local government, you need to find a question about local government that really interests you. If your boss wants a report on how to improve the mailroom, you need to start with a question that pinpoints the imbalance between the way the mailroom ought to be and the way it is.

Exercise A

For each of the following subjects, try to generate a good starting question. Look at your own expectations and values in connection with the subject (the inside perspective). Then look at the ways in which the actual situation fails to meet or exceeds your expectations (the outside perspective).

1.   Your relationship with a member of your family

Inside Perspective   *Outside Perspective*

Starting Question:

2. Choosing a college

    Inside Perspective   *Outside Perspective*

    Starting Question:

3. An issue that's important to you and that you have had some experience with

    Inside Perspective   *Outside Perspective*

    Starting Question:

4. Sports

    Inside Perspective   *Outside Perspective*

    Starting Question:

5. Jobs

    Inside Perspective   *Outside Perspective*

Starting Question:

EXPLORING THE SUBJECT

Once you have framed a good starting question, you can begin to explore the subject you are writing about. Using the question as a guide, answer it in as many ways as possible. For instance, suppose you were exploring the question:

How can people be encouraged to take care of their health?

You should just write down whatever comes into your mind in response to this question. This process is often called brainstorming. Your brainstorming list on health care might look like this:

- prepare a list of area doctors for newcomers
- set up free clinics
- publicize local health organizations
  - e.g. Mental Health Association
  - Cancer Society
- health column in newspaper
- * Civic Association could sponsor a health fair for adults
- what do children get in school?

   If the health-fair idea seems the most promising to you, you might want to brainstorm about it separately, listing whatever details you can think of that might be related to holding a health fair in your community. You could also list questions that you have about holding a health fair.

   Sometimes, you may get stuck when you are trying to brainstorm a subject. Every writer hits blocks from time to time, and you can help yourself get around such blocks by using a list of questions to help get your thinking started.

Questions for Exploring Subject

Who?
What?
Where?
Why?
When?
How?
How much?

   Suppose you are writing a term paper in political science and your starting question is:

What effect does a mayor have on local residents?

Using the questions above, you might brainstorm like this:

Who

Can anybody run for mayor?
everybody pays taxes-does mayor affect taxes?
mayor vs. city council

What

mayor as P.R. for city, ceremonial office
zoning, taxes, budget
relationship to state, federal gov't?
strong mayor system vs. strong council

Where

Our county - mayors in Allentown
Liston
St. John
Fayette
are there cities without mayors ?

When

no cities established here after 1930.
when mayoral elections held ?
has the role of mayor changed
in last 20 years ? 100 years ?
mayor used to have more personal power.

Why

power concentrated in mayor
why does one mayor have more power
than another ?
why are some mayors not taken
seriously ?
- e.g. Birkett in Liston

How

mcmanus held office 40 years - how ?
apathy, efficiency, political organization

How much

mayor's salaries ?

Studying this list might help you discover a way to answer your starting question by focusing on the career of the man who was mayor for 40 years, for example, or by showing the difference between a mayor's power and a council member's power. You probably would want to go back then and brainstorm these subjects separately. But since the list shows as many questions as answers, this brainstorming might also suggest that you don't know enough yet to answer your starting question. Besides showing you what you know, brainstorming can also show what you don't know. In this case, to get more information you might check political science books and journals in the library or interview some local mayors.

Exercise B

Brainstorm the starting questions you constructed in Exercise A. For each question, brainstorm twice. The first time, list as many possibilities as you can for answering the question. The second time, focus on the one area you think will be most fruitful for writing. If you want to, use the *who?*, *what?*, *where?* signals to get your brainstorming started. If your first brainstorming shows that you don't know enough to answer your starting question, ask your teacher or your librarian where you can get more information on the subject.

EXAMPLE:

Health Care
Starting Question: How can people be encouraged to take
care of their health?

Broad Exploration	*Narrow Exploration*

Broad Exploration

list of doctors for newcomers

set up free clinics

publicize local health

organizations

   — Mental Health

   — Cancer Society

health column

health fair

school programs

Narrow Exploration

<u>Health Fair</u>

who?   Civic Asso. sponsor
invite local doctors and
health organizations
all adults invited

what?   eye exams, hearing tests,
blood tests, diabetes,
health literature,
health counselling

where?   school auditorium

when?   1 day - late spring

how much?   <u>free</u>

how?   need 30-40 volunteers

1. Relationship with family member

   Starting Question:

Broad Exploration   *Narrow Exploration*

2.   Choosing a college

Starting Question:

Broad Exploration   *Narrow Exploration*

3. Important issue

    Starting Question:

Broad Exploration   *Narrow Exploration*

4. Sports

Starting Question:

Broad Exploration   *Narrow Exploration*

5. Jobs

    Starting Question:

Broad Exploration   *Narrow Exploration*

EXPLORING THE AUDIENCE

Sometimes, you have no choice about your audience. You may know from the beginning, for instance, that the report you are preparing will be read by your supervisor. Other times, you are free to choose the most suitable audience for what you want to say. Would your ideas on solar power have more impact on your representative in the legislature or on a group of local business people?

In any case, to write well, you must consider who will be reading what you write. Is it a person you know well, like your brother? Or is it a group of people you don't know personally—the members of the City Council, for example? Is your audience already interested in the subject you are writing about—a group of fellow skindivers, perhaps? Or do you have to convince your audience of the importance of your idea—for instance, potential contributors to your club's fund raising project?

For each kind of audience—personal or public, knowledgeable or uninformed—you have to write in a somewhat different way. You would choose different arguments, use different words, take a different attitude, depending on your audience.

For example, if you were writing something about inflation for the local food co-op newsletter, you would want to choose examples that your audience could immediately recognize, like food prices. If you were writing about inflation for your economics class, though, you would have to choose other kinds of examples since members of this audience might not do the family grocery shopping.

Also, your language would be different for each group. For the food co-op members, you would try to use fairly nontechnical terms so that you could be easily understood by everyone. Your economics class, on the other hand, should be more familiar with the professional language of economists, and so you could use words like "commodities market," "the Fed," and "prime rate" and expect to be understood.

In brainstorming about your audience, you might consider such factors as:

1. Familiarity with subject
2. Attitude toward subject
3. Age, sex, race, marital status, other personal data
4. Socioeconomic background
5. Organizational memberships
6. Geographic location
7. Educational level
8. Relationship to writer
9. Religious and political affiliation
10. Professional or work experience

Suppose you want to write a letter to your City Council about the need for public day care facilities in your area. You might brainstorm your audience like this:

Who are Council members?
- Clarke - Chairman
- Nolan - my district
- Barrett
- Freeson (?)
- Ventre - female
- One other?

how many have children?
Clarke said in newspaper he would
introduce day care bill
don't know how others feel
All Council members Democrats
Public hearing scheduled - 2 weeks
So all members know of proposal
Professional background of council members
- Barrett - tax lawyer
- Clarke - in insurance
- others - don't know

met Nolan once at high school graduation
he gave talk on necessity for future education
- relate this to need for day care?
only existing city center is in Clarke's district

This brainstorming has revealed several things that you need to consider. First, there are some significant gaps in your knowledge of your audience. You are not sure of all the names. You don't know how many council members have children. You don't know the professional backgrounds of the council members. But you need this information to compose an effective letter. Therefore, you're probably going to have to go down to the Public Library or call City Hall to get some more information about your audience.

Brainstorming has also shown that it may not be possible to write just one letter that will appeal to the interests of all six council members. So you may decide to write just one letter, addressed to the chairman and appealing to him, and to send copies to the other members. More time-consuming, but more effective, would be six different letters, each using what you know about that recipient to gain his or her support.

For instance, since Nolan is from your district and you have heard him speak, you might make your appeal to him a little more personal than one to those members whom you do not know at all. Since Clarke is the sponsor of the bill, you know he is already very interested in the subject. Your letter to him could be a simple statement of support and encouragement, or it might include any suggestions you have for improving the bill. Barrett, a tax lawyer, might be appealed to on the basis of economic benefits to the city. If Ms. Ventre is a mother, you might appeal to a sense of fellowship with the plight of working women with children. And so on for each council member.

Notice how your knowledge of your audience affects the content of your writing.

Exercise C

Try to brainstorm each of the following audiences. In each case, assume that you want to write an evaluation of the orientation (or lack of one) given to freshmen at your college.

1. The President of the college
2. Your parents
3. Your best friend
4. The President of the Student Government
5. Your favorite high school teacher

EXPLORING PURPOSE

Closely related to your consideration of the audience for your writing is an analysis of the effect you wish to achieve with a particular piece of writing. As with audience, your purpose in writing may be given to you as part of the writing situation, or you may have some choice in what purpose you want to achieve.

Do you want members of the food co-op to understand what the term *inflation* means? Do you want to show them some ways they can get the most for their money? Do you want to convince them that inflation is not really a serious problem? Do you want them to support some piece of legislation designed to curb inflation? Each of these possible purposes for an article on inflation would demand a different writing strategy.

To explain the meaning of *inflation*, you might give the derivation of the word and some historical examples of it. If you take the second purpose, you assume that the audience is already feeling the practical effects of inflation, even if they aren't too sure about its historical origins, and you proceed to give them some down-to-earth suggestions on how to cope with the problem. To convince this group that inflation is not really a problem, you might put inflation in this country next to inflation in another part of the world that would make U.S. inflation look less serious; or you might present inflation as only part of a larger problem that would diminish the seriousness of inflation by itself. Finally, if you wanted to move this audience to a particular action, like support of legislation, you would have to convince them that this legislation would produce a certain desirable effect and that supporting it would not be too difficult for them.

Whatever your purpose is, you should understand it clearly before you begin to write. If you understand why you are writing, you can better control what you say so that the paragraph does exactly and only what you intended.

There are four general purposes for writing:

To entertain: to make the subject enjoyable for the audience.

To inform: to fill in gaps in your audience's knowledge of the subject.

To interpret: to explain the meaning or significance of certain facts for your audience.

To persuade: to convince your audience to follow a certain course of action.

Of course, it frequently happens that you have more than one purpose in writing. You may want to entertain as well as inform or inform as well as persuade. In cases like these, you should decide which purpose is most important so that you will be able to emphasize it in your writing.

Another part of brainstorming the purpose of a piece of writing is to find an appropriate strategy for carrying out that purpose. Some of the most frequently used strategies are:

Telling a story about
Describing physical characteristics of
Breaking into parts, or categories, or steps
Listing examples of, or reasons for, or causes of
Showing similarities to or differences from

Any of these strategies may be used for any purpose. You need to think about which strategy will work best with the subject and audience you have in mind. (Some suggestions for using these strategies are presented in Chapter 10.)

Suppose, for instance, that you are a member of the local Board of Education. One of your tasks this year has been to study the reading program in elementary schools. Now you want to write a report for your fellow board members, none of whom is too familiar with the reading program.

Your brainstorming list on purpose and strategy might look like this:

- inform
     what is the reading program like ?
        - use story of typical reading class
        - compare to other systems

- interpret
     give plan of action - time order steps
     why our program doesn't work - list reasons
     how did we get to this program ?
               (historical approach)
     disadvantages of sight reading

- persuade
        get new texts
          (show advantages)

From a list like this, you would have to choose what you thought was your most important purpose, or which purpose you should deal with first. Should you just explain the instructional method being used? Or should you attack the present method? Or should you try to get the Board to act right away to solve the problems you discovered?

Here is one paragraph that might be part of your report. What is its purpose? What strategy does it use to achieve that purpose?

> Most children are taught to read by one of two basic methods: sight-reading or phonics. With sight-reading, children learn to read by reading. They are given short stories containing the most common English words. Gradually, through repetition, the students begin to recognize certain words. A sight-reading text might contain a sequence like this: "Here is Bob. Here is Rosa. Bob runs. Rosa runs. Run, Bob, run! Run, Rosa, run!" At the end of a year of sight-reading instruction, children should have a reading vocabulary of about 350 words. With the phonics system, on the other hand, children begin with letters rather than words. Children learn the 26 letters of the alphabet and the 44 sounds those letters stand for. The letters and sounds are taught in a planned order, and students see only those words whose sounds they have already mastered. A beginning phonics reader who knew some basic consonant sounds plus the short *a* sound might be given a sentence like: "Dan can fan the man." At the end of a year of phonics instruction, children should have a reading vocabulary of about 5,000 words. Sight-reading and phonics are the basic choices the Board of Education has when it establishes a reading program.

The basic purpose here seems to be to *inform*. The strategy is to show differences between the two methods in order that the Board can understand what each method does. Sight-reading might sound okay if the Board doesn't know about phonics.

Once the Board has this information, you can go on in other paragraphs to interpret or persuade. Each paragraph of the report should have its own clear purpose and strategy.

Here is another paragraph that might appear in the report. What is its purpose? What is its strategy?

> Because the sight-reading method of teaching reading has been a dismal failure, the Board of Education should act immediately to replace it with the phonics method of instruction. First, the Superintendent of Schools should inform all principals of the decision. Then, a committee of reading teachers should be charged with preparing a plan for the implementation of phonics instruction. Money should be set aside in next year's budget for the purchase of new textbooks. And finally, the Board should hold a series of informational meetings for parents and taxpayers to explain the reason for the change in emphasis. After a phonics reading program is established, the Board should expect a significant improvement in the reading abilities of students in this school district.

This paragraph assumes that the Board has already been persuaded to take some action. So the purpose here seems to be *interpretation* of what to do next, and the strategy is to break down the proposed solution into a series of steps to be taken in a certain order.

Exercise D

Do some brainstorming about purpose and strategy for each of the following writing situations. List all the possible purposes you might want to achieve. Then, for each purpose, list some possible strategies. When you have finished brainstorming, be prepared to discuss which purpose and strategy you would finally choose.

1. Your brother's Cub Scout troop has asked you to write something about your hobby for the next newsletter, which is going to be about various kinds of leisure activities.
2. Your English teacher has given you the topic, "How I Spent My Summer," for your first writing assignment. He encourages you to be creative in approaching this subject.

VOICE

In every writing situation, as in every speaking situation, you use a certain voice to communicate with your audience. You try to sound a certain way to achieve a certain effect. If this quality of voice is based on your analysis of the audience, purpose, and subject of your writing, you are more likely to achieve the effect you intend.

For example, suppose that an automobile accident has occurred. One car is badly damaged. The other has only a small dent. No one has been injured. If you were a police officer writing a report on this accident, you would choose a voice that was impersonal, unemotional, and serious. You would know that your purpose was to record the factual details of the accident as clearly as possible and that your audience (e.g., your superior officer, the participants, insurance claim adjustors, the courts) would not be interested in your personal feelings about the accident. In fact, allowing emotion to show in your report might obscure the facts or lessen the degree of confidence the audience could place in your observations. So your report might sound like this:

At approximately 9:10 P.M. on Sunday, January 29, the first car, a tan 1979 Aspen station wagon, approached the traffic signal at Howard and Monroe Streets at a speed of approximately 50 mph. . . .

However, if you were the driver of the damaged car and you had to write your brother, who is the car's owner, explaining the accident, you would probably want a different voice to suit your purpose and audience. In this situation, a more personal and emotional voice might be more appropriate. Here, it is your interpretation of events and your relationship with your brother that will determine the effectiveness of the writing. So your letter might sound like this:

Dave, I'm sorry, but I have some bad news. Your Mustang has been damaged in an accident. Last Sunday, as I was going home after I had visited Dad in the hospital, some crazy driver ran the red light at the corner of Howard and Monroe . . .

In the actual writing process, voice is created by such things as sentence structure (see Chapters 2–6) and word choice (see Chapter 13). But consciously thinking about voice *before* you write can help you choose the most effective voice possible.

Questions for Choosing Voice

Do you want a personal voice (I, you, we, us) or an impersonal voice (he, she, it, they)?

An emotional voice or an unemotional voice? Which emotion—anger, sadness, joy, excitement?

A serious voice or a light voice?

A formal voice or an informal voice?

A knowledgeable voice or a questioning voice?

Exercise E

For each of the following writing situations, you are given two possible opening sentences. Decide which voice is better suited to the audience, purpose, and subject in each case and be prepared to explain your choice.

1. The editor of the Hometown Senior Citizens Newsletter has asked the president of the Hometown Historic Preservation Society to write her a short piece explaining some of the problems of preservation. Which of these openings seems more promising?

A. Ten dollars is a small price to pay for the many benefits of member-ship in the Hometown Preservation Society.

B. The current attempt to save the Sullivan Building on Crane Boule-vard illustrates many of the difficulties, legal and financial, that his-toric preservationists have to deal wiith.

2. You want a position as assistant manager of the local department store. Which of these openings is more likely to get you an interview?

A. I am a 37-year-old victim of polio, and if you don't hire me as the as-sistant manager of Spendo-Mart, my life will be ruined, and besides I will file suit against you for discrimination.

B. I believe that my 15 years of experience in retail management as well as my familiarity with this community make me well-suited to man-age the new branch of Spendo-Mart opening here next fall.

3. Your daughter's third grade teacher has asked each parent to write a para-graph or so about his or her work for the student's unit on lifestyles. You are a veterinarian. Which opening would be more suitable for your daugh-ter's class?

A. If you like helping animals and don't mind working at some unusual hours of the night, you could be a good veterinarian.

B. Veterinary medicine is a good career for people who have a strong sense of other-directedness and the intellectual ability to master ad-vanced principles of anatomy and physiology.

4. Your credit card company has just billed you for the fourth time for a round-trip ticket to Nairobi. You feel there has been a mistake and you want it straightened out. Which of these openings would be more effec-tive?

A. I know your efficient computers hardly ever make mistakes, but I should respectfully like to suggest that there is (maybe) a possible error in the bill you recently sent me, although I must admit you have given me fine service for the last three years and I am reluctant to be-lieve that you are mistaken, but I'm pretty sure I never spent that money.

B. On June 17, 1978, you billed my account #A–300–166 for $748.18 for a round-trip ticket to Nairobi, Kenya; however, I believe this billing is in error.

5. Your final exam in American History asks you to discuss the major causes of the Civil War. Which of these openings will be more impressive to your history professor?

A. Although it is difficult to pin down exact events that caused a major historical phenomenon like the Civil War, we can see general causes of the war in the economic conditions of the North and the South and in the relative political power of the two areas.

B. Basically the Civil War was fought by infantry and cavalry troops who each performed a distinct military function.

Exercise F

Evaluate each of the following openings for its effectiveness in the situa-tion presented for it. Which openings seem suited to the audience, subject, and purpose?

1. Since you teach guitar, *Folk Music* magazine has asked you to write a brief article on how to buy a guitar. Would this be a good opening?

    In buying a guitar, you should consider these five factors: resonance, type of wood, type of strings, string action, and tone.

2. A good friend who is visiting your city for the first time has asked you which of two restaurants she should take her client to for dinner. Is this an appropriate opening for your response?

    When evaluating a restaurant, you should consider the location, the type and quality of food, the price range, and the atmosphere.

3. You are spending your winter break backpacking through Europe. The college newspaper has asked you to write about your experiences in the various countries you visit. How would this be as an opening for one of your reports?

    The mean temperature in Belgium during January is a chilly −17° centigrade, and the precipitation is expected to total 20 inches for the month.

4. The adult education group at your church has asked each member to write a definition of *church* for the next meeting. Would this be a good opening?

    To me, the church is not a building of brick or wood, but rather the people caring for each other in God's love.

5. As part of your student nurse's training, you must write a report describing the patients you observed on the psychiatric ward during the last two weeks. Would this be an appropriate opening?

    While there were a few patients on the ward who showed definite signs of psychosis, most of the patients I observed displayed symptoms of neurosis.

Rewrite any of the unsatisfactory openings in the preceding exercise to make the voice appropriate for the intended audience, purpose, or subject.

WRITING PRACTICE

You have received an expensive gift (wedding, graduation, birthday, whatever). However, there is some flaw in the gift such as a faulty paint job, a missing piece, or a broken part. After doing some brainstorming, write the following:

1. A thank-you note to your favorite relative
2. A thank-you note to your least favorite relative
3. A letter of complaint to the manufacturer

REVIEW

Exploring the Writing Situation

1. Inside Perspective ↔ Outside Perspective
    Starting Question

2. Exploring the Subject

Who?	Why?
What?	When?
Where?	How?
	How much?

3. Exploring the Audience
    Familiarity with subject
    Attitude toward subject
    Personal data (age, sex, etc.)
    Socioeconomic background
    Organizational memberships
    Geographic location
    Educational level
    Relationship to writer
    Religious and political affiliation
    Professional or work experience

4. Exploring Purpose / Strategy

Entertain	tell a story about
Inform	describe
Interpret	break down into parts, steps
Persuade	list examples, reasons
	show similarities, differences

5. Voice
    Personal / Impersonal
    Emotional / Unemotional (which emotion?)
    Serious / Light
    Formal / Informal
    Knowledgeable / Questioning

Before Writing:
Organizing

9

After you have explored the audience, purpose, and subject of your writing, you probably have a lot of material to work into your paragraph or essay. Once you have done this preliminary thinking about your writing, you are ready to begin sorting through these ideas to see which ones you really want to use and in what order you want to arrange them.

FOCUS THE MAIN IDEA

One way to begin the organization process is to come up with a preliminary topic sentence which will focus your main idea for you. This sentence should be an answer to your starting question.

For instance, suppose that you work for an office furnishings company and want to interest potential clients in your new product line. You have decided that your strategy will be to describe an office filled with your products. Your brainstorming list for the description might look like this:

open rooms
few walls: free-standing partitions / file cabinets
upholstered desk chairs
chrome
sculpture

carpeting
no regular rows of desks
work modules
clean-looking desks
lighting
earthy colors—orange, yellow, brown

Now, looking at this list, you can try to decide on one word which most clearly defines the central impression you want your clients to have about the office you are describing. Brainstorming can be useful in this process too. Just list the words you think might fit:

flexibility
economy
✓ *openness*
spacious
freedom

Then think about your audience. Which word will your clients respond to most favorably? Try creating a topic sentence that will focus on whatever word you have chosen. Try using the key idea in several different positions in the sentence:

Subject	— *Openness* is the key in an office designed by Modern Furnishings, Inc.
Verb	— Modern Furnishing, Inc. *can open up* your office to the look of the eighties.
Complement	— An office designed by Modern Furnishings, Inc. will have *a feeling of openness*.

Exercise A

Using the lists you developed in Chapter 8, Exercise B, construct topic sentences for paragraphs on some aspect of Your Relationship to a Member of Your Family, Choosing a College, An Important Issue, Sports, and Jobs.

Your topic sentences should have a limited subject and a clear focus (the basic requirements presented in Chapter 7). They should also be suited to the audience and purpose/strategy you have selected.

Try to construct two possible versions of each topic sentence.

EXAMPLE:

Foreign Countries

Starting Question: What is the most significant difference between the U.S. and Cyprus?

Narrowed Subject: Cyprus standard of living

Audience: college sociology class

Purpose/Strategy: inform/contrast with U.S.

Focusing Idea: moderate, lower than U.S.

Topic Sentence A: The standard of living in Cyprus is much lower than that of the Untied States.

Topic Sentence B: The American standard of living makes that of Cyprus seem moderate.

1. *Relationship with Family Member*
    Starting Question:
    Narrowed Subject:
    Audience:
    Purpose/Strategy:
    Focusing Idea:
    Topic Sentence A: _____

    _____

    Topic Sentence B: _____

    _____

2. *Choosing a College*
    Starting Question:
    Narrowed Subject:
    Audience:
    Purpose/Strategy:
    Focusing Idea:
    Topic Sentence A: _____

    _____

    Topic Sentence B: _____

3. *Important Issue*
   Starting Question:
   Narrowed Subject:
   Audience:
   Purpose/Strategy:
   Focusing Idea:
   Topic Sentence A: _____

   _____

   Topic Sentence B: _____

   _____

4. *Sports*
   Starting Question:
   Narrowed Subject:
   Audience:
   Purpose/Strategy:
   Focusing Idea:
   Topic Sentence A: _____

   _____

   Topic Sentence B: _____

   _____

5. *Jobs*
   Starting Question:
   Narrowed Subject:
   Audience:
   Purpose/Strategy:
   Focusing Idea:
   Topic Sentence A: _____

   _____

   Topic Sentence B: _____

   _____

GROUP SUPPORTING DETAILS

When you have written a preliminary topic sentence, or at least decided on a preliminary focusing idea, you can begin to organize the supporting details for your paragraph.

First, you should study your brainstorming list on your subject and see which points seem to coordinate. For example, suppose that in brainstorming about muscles for a report in anatomy class, you have this list:

function movement
skeletal muscle - biceps, eyes
consists of protein and water
tendons
works by stimulation & contraction
voluntary
involuntary
over 600 muscles in body
smooth muscles - digestive system
40-50% total body weight
striated muscle
different shapes - sheetlike cylindrical
different sizes
connected to skelatal system
connected to nervous system

You have already decided that since your purpose is to inform, you will discuss the different types of muscles in the human body. Your preliminary topic sentence is:

Muscles can be classified into three types: striated muscle, smooth muscle, and cardiac muscle.

Your brainstorming list had included two of the categories, and you added the third coordinate group, cardiac, when you realized it was missing. (Filling in any gaps you may uncover is also part of the organizing process.) Now, what information do you have on your list that would fit under these coordinate subheadings?

Striated	*Smooth*	*Cardiac*
skeletal muscle	digestive system	heart
voluntary	involuntary	involuntary
shape—cylindrical	shape—sheetlike	shape—hollow
size—(another gap—	size—	size—
look this up?)		

Some of the other ideas on your brainstorming list relate to muscles in general, so you could create another group for these items.

All Muscles

function-movement
consists of protein and water
stimulation and contraction
40–50% total body weight
over 600 muscles
connected to skeletal & nervous systems

Frequently, you may find that some items on your brainstorming list don't fit into any group. This isn't a problem. Possibly you will see a use later in the writing process for one of these ideas, or perhaps some ideas that don't really suit your purpose or your audience this time can be saved for another time. You might want to keep a notebook of ideas that you can refer back to in future writing situations.

Exercise B

After each of the following brainstorming lists, there are several possible subheadings. Show which ideas from the list would fit with each subheading.

FAMOUS WOMEN°

a. Madame Curie
b. Golda Meir
c. Margaret Thatcher
d. Billie Jean King
e. Mary Leakey
f. Queen Isabella
g. Babe Didrikson
h. Indira Gandhi

° A good dictionary should give you information about these women.

     i. Mary Cassatt
     j. Harriet Tubman
     k. Maria Callas
     l. Elizabeth I of England
    m. Jane Austen
     n. Margaret Mead
     o. Wilma Rudolph
     p. Lady Murasaki

1. Scientists   _____

2. Artists _____

3. Politicians _____

4. Athletes _____

LIFE IN NEW YORK

     a. shrinking tax base
     b. zoos
     c. port facilities
     d. decaying centers
     e. neighborhood bars
     f. Puerto Ricans
     g. mayors
     h. poverty
     i. pollution
     j. little restaurants
     k. Blacks
     l. museums
    m. Hassidic Jews
     n. Chinese

1. Ethnic Groups   _____

2. Diversions _____

3. Problems _____

Of course, the way you group the ideas on your brainstorming list depends on the audience and purpose you have in mind. For instance, if you were writing on movies of the Seventies, you might arrange them according to subject (science fiction, comedy, serious social issues) if you were writing a report on the sociological trends of movies. For an audience interested in movie treatment of women, you might choose other groups (films with women heroes, films with women in major supporting roles, films with women as minor characters). For a cinematography class, you might arrange the movies according to camera techniques used. A number of logical arrangements are possible depending on your audience and purpose.

When the ideas on your subject list have been grouped into several coordinate categories, you should study the lists again to see if you now have more points to add to one or more of the groups. For instance, after you arranged the films of the Seventies according to roles given to women, you might be reminded of some other films not on your original list that would help you make your point.

Exercise C

Study each of the following brainstorming lists. Decide on an audience and a purpose for writing on that subject and then group the subordinate details in an appropriate way. You will need to put in the subheadings for your categories. If you can think of additional details in any category, add them.

EXAMPLE:

Things to Do in the City   Audience: Suburbanites
                                  Purpose: Inform

a. zoos
b. little restaurants
c. neighborhood bars
d. museums
e. symphony
f. small shops
g. parks
h. major league sports
i. theaters
j. ethnic food

I. *Stretch the Mind*   II. *Relax Outdoors*   III. *Eat*
    museums   zoos   little restaurants
    symphony   parks   neighborhood bars
    theaters   major league sports   ethnic food
    art galleries (added)   elegant restaurants
                                                         (added)
                                                         gourmet food (added)

1. Monsters   Audience:
                          Purpose:

    a. Dracula
    b. Godzilla
    c. The Alien
    d. Mr. Hyde
    e. The Thing
    f. Wolfman

I.   II.   III.

2. Sports   Audience:
                    Purpose:
    a. basketball
    b. gymnastics
    c. hockey
    d. figure skating
    e. football
    f. swimming
    g. golf
    h. tennis
    i. baseball
    j. soccer
    k. running
    l. horseback riding

I.   II.   III.

3. Reasons for Going to College   Audience:
                                    Purpose:
    a. make more money
    b. meet new people
    c. better jobs
    d. personal development
    e. more social life
    f. good sports
    g. explore different fields
    h. sense of independence

    i. career promotion
    j. satisfaction of greater achievement
    k. participate in clubs
    l. increase knowledge

I.   II.   III.

ARRANGE GROUPS LOGICALLY

The second stage of the grouping process is to arrange the subheadings in a logical order. For example, for the report on muscles, you had four coordinate groups: striated, smooth, cardiac, and all muscles. One logical way to arrange the four points would be to use the information about muscles in general as an introduction and then present the three kinds of muscles in an orderly pattern.

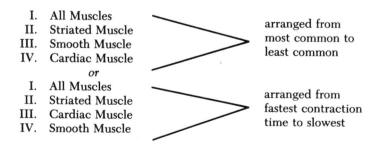

    I.   All Muscles
   II. Striated Muscle
 III. Smooth Muscle
 IV. Cardiac Muscle   arranged from most common to least common
           or
    I.   All Muscles
   II. Striated Muscle
 III. Cardiac Muscle
 IV. Smooth Muscle   arranged from fastest contraction time to slowest

Logical patterns of arrangement could be based on time (earliest event to latest event), space (farthest away to closest, top to bottom), or size (smallest to largest). If no other pattern of arrangement seems obvious to you, you can arrange points in order of importance, always beginning with the least important and ending with the most important.

Of course, the order in which you present your ideas depends, to some extent, on your audience and purpose. For instance, in the example shown above on muscles, an arrangement from most common type to least common would be suitable for an audience whose knowledge of muscles was not very specialized. The arrangement from fastest contraction time to slowest would be suitable if your audience had more detailed knowledge or if your purpose were to explain some research related to the contraction time of muscles.

Knowledge of audience is particularly critical when you arrange items in an order of importance. The most important point to one audience may not be the most important point to another. Suppose, for instance, that your employee group has three complaints about the job: low pay, poor working environment, and the difficulty of the work. If you were writing to the plant manager about these complaints, you might choose to end with (i.e., emphasize) poor working environment because that is the area that the plant manager can do the most about. A letter to fellow workers, on the other hand, might make low pay the item of greatest importance.

Whatever pattern of arrangement you choose, be sure that it is as clear to your reader as it is to you. This may require some use of signals in your writing to tell your reader what the organizational structure is. In the example above about muscles, you could say, "Striated muscle, which is the most common type, . . ." and "a smaller group is smooth muscle." Phrases like these would indicate to your reader the direction in which you were moving. (Chapter 12 on Coherence presents a full discussion of connectives between major ideas.)

Exercise D

Arrange each of the following lists of major supporting points in a logical order and explain briefly what principle you have used to organize them. Would a different audience or purpose require a different arrangement than the one you have chosen?

1. Description of Jane's face

nose	I.
chin	II.
hair	III.
eyes	IV.
lips	V.
cheeks	VI.

Explanation _____

_____

2. Advantages of a light rail system over a highway

saves fuel	I.
less pollution	II.
more orderly growth	III.
frees commuter from driving	IV.
less disruption to community	V.

Explanation _____

_____

3. Major American fiction writers

Nathaniel Hawthorne (1804–1864)	I.
Edgar Allan Poe (1809–1849)	II.
William Faulkner (1897–1962)	III.
F. Scott Fitzgerald (1896–1940)	IV.
Herman Melville (1819–1891)	V.
Ernest Hemingway (1898–1961)	VI.

Explanation _____

_____

4. Tour schedule

New York	I.
Los Angeles	II.
Denver	III.
Chicago	IV.
Boston	V.
Dallas	VI.

Explanation _____

_____

5.   Restaurant review

food****	I.
atmosphere/decor*	II.
price****	III.
service**	IV.

Explanation _____

_____

When the major groups have been arranged satisfactorily, you can arrange any supporting detail within each category. For instance, look at the details you had listed earlier under muscles:

Striated	*Smooth*	*Cardiac*
skeletal muscle	digestive system	heart
voluntary	involuntary	involuntary
shape—cylindrical	shape—sheetlike	shape—hollow
size	size	size

The supporting points under *Striated* could be related into two groups, like this:

Appearance	*Function*
shape	skeletal
size	voluntary

The supporting points in the other two categories could be arranged similarly. This organization of supporting details ensures that you will cover the same points for each kind of muscle.

OUTLINING

A formal way of presenting the organization of a piece of writing is an outline. It can be useful to you as a writer by clarifying the planning you have done, clearly showing the coordinate and subordinate relationships among your ideas. It can also be useful to your readers, especially for a long piece of writing like a term paper, by showing them what to expect from your essay.

An outline uses Roman numerals (I, II, III) to show major points. Capital letters (A, B, C) show supporting details for each major point. Arabic numerals (1, 2, 3) show any further examples under an A, B, or C.

Here is an outline of the report on muscles:

Topic Sentence: Although all muscles have certain properties in common, muscles can be divided into three distinct types: striated, smooth, and cardiac.

I.   All Muscles
   A.   Function—movement
   B.   Operation—contraction and relaxation
   C.   Composition—protein and water
II.   Striated
   A.   Appearance
     1.   Size
     2.   Shape
   B.   Function
     1.   Skeletal
     2.   Voluntary
III.   Smooth
   A.   Appearance
     1.   Size
     2.   Shape
   B.   Function
     1.   Digestive System
     2.   Involuntary
IV.   Cardiac
   A.   Appearance
     1.   Size
     2.   Shape
   B.   Function
     1.   Heart
     2.   Involuntary

Conclusion: Each of the three types of muscles is ideally suited to its own particular movement function in the body.

Notice that an outline moves from the most general idea, expressed in the topic sentence, to the most specific idea, here expressed as Arabic numerals 1 and 2. In an outline that goes only as far as Arabic numerals, you usually will not have a I without a II or an A without a B. Sometimes, if you are using only one example, there may be a 1 without a 2, but this is not the norm.

Be careful that your outline accurately reflects the weight to be given to each point. All Roman numeral items should coordinate. Similarly, all capital letter items should be of equivalent weight, but subordinate to the Roman numeral points.

What is wrong with this outline?

Topic Sentence: Good fishing can be found in both fresh and salt water.

I.   Salt Water
   A.   Barracuda

II.   Water that is Fresh
    A.   Trout
    B.   Carp
III. Tuna

Conclusion: Either kind of fishing can provide an exciting day on the water.

For one thing, *III. Tuna* is not coordinate with *I.* and *II. Tuna* shouldn't get a Roman numeral in this outline. *Tuna* is really a supporting example subordinate to *I. Salt Water.* Another problem with this outline is the order in which the major points are presented. The topic sentence gives them in one arrangement, but the outline does not follow that pattern. Finally, coordinate points should be phrased in a similar way to emphasize their relatedness. So *Water that Is Fresh* should be *Fresh Water* to emphasize its coordination with *Salt Water* in I.

Exercise E

Put the following lists of details into outline form. You may wish to do a rough grouping first, then a more formal outline.

1.   *T.S.* Human beings are amazing.

    a.   Eskimos in the Arctic
    b.   Build spacecraft
    c.   Protect orphans
    d.   Construct radio telescopes
    e.   Tuaregs in the Sahara
    f.   Live anywhere
    g.   Make marvelous tools
    h.   Computers
    i.   Altruistic
    j.   Provide for the helpless
    k.   Mourn the dead

Conclusion: Humans can be proud.

I.
    A.
    B.
    C.
II.
    A.
    B.
    C.

III.
    A.
    B.

2.   a. The setting is beautiful.
    b. Everybody should try rafting.
    c. It is good exercise.
    d. The rocks are dangerous.
    e. A rafter paddles constantly.
    f. Rafting satisfies in several ways.
    g. A rafter occasionally swims.
    h. It is challenging.
    i. The valley is green.
    j. The rapids are tricky.
    k. The river sparkles.

T.S.

I.
    A.
    B.
II.
    A.
    B.
III.
    A.
    B.

Conclusion:

3.   a. *Typee* was a bestseller.
    b. He went to sea young.
    c. He lost his father.
    d. Melville needed considerable strength.
    e. Melville had a complex life.
    f. It was marred by tragedy.
    g. *Omoo* was popular.
    h. He lived with cannibals.
    i. It was full of adventure.
    j. His career failed.
    k. It was marked by success.
    l. His son committed suicide.

T.S.

I.
    A.
    B.

II.
    A.
    B.
III.
    A.
    B.
    C.

Conclusion:

4.   a. Winning teaches generosity.
      b. Athletics build character.
      c. Drama cultivates acting ability.
      d. Student officers learn procedure.
      e. Meeting people encourages tolerance.
      f. College offers many learning activities.
      g. Social activities teach.
      h. Conflict sharpens wits.
      i. College isn't just classrooms.
      j. Teamwork inculcates discipline.
      k. Responsibility fosters leadership.
      l. Politics can instruct.
      m. Dating teaches tact.
      n. Cultural activities encourage growth.
      o. Losing teaches self-control.
      p. Attending exhibits builds perception.

T.S.

I.
    A.
    B.
II.
    A.
    B.
    C.
III.
    A.
    B.
    C.
IV.
    A.
    B.

Conclusion:

Case Study
Capital Punishment

A student is preparing for a debate (on capital punishment) in her speech class. Each student is to prepare a brief statement on some aspect of the subject.

Here is how one student does her assignment:

1. *Brainstorming*

Audience	*Purpose/Strategy*	*Voice*
speech class, debate	explain position	serious
hostile to death penalty?	arouse interest	not emotional
mostly 18 year olds	share knowledge	knowledgeable
middle class	impress teacher	
no involvement with crime	help debate	
uninformed	strategy - examples?	
no legal background		
possibly some religious attitudes		
conservative?		

Subject (before research)	*Subject* (after some research)
deterrent?	Old / New Testament
Supreme Court decision	Eye for an eye
cruel	Thou shalt not kill

Cheaper to tax payer
than jail
Speck
guy in California
ok to stop murder?
"an eye for an eye"

Does it stop crime?
Mercy
Supreme Court decision
Cruel and unusual punishment
(Bill of Rights)
Discrimination in
death penalty
Black/White Rich/Poor
(Time)
Mass Murderers
Richard Speck – Chicago
nurses – early 60's
Juan Corona – California
migrant workers

2. *Preliminary Topic Sentence*

Possible topics
—Supreme Court decision
—religious aspects of capital punishment
—punishment for mass murderers

The writer chose to go with the topic of the Supreme Court decision on
"cruel and unusual punishment." She could, of course, have made other
choices, but this was a sound one. The outstanding characteristic of her audience, a school class debating current issues, was its lack of information (uninformed). By choosing to discuss the Court decision, she has decided to give her
readers information which she can assume will interest them and which they
will need in order to carry on an informed debate.

She has also made a choice which satisfies several of the purposes she
listed. She is sharing information central to the debate, showing her knowledge, stirring up the group, creating a good impression on teacher and students, and helping the debate. Her other main choices would not have suited
the audience and purposes so well. The discussion of mass murder may have
been more sensational, but would not have been as central to the debate and
would have led the discussion off into a side issue. Likewise, her analysis shows

no particular interest in the religious aspects of the question, and a repetition of the familiar Ten Commandments and other Biblical quotations would probably not have given new, useful information to many members of the class.

Therefore, the student came up with the following list of possible focusing ideas related to her audience's lack of information.

> The decision was wrong.
>
> The decision has been misunderstood.
>
> The decision caused a rise in crime.
>
> The decision has caused a lot of confusion.
>
> The decision went against the people's opinion.

Topic Sentence #1:

> The Supreme Court confused everybody with its decision on capital punishment.

Thinking about this sentence, the student decides that it is not quite accurate. She, after all, understood the decision as soon as she took the trouble to read about it.

Topic Sentence #2:

> People have not taken the trouble to find out what the Supreme Court's decision on capital punishment was all about.

The student doesn't want to attack her audience, so she tries again.

Topic Sentence #3:

> Many people do not understand the real basis of the Supreme Court's decision on capital punishment.

3. *Finding the Major Supports*

Looking at her topic sentence, the writer on capital punishment checks her subject list to see which items pertain to the topic she has chosen—understanding the Supreme Court's decision. She comes up with this list:

Cruel and unusual punishment – Bill of Rights

discrimination in death penalty

black / white   rich / poor – (time)

morality

mercy

does it stop crime? (deterrent)

All these things represent different ways in which the decision has been understood by different people.

Studying the list a little further, she sees that some of these ideas can be grouped together.

Morality
Mercy   ⟩ Misunderstandings
Deterrrent

/Cruel and unusual punishment
Discrimination
Real reasons ⟨ Black/white, rich/poor

4. *Constructing an Outline*

> *TS:*   Many people do not understand the real basis of the Supreme Court decision on capital punishment.

> I. Misunderstandings
>   A. Morality
>   B. Mercy
>   C. Deterrent
> II. Real Basis—Discrimination
>   A. "Unusual punishment"
>   B. Black/white
>   C. Rich/poor

> *Conclusion:*   Understanding the reason for the Court's decision will help make discussions of capital punishment clearer.

5. *Finished Paper*

Many people do not understand the real basis for the Supreme Court's decision on capital punishment. Some think the Court thought the death penalty was *immoral*. Others believe the Court stopped capital punishment because it violated our ideal of *mercy*. Still others argue that the Court believed the death penalty was not a useful *deterrent* to murder. Actually, the Court found that the penalty was being applied in *discriminatory* ways. It was, therefore, unconstitutional since the Bill of Rights forbids *"unusual" punishments,* and the Court felt that discrimination was making the death penalty unusually severe on certain groups. For example, according to *Time* magazine, statistics presented to the Court showed that for the same kind of murder a *black* American would be executed while the *white* killer would get life in prison. Studies also indicated that *rich* murderers did not go to the gas chambers, but *poor* ones did. Understanding the reason for the Court's decision will help make discussions of capital punishment clearer.

PREWRITING: SUMMARY

By thinking about and planning your writing before you start putting sentences on paper, you can make sure that the finished piece of writing really says what you want it to say. You aren't in the position of getting halfway through a paragraph or essay and then wondering what you are going to say next. The prewriting process lets you see the end of your work before you even begin writing. The work of prewriting also frees you to concentrate on *how* you are going to present your ideas rather than on *what* you are going to say. When you have done the necessary brainstorming and organizing, you know what you need to write and you can concentrate your energy on choosing the best possible words and sentence structures to convey your ideas effectively to your readers.

Organizing Your Writing

1. Explore audience, subject, and purpose.
2. Construct a sentence that focuses your main idea.
3. Group the supporting details under several coordinated headings.
4. Fill in any gaps you find.
5. Arrange the headings in an effective order.
6. Make a formal outline. (Optional)

Exercise F

Using the subject lists that you brainstormed for Family Relationship, Choosing a College, Important Issue, Sports, and Jobs, take at least one of these subjects through the entire prewriting process. Brainstorm your audience and purpose, construct a topic sentence, group the supporting details, fill in any gaps that show up, and put together an outline.

Now you are ready to write a first draft of your paper.

Practice
in Composing
Paragraphs

10

As you have seen in previous chapters, you can choose any one of several strategies for developing a paragraph.

> telling a story
> describing physical characteristics
> listing examples, reasons, or steps
> breaking down into parts or categories
> showing similarities or differences

In this section, you will have a chance to work out some paragraphs using each of these strategies. In doing these exercises, assume that you have already decided on an audience and purpose for which these strategies are appropriate.

STRATEGY: TELLING A STORY

A. Focus on one specific incident. Don't try to tell about your whole vacation, for instance, in one paragraph.

B. Be sure that your topic sentence explains the significance of the story.

EXAMPLES:

Last summer's weekend trip on the Bay turned into a *nightmare for our family*.

Jerry's behavior at the party just shows *what a gentle person he is*.

I've never been so embarrassed as I was the day I took my driver's test.

C. Arrange events in a logical time order, making sure that no important part of the story is left out.

D. Use joining words like *after, next, while, then, before* to emphasize time relationships between events.

E. Use sentences with strong verbs to emphasize action in telling a story.

EXAMPLES:

Weak verbs

There *was* a certain tension in the air before the race.

Millie *put* the package on the table.

Strong verbs

Tension *crackled* in the air before the race.

Millie *slammed* the package down on the table.

F. Try to put an action in each base sentence.

EXAMPLES:

Action not emphasized

It was late summer in 1963 when we set out for a sail in our new boat.

The sun shone cruelly overhead as the drivers clocked mile after mile.

Action emphasized

In late summer 1963 *we set out in our new sailboat*.

The drivers clocked mile after mile as the sun shone cruelly overhead.

G. Use a concluding sentence to reemphasize the significance of the story.

EXAMPLES:

At last, the nightmare was over.

Jerry's compassion that night touched everyone in the class.

With my family, I've never quite been able to live down my "run in" with the Department of Motor Vehicles.

Exercise A

Keeping in mind the hints suggested above, combine the following groups of sentences to produce a paragraph that makes its point by telling a story.

1. I take Danny out to dinner.
   I take Bob out to dinner.
   Danny and Bob are my sons.
   We go to a nice restaurant.
   This is not my idea of an evening.
   The evening is one of enjoyment.

   Although this is not my idea of an evening of enjoyment, I took out my sons Danny & Bob to dinner to a nice restaurant.

2. We have to struggle.
   The struggling is over baths.
   We have to tear the house apart.
   The searching is for two clean shirts.
   The searching is for two clean pairs of trousers.
   The searching is for socks.
   The socks should match.
   All this happens before we can even leave the house.

   We had to struggle over baths, we had to tear the house apart searching for two clean shirts, two pair of trousers or matching socks. And all this happened before we can even leave the house.

3. Danny has to go to the bathroom.
   We arrive at the restaurant.
   We are seated at our table.

   After we arrived at the restaurant and were seated at our table, Danny had to go to the bathroom.

4. I am with Danny.
   Bob takes bites.
   The bites are out of all the rolls.
   The rolls are in the basket.
   He opens the sugar packages.

   When I was with Danny, Bob opened the sugar packages and took bites out of all the rolls which were in the basket.

5. We order our dinner.
   Of course, the boys hate everything on the menu.
   They tell the waiter this.
   They speak in loud voices.

   When ordering our dinner the boys told the waiter that they hated everything on the menu in loud voices.

6. Finally, their hamburgers arrive.
   Danny insists that Bob's is bigger.
   Danny refuses to eat the "small" hamburger.

   Finally when their hamburgers arrived, Danny insisted that Bob's was bigger and refused to eat the "small" one.

7. The clean shirts are covered.
   Chocolate sauce and mustard cover them.

   →

The clean faces are covered too.
By this time, dinner is over.

8. My coffee is cold.
   My shrimp is untouched.
   My stomach is upset.
   I wonder.
   Does the zoo take reservations for dinner?

(Handwritten right margin:)

(During the dinner)
The clean shirts were covered with chocolate sauce and mustard. But by the time the clean faces were covered too the dinner was over.

(Now that) My coffee is cold, my shrimp untouched, my stomach upset, and I wonder if the zoo takes reservations for dinner...

STRATEGY: DESCRIBING

A. Focus on one person, place, or thing.

B. Be sure that your topic sentence presents one central impression you want to give your reader.

> EXAMPLES:
>
> My brother's room is always *a mess.*
>
> Shirley looked *exhausted* after her first day at work.
>
> The kitchen is the *most cheerful* room in the home.

C. Reinforce that central impression by using details that will appeal to the senses. Show your reader what the subject looks like, sounds like, smells like, tastes like, and/or feels like.

D. Use vivid adjectives to get your reader really involved in your description. Show your reader the exact color, size, shape, position, etc. of each detail.

E. Put these descriptive details into your base sentences.

> EXAMPLES:
>
> *Description not emphasized*
>
> Her desk, *which is covered with books, papers, and half-eaten food,* stands near the door.
>
> He ran into the alley, *where the tantalizing smell of pizza overwhelmed him.*
>
> *Description emphasized*
>
> *Open books, scattered papers, and half-eaten food littered her desk,* which stood near the door.
>
> *The tantalizing smell of pizza overwhelmed him* as he ran into the alley.

F. Arrange the descriptive details in a logical order, such as top to bottom, left to right, or far away to close up.

G. Use transitions like *beside, under, against, where, on* to emphasize the spatial relationships between details.

H. Restate the central impression in the conclusion.

EXAMPLES:

Fred's room is a *man-made disaster area.*

Altogether, Shirley's fatigue *completely obscured her natural good looks.*

With its bright colors and open layout, *the kitchen lifts everyone's spirits.*

Exercise B

Keeping in mind the suggestions above, combine the following groups of sentences to produce a paragraph that describes:

1. The face reveals suffering.

   The face belongs to Jim Wood.

   The suffering has marked his whole life.

   Jim Wood's face reveals suffering which has marked his whole life.

2. His hair sticks straight up.

   His hair is short.

   His hair is graying.

   He looks like he is terrified.

   The terror is unending.

   His short, graying hair sticks straight up making him look like he is unendingly terrified.

3. Eyes look out of his face.

   The eyes are pain-filled.

   The eyes are brown.

   The face is lined.

   The face is leathery.

   His brown, pain-filled eyes look out of his lined, leathery face.

4. A scar runs down.

   The scar is crooked.

   It is on his left cheek.

   His nose is bent.

   The bending is at an angle.

   The angle is queer.

   The nose has been broken.

   This has happened several times.

   (And) *A crooked scar runs down on his left cheek. His nose which has been broken several times is bent at a queer angle.*

5. His mouth is half-open.

   His mouth displays rows.

   The rows are of teeth.

   The teeth are yellowed.

   There are many gaps in the rows.

   His half-opened mouth displays many gaps in the rows of yellowed and rotted out teeth which have been knocked-out in fights.

Teeth have rotted out.

Teeth have been knocked out in fights.

6. A beard meanders.

    The beard is pathetic.

    The beard is scraggly.

    The meandering is over his chin.

7. Jim Wood's face tells the story.

    The story is of his life.

    The life is luckless.

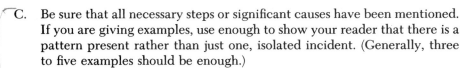

(And)

A pathetic, scraggly beard meanders over his chin.

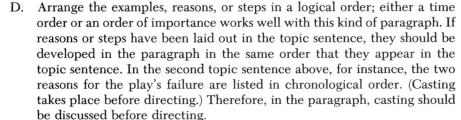

(As you can see)

Jim Wood's face tells the story of his luckless life.

STRATEGY: LISTING EXAMPLES, REASONS, OR STEPS

A. Focus on a process or event that you are familiar with so that you will know the examples, causes, or steps involved.

B. State the subject as clearly as possible in the topic sentence and try to indicate the examples, causes, or steps you will be discussing.

> EXAMPLES:
>
> The Drama Club's production of *As You Like It* failed *because of poor casting and poor directing.*
>
> You can make a wreath for your front door *in five simple steps.*
>
> Throughout American history, *women have had to struggle for educational opportunities* that men took for granted.

C. Be sure that all necessary steps or significant causes have been mentioned. If you are giving examples, use enough to show your reader that there is a pattern present rather than just one, isolated incident. (Generally, three to five examples should be enough.)

D. Arrange the examples, reasons, or steps in a logical order; either a time order or an order of importance works well with this kind of paragraph. If reasons or steps have been laid out in the topic sentence, they should be developed in the paragraph in the same order that they appear in the topic sentence. In the second topic sentence above, for instance, the two reasons for the play's failure are listed in chronological order. (Casting takes place before directing.) Therefore, in the paragraph, casting should be discussed before directing.

E. Use transitions like *next, then, even more important, another example, a hundred years later, most significant of all* to show the logical connections between your examples, causes, or steps.

F. Put important examples, causes, or steps into your base sentence.

EXAMPLES:

Unimportant idea emphasized

The first computers, which had vacuum-tube memories and oc-cupied an entire room, *were developed in the 1940's.*

Next, a *medicated pad,* which should be wiped over the entire face, *can be very effective.*

Important idea emphasized

The first computers, developed in the 1940's, *had vacuum-tube memories and occupied an entire room.*

Next, *a medicated pad,* which can be very effective, *should be wiped over the entire face.*

G. Use specific, concrete statements rather than general or abstract ones.

EXAMPLES:

General

Cars today are more efficient.

Tighten the bolts.

The *Ohio* is a big submarine.

Specific

A 1980 Citation averages 30 miles per gallon.

Use an eight-centimeter torque wrench with a rubber handle to tighten the bolts.

The nuclear submarine *Ohio* is 560 feet long and has an 18,700-ton displacement.

H. Make the conclusion a restatement or summary of your main point.

EXAMPLES:

Although the sets were elegant, poor casting and poor direction ruined this play.

With little more than an hour's work, you can hang this decoration on your door.

So, little-known women like these have forced open the doors of American educational institutions.

Exercise C

Keeping in mind the techniques above, combine the following sentences to produce a paragraph that lists reasons and examples.

1. I am qualified.

    The qualification is full.

    It is for a computer programming job.

I'm fully qualified for a computer programming job.

2. I have the background.

The background is in education.

You require the background.

I have the required educational background.

3. I graduated from Bayside College.

I received my A.A.

The degree was in computer programming.

I mastered COBOL.

I mastered Basic.

I mastered FORTRAN.

I graduated from Bayside College and received my A.A. in comp. programming. I mastered Cobol, Basic and Fortran.

4. I also have experience.

My experience is extensive.

My experience was gained on the job.

I also have extensive experience gained on the job.

5. I worked for CompuData, Inc.

I worked as a programmer.

We handled the accounts of several large businesses.

I worked there for two years.

I worked for 2 years for CompuData inc. as a programmer, handling the accounts of several large businesses.

6. I am working for the Social Security Administration.

I have worked there for a year and a half.

I work in Claims Verification.

I am working there now.

I have worked for a year and a half for the Social Security Administration, and now I'm working in Claims Verification.

7. My education gives me qualities.

My experience gives me qualities.

You need these qualities.

My education & experience gives me the qualities I need.

STRATEGY: BREAKING DOWN INTO CATEGORIES

A. Focus on a group of people or objects that you are very familiar with so that you will know the various types within the group.

B. Find some principle that you can use to classify the members of the group you are writing about. Teachers, for example, might be classified according to how strictly they grade. Restaurants might be classified according to price or according to kind of food served. Be sure this classification principle reveals some *significant* similarities or differences among members of the group. (Most people would not be interested in a division of teachers according to height, for instance.)

C. If possible, name the major categories (usually three to five) in your topic sentence.

EXAMPLES:

Three kinds of students roam the halls of Southern High School: *the scholar, the jock,* and *the loner.*

Nervousness, calm, and *enjoyment* are the three stages in learning to dance.

Children's games require *varying degrees of athletic skill.*

D. Explain each category and/or give examples of items that would fit in each.

E. Present the categories in a logical order: from smallest group to largest, from most expensive to least expensive, from first stage to last stage.

F. Use transitions that will emphasize your principle of classification: *slightly more expensive, the highest degree of skill, most boring of all, last.*

G. Use a conclusion that will sum up the whole classification system, not just the last point.

EXAMPLES:

Though the actual students change from year to year, *the same types seem to appear again and again.*

It is a rare dancer who does not pass through *each of these stages* in the course of his or her development.

Children have devised games that *suit every level of athletic skill* from none at all to super jock.

Exercise D

Using the suggestions above, combine the following groups of sentences to produce a paragraph that could introduce a study of architectural styles.

1. There have been four traditions.

    The traditions are in architecture.

    The architecture is of the West.

    The traditions are major.

    These traditions have influenced architecture.

    The traditions are from Egypt.

    The traditions are classical Greek and Roman.

    The traditions are Medieval.

    The traditions are of the Renaissance.

    There have been four major traditions influencing the architecture of the West. These traditions are from Egypt, classical Greek & Roman, Medieval and from the Renaissance

2. Architects learned about ornamentation.

    The ornamentation was decorative.

    The learning was from palaces, temples, and tombs.

    These structures were in ancient Egypt.

    Architects learned about decorative ornamentation and the value of the scale from palaces, temples and tombs in ancient Egypt.

Architects learned about the value of scale.

This learning was also from palaces, temples, and tombs.

(On the other hand)

3. The effect can be felt.

The effect is of classical Greece.

The effect is of classical Rome.

The feeling is in the practicality.

The practicality is elegant.

The practicality is of columns.

The feeling is in walls.

The walls are punctuated.

The punctuation is with arches.

The effect of classical Greece and Rome can be felt in the elegant practicality of columns and walls punctuated with arches.

4. Architecture was enriched.

The enrichment was by towers.

The enrichment was by spires.

The enrichment was by sculpture.

The sculpture was used for decoration.

These elements were developed mainly in cathedrals.

The cathedrals were in Europe.

They were great.

This took place during the Middle Ages.

(Later)

Architecture was enriched by towers, spires and sculpture used for decoration. These elements were developed during the Middle Ages in the great cathedrals of Europe.

5. Architecture grew in richness.

Architects developed skill.

The skill was technical.

The skill grew greater and greater.

The Renaissance developed an architecture.

The architecture was of expression.

The expression was of individual architects.

Architecture grew in richness and architects developed their technical skills which grew greater and greater. (And in addition) The Renaissance developed an architecture of expression of individual architects.

(And)

6. Every aspect developed.

The aspects are of architecture.

The architecture is modern.

The development has been out of these traditions.

Or the development has been in response to these traditions.

Every aspect developed modern architecture out of, or in response to these traditions.

STRATEGY: COMPARING OR CONTRASTING

A. Focus on two subjects between which you see some clear differences or similarities that will be of interest to your readers.

B. Name both subjects in the topic sentence and define the similarity or difference as clearly as you can.

> EXAMPLES:
>
> The *computer* **differs** from the *human brain* in its **speed of operation, number of components,** and **degree of free will.**
>
> *College* is much **more academically demanding** than *high school.*
>
> *My mother* and *my father* share the **same easygoing temperament.**

C. List several examples of the similarity or difference you are emphasizing. Make sure that your two subjects are developed in equal ways with just about the same space given and the same ideas developed for each subject. You can't, for example, compare two stories by writing two sentences about the plot of one story and ten sentences about the characters in the other.

D. Arrange the points of comparison or contrast in the block pattern or the alternating pattern.

> EXAMPLE:
>
> *Block pattern*
>   I. High School
>   A. Classwork
>   B. Homework   block of information
>   C. Long-term projects   on
>   high school
> II. College
>   A. Classwork   block of information
>   B. Homework   on
>   C. Long-term projects   college
>
> *Alternating pattern*
>   I. Classwork
>   A. High school
>   B. College
> II. Homework
>   A. High school
>   B. College
> III. Long-term projects
>   A. High school
>   B. College

Also consider the order in which you present the major points. High school, for instance, would logically be discussed before college; classwork might (since it is less demanding) logically come before long-term projects.

E. Use transitions like *similarly, likewise,* or *compared to* to suggest similarity between ideas. Use transitions like *on the other hand* or *however* to suggest contrast between ideas.

F. Put the similarities or differences you are trying to emphasize into the base sentence.

> EXAMPLE:
>
> *Similarity emphasized*
>
> Although I like to think of myself as more liberated than my grandmother, *our ideas about marriage are remarkably alike.* While we disagree about the methods to use, we *both think that communication between spouses is crucial to a good marriage.*
>
> *Difference emphasized*
>
> Although our ideas about marriage are remarkably alike, *I consider myself more liberated than my grandmother.* While we both agree that communication between spouses is crucial to a good marriage, *we disagree on the methods of communication.*

G. Use concrete, specific language rather than vague or abstract words to point out similarities or differences.

> EXAMPLE:
>
> *Vague language*
>
> Carol is nice like her mother.
>
> Summer is pleasanter than winter.
>
> *Specific language*
>
> Like her mother, Carol always has a smile and a kind word for everyone who comes to her door, even salespeople.
>
> With its drowsy, mint-julep evenings, summer in Atlanta is far more attractive to me than the cold, harried evenings up North when school is in session.

H. Restate the two subjects and the main points of similarity or difference in the conclusion.

> EXAMPLE:
>
> In **speed, complexity,** and **autonomy,** the *computer* is still not the equal of the *human brain.*
>
> Anyone who says that *college* is just another four years of *high school* hasn't looked carefully at the **academic demands** of college.
>
> Two more **evenly matched, unflappable** personalities than *Mom* and *Dad,* I could never hope to find.

Exercise E

Keeping in mind the suggestions above, combine the following groups of sentences to produce a paragraph that contrasts Baltimore and Washington, D.C.

1. Baltimore and Washington are only 45 miles apart.
   They share the Mid-Atlantic Piedmont.
   They are different.

2. Baltimore grew around a port.
   Its port is the second largest on the East Coast.
   It is the foundation of the city's economy.

3. Washington has no "natural" function.
   It was created to be a government center.
   It was deliberately put where no town had taken root.

4. Baltimore is mainly a blue-collar city.
   It works at heavy industry.
   One industry is steel.
   Another industry is automaking.
   Another industry is railroading.

5. Washington is primarily a white-collar city.
   It is dominated by huge office buildings.
   These buildings house the federal bureaucracies.

6. Baltimore is a city of ethnic neighborhoods.
   There is a large Polish population.
   There is a large Jewish population.
   There is a sizable Ukranian population.
   There is an established German community.

7. These groups live in areas.
   The areas are identifiable.
   Families have stayed there for generations.

8. The Washington area is peopled by professionals.
   They come from all over the country.
   They come to represent their hometowns and states.
   They come to work at the center of the government.

9. Baltimore belongs to its region.
   Washington belongs to the nation.

Exercise F

Combine each of the following groups of sentences to produce a complete paragraph. In some cases, you may have to add a topic sentence or a conclusion or transition words. In other paragraphs, you may have to rearrange the sentences to get the most effective order. In writing these paragraphs, use whatever techniques are appropriate to the strategy being used.

Emergency Room Report

1. The patient was admitted.
   The admitting was at 7:10 A.M.
   It was in the emergency room.
   The patient was complaining of severe pain in his ankle.

2. The region was swollen.
   The region was below the left distal fibula.
   The region was discolored.
   The discoloration covered an area.
   The area had a diameter of 7 centimeters.
   The area was circular.

3. The right side showed swelling.
   There was no discoloration.

4. The patient made a statement.
   He has pain when he moves the foot.
   The movement is from side to side.
   The pain is sharp.

5. The swollen area is tender.
   The tenderness is to the touch.
   The patient complains about it.

6. No signs appear.
   The signs are of injury.
   The appearance is on the leg above the ankle.
   The appearance is on the foot.

7. X-rays are needed.
   The need is to determine the extent.
   The extent is of the injury.
   Bones may be broken.

Boning a Trout

1. There is a way to bone a trout.
   The way is neat.
   The way is efficient.
   It can be learned in a few minutes.
2. Lift the fish by its tail.
   Make a cut on the underside.
   The cut should be small.
   It should be near the tail.
   This should be done first.
3. Hold the tail.
   Insert the tines of a fork into the cut.
   Separate the meat from the bones.
   The separating should be gentle.
4. You reach the gills.
   The filet will drop onto the plate.
   The filet will be unbroken.
5. Turn the fish over.
   Repeat the process.
   This may be done next.
6. You will have two filets.
   They will be perfect.
   You will have the backbone.
   The tail will be attached to the backbone.
   The head will be attached to the backbone.
   Head, tail, and backbone will be ready to throw away.
   You are done.

Visiting the Sierras

1. We always drove.
   The drive was up the Owens Valley.
   Mt. Wilson was on the left.
   It was bare.
   It was stark.
   Death Valley was on the right.

2. We left early.
   We saw the dawn.
   The dawn moved down the slope.
   The slope belonged to Mt. Wilson.

3. We passed through Lone Pine.
   We passed through Independence.
   We passed through Bishop.

4. There was a chain of lakes.
   It was high in the mountains.
   The lakes were perfect for fishing.
   They teemed with trout.

5. The lakes mirrored crags.
   The crags were covered with snow.
   The lakes were rimmed with pine.

6. We would rent a boat.
   I would row.
   My grandfather would flyfish.

7. I can see him.
   He would stand in the back of the boat.
   He was dressed in a flannel shirt.

8. He would catch the trout.
   My grandmother would cook them.
   The cooking was quick.
   They would be brown.
   They would be crisp.
   They would be delicious.

9. I will never forget those visits.
   The visits were to the Sierras.
   I went with my grandparents.

Finding "Real" Parents

1. Children should not be allowed to track down parents.
   The children are adopted.
   The parents are natural.
   There are emotional arguments.
   The arguments go against my opinion.

I feel this opinion.

My feeling is strong.

2. The parents have a right.

The parents are the natural ones.

The right is the one of privacy.

3. They may have built lives.

They may not want these lives disturbed.

The disturbance is by a stranger.

The stranger comes uninvited.

He comes from the past.

4. Most parents were assured.

These parents put children up for adoption.

The assurance was that the records would be sealed.

5. Some want to change this rule.

The change would come in the middle of the game.

This wouldn't be fair to people.

These people signed up under the old rules.

6. The parents have a right.

The parents adopted the child.

Their right is to be respected.

7. Their care should not have to compete.

Their love should not have to compete.

The competition is with an idea.

The idea is of identity "in the blood."

The idea has no basis in science.

The idea has no basis in law.

8. Curiosity is understandable.

Hurting people close to you has no excuse.

9. The privacy of natural parents outweighs it.

The feelings of adoptive parents outweigh it.

It is the curiosity about one's "blood" identity.

Natural Adaptation

1. They rush to make use of the abundance.

The females incubate the eggs in their bodies.

The newborn feed on the body.

2. The Irish elk grew antlers.
   The antlers were enormous.

3. Adaptations can be fascinating.
   The adaptation is natural.
   The fascination is in variety.
   The fascination is in subtlety.

4. One species of insect eats its mother.
   The insects are called gall midges.

5. Some antlers reached a span of twelve feet.
   The antlers were part of a display.
   The display was for mating.

6. Nature contains adaptations.
   The adaptations are unusual.
   They range from the tiny to the oversized.

7. Cicadas reproduce in long cycles.
   The cycles last 17 years.
   The cycles confuse their enemies.
   The abundance in one year ensures survival.
   The survival is that of some offspring.

8. They hatch from eggs.
   This kind of hatching is usual.
   Sometimes the food supply is particularly abundant.
   Then the midges reproduce as fast as possible.

9. Some scientists thought the antlers made the elk extinct.
   They became too big to support.
   This conclusion was false.
   Climatic changes killed the species.

Why Writing?

1. Only writing allows for independence.
   Only writing allows for records.

2. Students must grow beyond these tests.
   They must prepare themselves.
   The preparation is in setting their own questions.
   The preparation is in answering their own questions.

3. Writing is a tool.
   The tool is useful.

Students must learn to use it.

Their use must be for their own advantage.

4. They take enormous amounts of time.

They leave no records.

They cannot be reviewed for fairness.

5. Other ways do exist.

Objective tests are one way.

Oral exams are one way.

6. Some people resent writing for grades.

They say it is unfair.

They are wrong.

Writing is the only efficient way of testing a person's independence.

7. Oral exams do test independent thought.

They are inefficient.

The inefficiency is incredible.

8. Objective tests are efficient.

They require no writing.

Someone must always make up the questions.

Someone must always make up the answers.

The students get no practice in independence.

9. Students can answer questions in their own way.

They can even form their own questions.

Teachers can read the papers easily.

Papers provide proof of grading fairness.

Exercise G

In the following exercises, you are given a group of sentences to combine into an effective paragraph. When you have finished combining, you will have the first of a pair of paragraphs. Using it as a guide, write the second paragraph.

A. There are reasons for exercising.
The reasons are two.
One reason is appearance.
The other reason is health.
Most people look better when fit.
Exercise keeps weight down.
Exercise burns up calories.
The calories are excess.

Exercise increases circulation.
Increased circulation improves complexion.
Exercise develops coordination.
Coordination gives precision and grace to movement.
Exercise tones muscles.
The tone improves posture.
Exercise has other effects.
These effects go beyond cosmetics.
Exercise also affects health.

B.   Movies tell their stories with moving, talking pictures.
TV dramas tell their stories with moving, talking pictures.
Movies and TV dramas are very different.
You have to go out to the movies.
Going out costs money.
Movies have to give something you can't get at home.
Movies don't have to worry about sponsors.
Movies don't have to worry about children watching.
Movies can be controversial.
Movies can deal with adult material.
People are willing to pay for these qualities.
Movies cannot serialize a story effectively.
Only TV can create long serials.

C.   The shadow glided along the wall.
It was silent.
The wall belonged to the old castle.
The shadow continued until it reached a window.
A hand opened the sash.
The hand was gloved.
The opening was carefully done.
A figure slipped into the room.
The room was where Sabrina usually slept.
The shadowy figure moved toward the bed.
There was no sound.
The hand reached for the bed-curtain.
A voice said, "Don't move."
The voice added, "I have a pistol."
The voice was soft.
The voice was cool.

REVISING

P
A
R
T

3

Because any piece of writing involves so many considerations—audience, purpose, organization, sentence structure, word choice—it is almost impossible for any writer to keep all these factors in mind at once.

Because of this complexity, most writers will do some planning before writing, then write a draft of the paper, then work on revising that draft.

Re-vision means *seeing again*. In revising a piece of writing, you go back to it, perhaps several times, looking at it from different perspectives. One time, you might be looking to make sure you have stayed with your main idea. On another reading, you might be checking that connections have been established between ideas. Looking a third time, you might concentrate on whether the particular words you have chosen are suitable for your audience and purpose.

During the revision process it is often helpful to have someone else read your paper: your roommate, your teacher, your English lab instructor, a friend, a classmate. Someone else may see problems in organization or wording that you have overlooked because you are so familiar with the ideas you are writing about.

A final version of your paper may come only after several revisions. There is nothing out of the ordinary about this. No writer sits down and produces a perfect paragraph, essay, or report on the first try. It's important, then, that you allow yourself plenty of time for revision. That way, your final copy will present your idea as accurately and convincingly as possible. Time spent in revising your writing is time well spent.

Unity

11

One way to begin the revision process is to evaluate the unity of your writing. How well does this piece stick to the main idea?

By the time you have finished your first draft, you should have pretty well committed yourself to dealing with a particular, limited subject in a particular, limited way.

RELATING SUPPORT TO TOPIC SENTENCE

The topic sentence of your paragraph is your written commitment to your audience of what you are going to do in a certain piece of writing. For instance, if your topic sentence has told the audience that you are going to write about the costs of opening a new dental practice, you can't turn around and discuss the rewards of dentistry as a profession. You must deliver to your reader what you promised in the topic sentence.

Look at this paragraph:

> Fictional detectives are frequently presented as smarter than ordinary human beings. For instance, Poe's classic hero, C. Auguste Dupin, in *The Purloined Letter,* quickly finds a stolen document that the police have spent months searching for in vain. Sir Arthur Conan Doyle's famous sleuth, Sherlock Holmes, baffles client after client by telling them what they have come for before they have said a word. In the twentieth century, Agatha Christie's Belgian detective, Hercule Poirot, prides himself on his ability to use his "little gray cells" more effectively than the police use theirs. No mere human villain can hope to outwit these superhumanly clever investigators.

What does this paragraph promise the reader? How does it keep that promise?

Well, the topic sentence limits the discussion to fictional detectives. The topic sentence also requires that the paragraph discuss only the intelligence of these characters, not their physical prowess or their social status. In addition, the topic sentence suggests that fictional detectives will be compared to ordinary people.

The topic sentence's promise is kept by the writer's giving three fictional detectives as examples and discussing the mental abilities of each one as compared to other people—the police or the client. So the paragraph does stick to the subject and focus set up in the topic sentence.

Because the focus part of the topic sentence exerts such control over what happens in the rest of the paragraph, it is frequently referred to as the controlling idea of the paragraph.

Now look at the paragraph below, which is presented without a topic sentence. If the support and the conclusion are doing what the topic sentence promised, you should be able to figure out the subject and the controlling idea and construct a suitable topic sentence.

At a minimum, all the rooms in the center should be well-lighted and clean. It should have fire extinguishers and clearly marked exits as well as smoke alarms. Windows on upper floors should be locked or made secure with screens or bars. Stairways should have handrails. All play equipment should be in good repair. Also the outside play area should be fenced and free of hazardous debris. Finally, a safe day care center should provide enough staff supervision to keep childish exuberance or inexperience from causing a serious accident. The safety of the children is an important factor in choosing an acceptable child care facility.

After reading this paragraph, you should see that the subject is a day care center (references circled) and that the focus is on safety features (references underlined). Notice that every sentence in this paragraph makes some reference to either the subject or the controlling idea or both.

A suitable topic sentence for this paragraph might be:

Safety must be considered in choosing a day care center.

or

In a good day care center, parents should not have to worry about the safety of their children.

A paragraph in which the support fits the topic sentence is said to have *unity.* In a unified paragraph, all the supporting sentences relate directly to the subject and the controlling idea presented in the topic sentence.

Exercise A

Here are several more paragraphs that are unified but lack topic sentences. Read the support and conclusion parts of the paragraphs and see if you can construct a topic sentence that will fit the subject and the focus of each paragraph. Circle all the references to the subject in each paragraph and underline all the references to the focus or controlling idea.

1. _____

   _____

   Many of Ellington's thousands of pieces were songs like "Sophisticated Lady" or "I Let a Song Go Out of My Heart." He also wrote impressionistic mood music like "Azure" and "On a Turquoise Cloud." Social commentary was part of his repertoire in works like "Harlem Speaks." In addition he composed religious music, ballets, and film scores. Finally, and perhaps most significantly, he innovated new jazz concepts in works like "The Mooch" and "Ko-Ko." It is this kind of versatility that made Duke Ellington one of America's greatest composers.

2. _____

   _____

   For one thing, El Mirador is much larger than Tikal. Archeologists estimate that the newly uncovered city supported close to 80,000 people, twice the population of its neighbor to the south. El Mirador is also some 350 years earlier than Tikal, which was inhabited by the Mayans in the eighth century. The architecture and pottery of the two sites also show some significant differences. El Mirador's pyramids are much larger than those at other Mayan sites, and its houses don't have the triangular, arched roofs found at Tikal. The pottery at El Mirador lacks the painted scenes found on other Mayan pieces. Archeologists are hoping that the study of these differences may unlock the secret of the fall of the Mayan civilization in Central America.

3. _____

   _____

   One type of information furnished by an accounting system is that which shows whether an organization is performing well or badly over some period of time. Are its sales increasing? Is it reaching more people? These data can be used by the management to plan and control current operations. Stockholders and government agencies can use such data for investment, funding, or tax purposes. Another kind of information generated by an accounting system is that which calls attention to a problem in the organization. Is one department working less effectively than the others? Closely related to the performance data, this attention-directing information lets management focus quickly on areas of possible improvement. Finally, a good accounting system provides problem-solving information. It can quantify the relative merits of several courses of action. Can more money be saved by switching to new packaging or by moving the storage facility? If the company lowers the employees' medical benefits, can it afford to fund a dental plan? Thus, an effective accounting system has to be able to serve more than one purpose.

4. _____

    _____

Once a master builder had been hired and a design for the cathedral approved, the master carpenter could begin cutting the timber, and the master quarryman could begin cutting the stone. The laborers, meanwhile, cleared the site and dug the hole for the foundation, a process which could take up to a year. Another ten to fifteen years would be spent constructing the foundation and the main support piers and buttresses. It would take another five years or so to complete the main walls. Then work could start on the roof, which was made of a series of wooden trusses covered with lead sheets. In another five years, work might begin on the vaulted ceiling of the interior. After about fifty years of building, the cathedral would be ready for the glassmakers to prepare the stained glass windows. While the windows were being installed, sculptors would finish the decorative carving inside, and masons would lay the stone floor. Eighty years after the cathedral had been started, it might be ready for the finishing touches: a bell, doors, a spire. All told, a hundred years was not an unreasonable building time for a twelfth-century cathedral. And if the conditions were less than ideal, if there were financial or structural problems, the building might well take two hundred years from start to finish.

5. _____

    _____

Behind me I was sure I heard relentless, ghostly footsteps, accompanied by a low, eerie laugh. Although the sounds seemed to be growing louder, I didn't dare turn around to see if *it* was catching up to me. Suddenly my chest felt too cramped to hold my heart, which was racing wildly. My palms were sweaty, but my mouth was dry, and when I tried to call out, no sound came except a faint croak. As the moaning laugh chased me down the hall, my bones seemed to have turned to jelly. I stumbled and choked in the rising dust. Finally, after what seemed like hours, my groping hand found the door and pulled frantically at the knob. Slamming the heavy door behind me, I collapsed against the wall, a quivering lump of fear.

One way of ensuring unity in a paragraph is to eliminate, either in prewriting or in revision, any details which don't directly support the topic and controlling idea you have chosen.

Exercise B

In each of the following exercises, you are given a topic sentence and some possible supporting details. In each case decide which details would fit in a unified paragraph and be prepared to explain why.

1. The reference books of the library can be a great help to a student.
    a. A good encyclopedia can give a student a general overview of a subject.
    b. The card catalog shows a student all the holdings the library has in any subject area.
    c. The card catalog is usually located near the main desk.
    d. The *Reader's Guide to Periodical Literature* can help a student find magazine articles on almost any topic.
    e. *Current Biography* can give a student background information on anyone who is in the news.
    f. This helpful reference tool is issued in monthly volumes.
    g. *Book Review Digest* tells the student the critics' views of major new books.
    h. The *Digest* covers only the twentieth century.
    i. The *Oxford English Dictionary* tells a student what a word means.
    j. It also can tell how the meaning of a word has changed over the years.
    k. The library has to spend a great deal of money to maintain a good reference collection.
2. Midwifery is making a comeback in the United States today.
    a. Over 20 hospitals in the New York area offer midwife services.
    b. In 1960 only two hospitals offered such services.
    c. Many midwives have graduated from nursing school.
    d. Almost all states now license nurse-midwives.
    e. The Department of Health and Human Services has encouraged federally funded institutions to employ these practitioners.
    f. In the past, midwives were a rural phenomenon.
    g. They were the symbol of inferior health care.
    h. Many women today believe that midwives offer a more personal, less technological approach to childbirth.
    i. There are over 500,000 births a year in the United States.

> j. All over the country, women are turning to midwives instead of traditional obstetricians.
>
> k. Expectant mothers ask midwives for advice on diet during pregnancy.
>
> l. They ask midwives for advice on contraception after delivery.

Exercise C

From each set of sentences below, you should be able to put together a unified paragraph. However, in some sets, you may find certain details which don't fit the subject and/or the controlling idea presented in the topic sentence. Leave these details out of the finished paragraph and be prepared to explain why they did not fit.

> EXAMPLE:
>
> (not a complete paragraph)
>
> *Topic Sentence*
> Mildred Didrikson was a female athlete.
> Her nickname was "Babe."
> As an athlete, she was the greatest.
> Her greatness was in modern times.

1. She excelled.
   Her excellence was in basketball.
   Her excellence was in track and field.
   Her excellence was in golf.

2. She was a basketball player.
   She played in 1930.
   She was an All-American.

3. She won eight events.
   She tied for a ninth.
   The events were in the championships.
   The events were in track and field.
   The events were for women.
   The winning took place between 1930 and 1932.

4. Wilma Rudolf was a runner.
   She competed in the Olympics.
   She was also a female.
   She was also a great athlete.

POSSIBLE PARAGRAPH: (incomplete)

Mildred "Babe" Didrikson was the greatest female athlete in modern times. She excelled in basketball, track and field, and golf. In 1930, she was an All-American basketball player. Between 1930 and 1932, she won eight events and tied for a ninth in the women's track and field championships. . . .

(Notice that the sentence about Wilma Rudolph should be left out of this paragraph since it does not relate to the subject set up in the topic sentence.)

Types of Human Activity

Topic Sentence

The thinkers classified all human activity.

The thinkers were in ancient India.

The classification was into spheres.

There were four spheres.

They were complementary.

1. *Artha* connotes wealth.

   It connotes power.

   The wealth is material.

   Artha connotes possessions.

   The possessions bring physical comfort.

   They bring security.

2. Wealth is a part.

   The wealth is individual.

   The part is of *Artha.*

   The economy is a part as well.

   The economy is of the state.

3. This classification is similar.

   The similarity is to a system.

   The system was developed in Japan.

   The system was developed by Buddhists..

4. *Kama* is the second area.

   The area is of human acitvity.

   Kama means gratification.

   The gratification is sensual.

5. *Kama* includes not only sexual love.

   It includes not only romantic love.

   It also includes regulation.

The regulation is of marriage.
The regulation is of the family.

6. Many Indians have families.
   The families are large.
   The father is the ruler.
   His rule is absolute.

7. *Dharma* encompasses a sphere.
   Dharma means Law.
   The sphere is of customs.
   The sphere is of morals.
   The sphere is of duty.
   The duty is religious.

8. The Law is applicable to everyone.

9. *Moksha* is the goal.
   The goal is of human existence.
   Moksha means release.
   The goal is final.

10. Its object is not success.
    The success is in worldly life.
    Its object is liberation.
    The liberation is from limitations.
    The limitations are of that life.

Conclusion
All human activity has a place.
The place is in the Indian system.
The system is of thought.
The system is well-ordered.

What Is a Symbol?

Topic Sentence
A symbol is an object.
A symbol is a name.
A symbol is a picture.
This thing is familiar.
The familiarity is in daily life.
This thing also conveys meaning.
The meaning is beyond the literal.

1. For example, the flag is symbolic.
   The flag is American.
2. The flag is some pieces.
   The pieces are of cloth.
   This flag exists on a literal level.
   The cloth forms a certain design.
3. However, the American flag has meaning.
   The meaning is more than just a piece of cloth.
   The piece is ordinary.
4. It can convey feelings of pride.
   It can convey feelings of hatred.
   The feelings depend on who uses the symbol.
5. A symbol is like a metaphor.
   A symbol is more complicated.
6. Another example is the lamb.
   The example is of symbolism.
   The lamb is used to represent Christ.
   The representation is as the perfect sacrifice.
   The symbolism is used in Christian writing and art.
7. The Lamb of God was a sort of subject.
   The subject interested painters.
   The painters were in the nineteenth century.
   The painters were romantic.
8. Even very primitive people use symbolism.
9. Painted animals are killed.
   The killing is symbolic.
   The killing is to ensure the death.
   The death is of the real animal.
   The death is in the hunt.
   This killing is done in some African tribes.
   Conclusion
   Symbols are one way.
   Human beings have used that way.
   The human beings are in all ages.
   The way is for dealing.
   The dealing is with a world.
   The world is complex.

Choosing a Brand Name

Topic Sentence
The key is simplicity.
The key is adaptability.
The key is to a good brand name.

1. The name should be short.
   One or two syllables are preferable.
   Examples are "Band-Aid" or "Souptime."

2. The name must also be easy.
   The ease is in reading.
   The ease is in pronunciation.

3. Brand names are developed.
   The development is by computers.
   This is done often.

4. The name is pronounceable.
   The pronunciation is in only one way.
   This brand name is best.

5. These characteristics will help a name.
   The characteristics are of simplicity.
   The help will be in adaptability.

6. Easy pronunciation will help.
   The pronunciation is in all languages.
   The product is to be marketed.
   The marketing is in foreign countries.

7. "Coke" is a good example.
   The example is of such adaptability.
   The adaptability is to other languages.

8. Simplicity also helps a name.
   The help is in fitting requirements.
   The requirements are for different packages.
   The requirements are for different labels.

9. Finally, simplicity means a name can be used.
   The use is with media.
   The media are for advertising.
   The media are several.

The media are different.

The media are print, TV, or radio.

10. In addition, brand names should not make suggestions.

The suggestions are negative.

The suggestions are offensive.

Conclusion

Simplicity can make the difference.

Adaptability can make the difference.

The simplicity and adaptability are of a brand name.

The difference is between a product and a failure.

The product is successful.

The product is new.

Tracing Your Family Tree

Topic Sentence

Genealogy is the study.

The study is of histories.

The histories are of families.

Genealogy should be done in a way.

The way is organized.

1. The first step is to make charts.

An alternative is to buy charts.

The charts are to record information.

The recording is systematic.

The information is about everyone in the family.

The information is such as complete names.

The information is such as dates.

The dates are of birth.

The dates are of marriage.

The dates are of death.

2. Then fill in the charts.

The filling should be with names.

The filling should be with dates.

You already know the names and dates.

The names are like your own.

The names are like your brothers' and sisters'.

The names are like your parents'.

The dates are like your birthdate.

The dates are like your brothers' and sisters' birthdates.

The dates are like your parents' birthdates.

3.   Next you should ask your parents.

You should ask your aunts and uncles.

You should ask your grandparents.

They can give you more names.

They can give you more dates.

The names are for your chart.

The dates are for your chart.

4.   The tradition has been exhausted.

The tradition is oral.

Look for records.

The records are written.

The records are of the family.

The records are like Bibles.

The records are like diaries.

The records are like letters.

These may give you clues.

The clues are valuable.

The clues are about dates.

The clues are about family relationships.

5.   Such records are valuable.

This value is frequent.

They can be sold to dealers.

The dealers are in antiques.

The sale can be for a profit.

6.   Begin to check agencies.

The agencies keep records.

The agencies are like courthouses.

The agencies are like churches.

This should be done after the family sources.

7.   These records are official.

These records will verify information.

These records will add to information.

You have already discovered information.

8. Finally, you have checked deeds.

You have checked wills.

You have checked marriage licenses.

You have checked birth and death certificates.

You have checked as many as you can.

Turn to a library.

The library is historical.

Or it may be genealogical.

The turning is to locate information.

The turning is to locate sources.

The information and sources are additional.

9. There are local libraries.

There are state libraries.

Besides these, you might want to try the Library of Congress.

You might want to try the Daughters of the American Revolution Library.

You might want to try the National Genealogical Society.

All of these are in Washington, D.C.

Conclusion

You use a method.

The method is orderly.

The method is for researching.

The method is for recording.

The researching and recording are of your family tree.

This makes it easier.

You find your ancestors.

UNIFYING THROUGH SUBORDINATION

In the paragraphs you just worked on, you were instructed to omit any details which did not refer directly to the topic and controlling idea set up for the paragraph. There is, however, another way of dealing with such material. Some details that are interesting but not directly related to the controlling idea may be included in your writing through the use of subordination.

For example, suppose that you are writing to a friend to tell him or her about how you are doing in school. Perhaps your topic sentence is: *Last semester went well for me.* You have these three facts to report:

I had trouble in English.
My math grades were good.
My history grades were the best I have ever earned.

If you just leave out all mention of English, you're not giving an entirely accurate picture of the semester. On the other hand, having trouble in English doesn't really support the impression of success you want to create.

One way of handling this difficulty is to emphasize your success in math and history by putting those ideas into the base sentence and to deemphasize your trouble in English by putting that in a subordinate word group.

> Even though I had trouble in English, *my math grades were good, and my history grades were the best I have ever earned.*

Here is another situation that calls for the use of subordination. Suppose you are reviewing a new restaurant for the local paper. In your opening sentence, you want to convey your favorable impression of the place and also mention its location. Since the main purpose of the review is to give your opinion, you don't want to give too much emphasis to the location. However, the location is certainly important information to your readers. The solution is to subordinate the location.

> *Paul's Pizza Palace,* located at 17 W. Tilman Street, *offers good, but not elaborate, Italian food at reasonable prices.*

This sentence emphasizes your favorable attitude by putting it in the base sentence. You have not destroyed the unity of your article by having a base sentence with information that does not directly support the controlling idea.

The techniques of subordination are presented in Chapter 4; you may wish to review them before doing the exercises that follow.

Exercise D

For each of the following paragraphs, you are given a topic sentence with the controlling idea italicized. Combine the sentences to produce unified support for the topic sentence. Every base sentence should be directly connected to the controlling idea.

Wye Castle

T.S.   Wye Castle has a *sinister* reputation.

1.   The Castle belonged to the Wye family for centuries.

The Castle is on a hill in Shropshire.

The hill is near the Welsh border.

Many legends tell of dark deeds in the Castle.

2. Moonlight shines on the floor.
   The floor is in the Duke's bedroom.
   A stain appears on the stone.
   The stain looks like blood.

3. The blood is Esmeralda's.
   She was the Duke's mistress.
   She was a peasant.
   She was beautiful.
   The Duke set her above his family.

4. There is a mirror.
   It stands in the bedroom.
   One can see them in it.
   One son is stabbing Esmeralda.
   The other holds her.
   Their mother watches.
   Their mother is the Duchess.

5. There is another room.
   The walls glow.
   The air is cold.
   The cold is like ice.

6. No one knows it.
   It happened in that room.
   It must have been awful.
   Everybody has some explanation.

7. There is also the cellar door.
   Someone taps on it.
   Someone asks to be let in.
   This happens every New Year's Day.

8. The door is opened.
   The opening is done by a foolhardy soul.
   No one is there.
   This happens every time.

9. The Castle is quite attractive in daylight.
   No one lives there now.

Job Application

T.S.   I am *fully qualified for* the position you advertised *teaching Spanish.*

1. I attended from 198– to 198–.

   I attended Middle States University.

   I received my Bachelor of Arts.

   My B.A. is in Spanish.

2. My overall grade point average is 3.75.

   I was graduated with these grade point averages.

   My grade point average in Spanish is 3.90.

3. I have experience.

   The experience qualifies me to teach Spanish.

4. Middle States University offers internships.

   One internship is in foreign language teaching.

   I took this one.

   It was in fall semester, 198–.

5. The school was in Capitol Heights.

   It was an elementary school.

   I had a class of twelve students.

   Their ages were from 8 to 10.

   I taught them the basics.

   The basics were of Spanish.

6. My students did well.

   I enjoyed myself.

   My supervisor was pleased.

7. I earned the money for my college expenses.

   I did this every summer.

   The program was run by the Parks and Recreation Department.

   I taught Spanish songs to children.

   The teaching was in a program.

8. I combine education and experience.

   I would be an excellent choice for your school.

   My combination is unique.

The Odyssey

T.S.   Homer celebrated *cunning* and *cleverness* in the *Odyssey.*

1. Athena is one figure.
   (pronounced *uh-THEE-nuh*)

Odysseus is the other figure.
    (pronounced *oh-DIS-ee-us*)
Two figures dominate the poem.
The figures are intelligent.
Their intelligence is extreme.

2.   Odysseus is trying to get home.
He wants to see his wife.
He wants to see his son.
He is the cleverest man alive.

3.   Odysseus conquered Troy.
Other heroes fought.
They fought for ten years.
They were trying to take the city.
He used a strategy to do it.
The strategy was clever.
Homer calls him "The man who is never at a loss."

4.   Several gods were against him.
His crew was disobedient.
He continued to get home.
It took him ten years.

5.   Athena is gray-eyed.
Athena is courageous.
Athena is the goddess of wisdom.
Athena is the other example.
The example is of cunning.

6.   She tricks her father.
She outwits her uncle.
Her uncle is the sea-god.
She fools everyone.
Her father is chief of the gods.

7.   She meets Odysseus.
They argue.
The battle of wits is unmatchable.

8.   Athena's cleverness brings peace.
Odysseus' craftiness brings peace.
This happens in the end.
The peace is to the world of the poem.

9. Homer respected courage.

   Homer admired honesty.

   Homer felt intelligence was greater.

Los Angeles

T.S.   Los Angeles is a *latecomer* among American cities.

1. Los Angeles is old.

   Los Angeles was founded by the Spanish.

   They founded it in the seventeenth century.

   Los Angeles was a village.

   The village was sleepy.

   This condition lasted for most of Los Angeles's long life.

2. San Francisco was growing rapidly.

   The Gold Rush helped San Francisco grow.

   The Gold Rush was in 1849.

   Los Angeles grew.

   The growth was slow.

   Los Angeles became a center.

   The center was agricultural.

3. The movies came.

   They were drawn by the climate.

4. The aircraft industry came.

   It came for the same reason the movies came.

5. War broke out in 1940.

   Los Angeles supplied planes and movies.

   Los Angeles's industries grew.

   The growth was enormous.

6. The war was over.

   L.A.'s population boom continued.

7. San Franciscans watched.

   Their watching was in disbelief.

   Los Angeles was the fourth largest city in the United States.

   This was by the early Fifties.

8. Los Angeles overtook Philadelphia.

   This happened in the late Fifties.

   Los Angeles became the third largest city in the United States.

The smog grew worse.

The freeways were born.

9. The village had become L.A.

The village was named after Our Lady, Queen of the Angels.

L.A. was a city.

The city was thriving.

The city was gigantic.

The city sprawled.

The sprawling is over the land area.

The land area is urban.

The land area is the largest in the world.

Coherence

12

To communicate an idea clearly to an audience, it is not enough that a paragraph concentrate on developing one idea. A paragraph may be unified and well-organized and still be unnecessarily difficult to read because the relationships among the sentences are unclear. In revising a piece of writing, you should pay particular attention to establishing the connections between your ideas.

For instance, look at the two paragraphs below. Which one is easier to follow?

A. The link between intelligence and heredity has not been proven to be as important as some people have claimed. We have no solid definition of what intelligence is. Those who believe there is an important connection base their idea on IQ tests. IQ tests are intended only to predict an individual's success in school. Academic achievement is a poor definition of intelligence. Good research on the in-

B. The link between intelligence and heredity has not been proven to be as important as some people have claimed. First, we have no solid definition of intelligence. Those who believe there is an important link base their claim on IQ tests, but these tests are intended only to predict an individual's success in school, and academic success is a poor definition of intelligence. Second, we have no good research on the inherita-

heritability of mental ability doesn't exist. The only sound evidence comes from studies of identical twins raised in different backgrounds. The information seems to show an important connection between scores on tests and heredity. The research doesn't take into account the influence of the shared age and sex in twins. Age and sex are known to be important on the tests. By themselves, they may account for the close scores achieved by the twins. The most famous twin study now appears to have been faked to fit the researcher's prejudices. We are not able to make a scientific generalization about intelligence and inheritance.

bility of intelligence. The only sound evidence comes from studies of identical twins raised in different backgrounds. These studies seem to show an important link between test scores and heredity, but they do not take into account the influence of the twins' shared age and sex, which are known to be important on the tests. By themselves, age and sex may account for the close scores achieved by the twins. In addition, the most famous twin study now appears to have been faked to fit the researcher's prejudices. As a result of the lack of a solid definition and good research, we are not able to make a scientific generalization about intelligence and inheritance.

Paragraph A is unnecessarily hard to read. To understand it, you may have to reread the paragraph several times, working to tie the ideas together, because the relationships between one sentence and another and between the topic sentence and all the supporting sentences are not clear. You may not have realized at first that the argument has two main parts: there is no solid definition of intelligence; there is no good research on the inheritance of intelligence. Even though the paragraph is organized into these two parts, the division is hard to see on a first reading.

What Paragraph A lacks is *coherence*, that is, the ideas do not stick together (cohere) well.

In the revised paragraph (B), on the other hand, four specific writing techniques have been used to show the relationships between ideas.

First, some sentences have been *combined* using methods familiar to you from exercises in earlier chapters.

Those who believe there is an important link base their claim on IQ tests, *but* these tests are intended only to predict an individual's success in school, *and* academic success is a poor definition of intelligence.

Second, some sentences have been tied into the paragraph by the addition of *transition signals* which explain their relationships either to the preceding sentence or to the topic sentence.

> *First,* we have no solid definition of what intelligence is.
>
> *In addition,* the most famous twin study appears to have been faked to fit the researcher's prejudices.
>
> *As a result of the lack of a solid definition and good research,* we are not able to make a scientific generalization about intelligence and inheritance.

Third, some sentences have been rewritten to give them *parallel structures* to point out their parallel function in the paragraph.

> First, *we have no solid definition* of what intelligence is.
>
> Second, *we have no good research* on the inheritability of intelligence.

And finally, the wording of some sentences has been changed so *key words and phrases are repeated* to help the reader follow the discussion.

> These *studies* seem to show an important link between scores and heredity. . . .
>
> In addition, the most famous twin *study* now appears to have been faked to fit the researcher's prejudices.

Revising to Help Readers See Connections

Sentence Combining

Transition Signals

Parallel Structure

Repetition of Key Words

SENTENCE COMBINING

You have been learning this technique since you began speaking, and you have been working at it ever since you opened this book. It is one of the most useful tools in achieving coherence because it employs the most common devices in the language for bringing out the relationships between ideas. Every time you modify a word, coordinate two ideas, or subordinate one idea to another, you are creating and explaining relationships. So fundamental are these devices that you could say the invention of the conjunctions (*so, if, or,* and others) was one of humanity's giant steps forward.

Careful combining of sentences helps the readers see precisely the connections you want them to see. Compare these examples:

> Those who believe there is an important link base their claim on IQ tests. These tests are intended only to predict an individual's success in school.

> Those who believe there is an important link base their claim on IQ tests, *but* these tests are intended only to predict an individual's success in school.

The addition of the conjunction *but* brings out the contrast between the use some people would put IQ tests to and the use for which they were intended. This contrast is the most important relationship between these ideas. In the first version, the relationship is there, but it is not immediately apparent. In the second version, the contrast is clearly indicated. Sentence combining is the basic stuff of coherence.

If you need to review any of the techniques of sentence combining, refer to Chapters 2, 3, and 4.

TRANSITION SIGNALS

This technique is closely related to sentence combining. You are adding a word or phrase to a sentence to make its connection to the preceding or following sentences clear. Words like *thus* or *in addition* serve as a sign to your readers of the way in which one sentence relates to another. Transition signals can help your reader follow more easily the pattern of your thinking. For instance, in the paragraph shown earlier in this chapter, the last sentence begins with the phrase, *as a result,* which lets the reader know that a conclusion is about to be drawn from what has been said before. Without that signal, the reader might be unprepared for a conclusion and might have to go back and reread the sentence once she has seen its function.

Each transition signal sets up a different kind of relationship between ideas. Here are some of the most common transition signals, grouped according to the kind of connection they establish between ideas.

Transition Signals

Adding On:	also, besides, first, second, furthermore, in addition, moreover, next, then, after, finally, last
Comparing:	similarly, likewise, in the same way
Contrasting:	however, on the other hand, nevertheless, instead, otherwise, yet
Giving Examples:	for instance, for example, specifically, in fact, in particular
Showing Result:	thus, therefore, consequently, as a result, accordingly, so
Summing Up:	in conclusion, in short, on the whole, in general, in summary, in other words
Moving in Time:	then, shortly, afterwards, in the meantime, soon, at last, now
Moving in Space:	nearby, overhead, opposite, on the left, on the right

Transition signals usually require punctuation since they are interrupting or preceding the base sentence.

> We met Sally and Dean at the movie. *Afterward,* we went to dinner.
>
> Billman has cheated the city; *therefore,* I will not vote for her.
>
> Their father leaves at 6 every morning. The children, *as a result,* rarely get a hot breakfast before school.

Exercise A

Use appropriate transition signals to show the relationship between the sentences in each of the following sets. Punctuate as needed.

1. The sponsors spent millions of dollars building historically accurate sets.
   The show should be worth seeing.
   I have to work that night.

   _____

   _____

   _____

2. Dan would never go there.
   That school is too far away from home.
   It doesn't have an agriculture program.
   It is far too expensive.

   _____

   _____

   _____

3. Mr. Levine is a thoroughly competent architect.
   Mr. Peters has a reputation for carelessness.

   _____

   _____

   _____

4. Many of Ross MacDonald's novels deal with the search for a lost parent.
   The Underground Man uses this theme. *The Blue Hammer* uses it.

   _____

   _____

   _____

5. Tennis is very popular in Sewall County.
   The Women's Tennis League has 500 members this year. The children's

program attracted 1,250 youngsters. Every school in the county offers tennis as a physical education option.

_____

_____

_____

_____

6. Computers are remarkable machines.
   Few people realize their ability to serve human needs.

_____

_____

_____

7. Martindale School has produced many successful women. Connie New-man became the vice-president of a major exporting company. Louraine Riser has published several widely acclaimed novels. Ann Terry is head of the State Association of PTA's.

_____

_____

_____

8. Amy is a lot like her mother.
   They both enjoy meeting people.
   Amy belongs to several social groups at school. Her mother belongs to two neighborhood social groups.

_____

_____

_____

_____

9. Kenny's yard was our favorite place to play. A huge tree shaded it. The sandbox filled with toys was always ready for us. There was a swing set and a sliding board. And it had a frontier fort complete with a lookout platform.

_____

_____

_____

_____

10. Ms. Delaney never arrives on time for work. She makes at least one mistake with her cash count every day. Several customers have complained about her rudeness. I would recommend firing her.

_____

_____

_____

_____

PARALLEL STRUCTURE

When you wish to show that two sentences do the same work or hold the same relationship to the topic sentence, arrange them in the same (*or parallel*) pattern.

For example, in the first version of the sample paragraph, the sentences announcing the main sections read: *We have no solid definition of what intelligence is* and *Good research on the inheritability of mental ability doesn't exist.* These sentences are doing the same work (indicating important sections of the paragraph), but their structure is not parallel, and the reader is not helped to see the similarity in the sentences' function.

In the more coherent version, the same sentences read: *First, we have no solid definition of intelligence* and *Second, we have no good research on the inheritability of intelligence.* Now both sentences begin with exactly the same three words (after the transition signal): *we have no . . .* , and both insert the topic they are introducing: *good research, solid definition;* then both end with the words *of intelligence.*

$$\text{We have no} \begin{cases} \text{solid definition} \\ \text{good research on the inheritability} \end{cases} \text{of intelligence.}$$

Now the parallel structure signals the parallel function and helps the reader see the underlying sameness of the sentence.

In the combining exercises earlier, you practiced all the major sentence patterns in English. You can apply your skill to create parallel structures when you want to give your reader a clearer sense of the underlying divisions of your paragraphs.

This device of parallelism can be used to stress the similarity of ideas within one sentence as well as between sentences.

For instance, in this sentence

In the evening, Jim likes *to read the newspaper*, to *drink a glass of wine*, and *to snooze before the fire.*

the three things that Jim likes are phrased in parallel ways—all using the *to* + verb construction.

Exercise B

Rewrite the sentences below using parallel structures to show the connection between related ideas.

1. Governor Von Mayer promised lower taxes, a legislature that is honest, and to make the state bureaucracy smaller.

   _____

   _____

   _____

2. Pairs skating is characterized by fancy lifts and showy turns. The skaters emphasize intricate footwork and precise movements in ice dancing.

   _____

   _____

   _____

3. A hospice administers carefully controlled medication that does not cure illness or prolong life, but is intended to relieve the pain of the slowly dying.

    _____

    _____

    _____

4. One of the major considerations in convention planning is the number of hotel rooms available. A city with less than 1,500 rooms can't compete very well for convention business. Selection of a convention site may also depend on the quality of the food service. Entertainment and sightseeing potential are also considered by convention planners.

    _____

    _____

    _____

    _____

5. Renting an apartment is certainly cheaper in the short term because of the lower costs. Tax advantages make home-owning more attractive in the long term.

    _____

    _____

    _____

6. Good photography depends on the skill of the photographer, having the best quality camera, and that you choose the proper film.

    _____

    _____

    _____

7. Her lips were full and self-indulgent; large, liquid eyes sat in her face; smoothness characterized her pale forehead.

_____

_____

_____

8. Sixty percent of the money goes to fund-raising costs. The Association takes 30 percent for administration. The poor receive only ten cents out of every dollar contributed.

_____

_____

_____

9. Franklin's success was due to his ability to work hard, the fact that he was curious, and because of his common sense.

_____

_____

_____

10. The first television sets were huge boxes with small, fuzzy images. Now tiny boxes that have images that are fuzzy and small are called televisions.

_____

_____

_____

REPETITION OF KEY WORDS

This important device consists of weaving the ideas of the paragraph together by repeating the words related to the topic and/or the controlling idea of the paragraph. Weaving is an appropriate image since this technique does not show relationships or organization; instead, it focuses the reader's attention on the "threads," the important ideas, as they move through the paragraph to make up the fabric of the discussion. For example, in the sample paragraph, the key words *intelligence* and *heredity* appear again and again, along with other important words (*study, claim, test*). These repetitions help the reader to see the main idea, sense the underlying unity of the argument.

Here is another paragraph that uses repetition of key words to achieve coherence. What are the key words in this paragraph? How many repetitions of them can you see?

America's attitude toward the handicapped has been undergoing a slow but definite change. For one thing, the handicapped have benefitted from a general shift in Americans' expectation of government. Since the Depression, this society has assumed that government ought to help people in trouble. More recently, handicapped Americans have followed the lead of other minorities in demanding not just government help, but their full rights as citizens. Another factor in the changing attitude toward the handicapped is their increased visibility. America's population is growing older, and thus more people are more subject to crippling diseases and injuries. At the same time, changes in medicine and technology have vastly increased the number of people, both young and old, who survive a disabling accident or disease. These changes in political philosophy and medical science have helped to move the handicapped out of hiding and into the mainstream of American life.

Exercise C

In the following sentences, change the wording of one of the pairs so the key idea in the two sentences is repeated. You may want to rewrite one sentence to parallel the other or add some transition signal if you feel these changes would add to the effectiveness of the sentences.

EXAMPLE:

Japanese art is characterized by an understanding of simplicity.

Making things simple also rules their music.

Japanese art is characterized by an understanding of simplicity. Simplicity also rules their music.

1. On Midsummer's Eve, everything is enchanted.
   Woods, waters, and winds seem filled with magical effects.

   _____

   _____

2. The gods help some people.
    Others have to aid themselves.

    _____

    _____

3. Money can't buy happiness.
    Contentment comes easier with a little wealth.

    _____

    _____

4. Everybody ages.
    Taking care of the old should concern all of us.

    _____

    _____

5. Money doesn't smell.
    If currency did, it would give off an odor of sweat.

    _____

    _____

6. The search for truth is long and hard.
    The looking isn't always rewarded.

    _____

    _____

7. Mervin told the neighbors he was a prophet.
    Nobody in the community believed his forecasts.

    _____

    _____

8. Sometimes people try to prove too much.
    They wind up demonstrating nothing.

    _____

    _____

9. You are in Rome.
    You should act as the people in the vicinity do.

    _____

    _____

10. Ask not what your country can do for you.
    Inquire about what actions you can take for the nation.

    _____

    _____

Part of the technique of repetition is the correct use of pronouns to help tie the paragraph together. For instance, proper use of *this* and *that* with words referring back to the key words helps the reader see the "threads" of your paragraph. Similarly, proper use of a pronoun like *it* to refer back to a key word creates coherence. However, using *this, that,* or other pronouns without clear reference back to the key word can destroy coherence.

> Connie is always late for work, and she cannot seem to be punctual for any appointment. This causes trouble.

In this example, the use of *this* hurts the coherence. What specifically does *this* refer back to? You can answer only with some awkward phrase like "her being late to work and for appointments." When you have this kind of situation in writing, pick a word that sums up what you are trying to say and use it with the *this* or *that* to make the meaning clear.

> Connie is always late for work, and she cannot seem to be punctual for any appointment. This *tardiness* causes trouble.

The same problem can exist with the use of any pronoun. When the pronoun does not refer back to any specific word before it, be careful! Replace the pronoun with a word or phrase that says exactly what you mean.

> We went to see *A Christmas Carol,* had a late supper, and dropped by some friends' place for eggnog. It was perfect.

We went to see *A Christmas Carol,* had a late supper, and dropped by some friends' place for eggnog. *Our date* was perfect.

(Making pronouns precise is discussed in more detail in Chapter 6.)

REVISION PRACTICE

The following paragraphs have unity and organization, but they lack any attempt to use the techniques which build coherence. Rewrite the sentences, combining sentences where appropriate, adding transition signals where necessary, changing sentences to form parallel structures, and repeating key words.

1. Japanese woodcuts had an important influence on Western art.

    The pictures arrived in Europe at the beginning of the nineteenth century.

    Japanese art came to the attention of the French Impressionists.

    The French learned several things from the Japanese works.

    The Japanese pictures represented the world flatly, without perspective.

    There was no central point to which all lines in the woodcut were directed.

    The size of an object was set not by its distance from the viewer but by its importance in the picture.

    Objects were made up of blocks of flat color.

    In Western painting, objects were modeled with precise shading.

    The body of a cat in a woodcut would be one solid, cat-shaped black blotch.

    Japanese painting delighted in everyday activities.

    Much European painting glorified historical spectacle and myth.

    French artists used all these techniques.

    The posters of Toulouse-Lautrec are the culmination of the borrowing.

2. Belinda lay listening for a moment.

    Belinda couldn't hear anything now.

    Belinda was certain she had heard a hinge squeal.

    Belinda threw back the covers.

    Belinda got out of bed.

    The floor was cold on her bare feet.

    Belinda thought out her situation carefully.

    Belinda groped for a candle and a match.

Belinda had some light.

Belinda made a slow circuit of the room.

Everything seemed normal.

Belinda came to the fireplace.

One of the hearth ornaments was crooked.

Belinda straightened the ornament.

There was the same squeal that had awakened Belinda.

A section of the chimney slid open.

There was an open section.

Inside there was a staircase.

Belinda didn't pause.

Belinda entered the secret passage.

Belinda started down the staircase.

Belinda held the flickering candle before her.

3.   The fall of Rome has been attributed to many causes.

Some historians have claimed the fall resulted from a massive case of lead poisoning.

Some historians have claimed the fall resulted from the persecutions of the Jews.

The most widespread myth links the fall of Rome and moral decay.

The sexual excesses and cruelty of Nero supposedly led to a decline in Roman strength.

Wild parties sapped the Empire's defenses.

This version simply isn't true.

Nero and the other famous party-givers actually lived before the greatest days of Rome.

The real "fall" was a long, dull economic breakdown.

There were no wild parties, no softening of morals.

Great landholders simply went back to their estates.

There the profits were secure.

The economies of Italy, France, and Spain stopped growing.

The Western Empire broke up.

The Western Empire was ripe for the coming of Germanic invaders.

The Eastern empire lasted another thousand years.

4.   There are several steps in preparing a report for any organization.

Make sure you understand the assignment.

Write down what you have understood of the assignment.

Ask the supervisor to check your notes with you.

Your resources should be checked.

Older employees may be useful sources of information.

The company files are invaluable.

Local libraries can be very helpful.

You should locate some models.

Trade journals often contain articles which can serve as models.

Previous reports should be examined for ideas.

Prepare a working outline.

Now is a good time to check back with the assigner.

Often a progress report at this stage is required.

You should not be afraid of going through several drafts.

Writing drafts seems time-consuming.

Trying to produce a perfect first draft is more wasteful.

Always proofread thoroughly.

The steps don't guarantee success.

They do help.

Choosing
Words

13

As you have discovered by now in working with sentence combining, one way of writing a sentence does not have the same effect on a reader as another way. Different structures convey different meanings. The same principle holds true with individual words. One word does not have exactly the same effect as another word. Therefore, in revision, you have to be as careful to choose the right words as you are to choose the right sentence construction, the right supporting examples, and the right pattern of arrangement for your subject, audience, and purpose.

EXACTNESS

One quality that you want in the words you use is exactness. You should choose a word or phrase that is as specific as possible in conveying the idea you have in mind.

For instance, what is the difference between these two words: *book* and *bible?* The word *book* can refer to any one of millions of items, while *bible* refers to a much more limited group. *The King James Bible* would be an even more specific reference. And *my grandfather's old King James Bible* would refer to only one item.

If you were describing the parlor in your grandparents' house and you said that *a book* lay on the table, your reader would repond in a different way than if you said that *a well-worn bible* lay on the table or *a new copy of the* **Sayings of Chairman Mao** lay on the table. Nouns need to be chosen with precision.

You also want to choose adjectives and adverbs carefully to help you convey an exact meaning. In this sentence,

Mrs. Dulaney was a *big* woman.

the adjective *big* does not make it clear whether you are talking about Mrs. Dulaney's size or her importance or her character. Another adjective such as *obese* or *generous* would help your reader focus more clearly on your idea. Or using a more specific detail like the following would clarify your idea.

Mrs. Dulaney *weighed three-hundred pounds.*

In this sentence,

I go to the dentist *often.*

your reader could take *often* to mean once a year, once a month, or once a week. You should choose a word that is more specific.

Verbs need the same quality of exactness as nouns and modifiers. To say,

Mr. Avery *talked* to me.

is not as exact as

Mr. Avery *reassured* me.
or
Mr. Avery *mumbled* at me from behind his newspaper.

The more exact you are in choosing nouns, verbs, and modifiers, the more likely your reader will be to respond just as you intended.

Exercise A

Revise the following sentences making each more precise.

1. There was something about him that I didn't like.

    His shifty eyes unsettled me

2. I have been in school for a long time.

    I've been in school 5 yrs now.

3. The animals walked across the yard.

    The pack of dogs cautiously

4. A car moved down the street.

    An orange Honda coupe bolted down the street

5. Because of something that happened, the people looked strange.

    Because of the obscurity of the lecture the ideas looked perplexed

6. The event was very uninteresting.

    The golf tournament was blufflingly dull

7. A person communicated with the president.

    A newspaper reported questions the school board pres.

8. Recently, they were in the area on business.

    Recently, Doctor Unger went to L.A. on official hospital business

9. The weather was not good.

    The Cleveland weather has been a constant blizzard for the last 3 days

10. The athlete did well.

    The decathlete won a silver medal.

Exact Connotation

One way of finding more exact words is to use a thesaurus, a book which lists words in groups related in meaning. For instance, for the word *small*, a thesaurus would list all these related words:

little	trivial
tiny	unimportant
short	petty
wee	puny
dwarfish	slight
undersized	weak
stunted	mean
minute	paltry
infinitesimal	pygmy
dainty	Lilliputian
petite	

Now, because all these words are related to *small*, does that mean you can freely substitute one for the other? No.

How would you feel if someone described your brand new baby daughter as *undersized*? Would you feel different if she were described as *dainty*? What is the difference between the two words? The distinction lies mainly in the feelings that are associated with each word. These feelings are called *connotations*. *Undersized* has negative connotations while *dainty* has positive connotations.

Here are some other examples of differences in connotation.

Neutral	*Positive*	*Negative*
inexpensive	thrifty	cheap
worker	craftsman	drudge
slowly	leisurely	sluggishly

In choosing words, then, you need to be sure that a word carries the right feelings for the subject, audience, and purpose you have chosen. For instance, if you were trying to give an unbiased report, you would choose words that do not have strong favorable or unfavorable connotations:

Dr. Lucas has six months of teaching experience.

If you were trying to criticize, you would choose words that have an unfavorable connotation:

Dr. Lucas is a raw beginner in the field of teaching.

If you were trying to praise, you would choose words with favorable connotations:

Dr. Lucas brings a fresh, new approach to teaching.

Exercise B

Using your own knowledge and/or a thesaurus, for each word below list as many words of similar meaning as you can. Group the words as neutral, positive, or negative.

1. look

neutral	positive	negative

2. woman

neutral	positive	negative

3. quickly

neutral	positive	negative

4. careful

neutral   *positive*   *negative*

Exercise C

In each of the following paragraphs, you are given two controlling ideas in the topic sentence. You must choose one by underlining it. Then, in the supporting sentences, choose between the paired words the one whose connotations fit your controlling idea. Cross out the word whose connotations don't fit. Use a dictionary for unfamiliar words.

EXAMPLE:

It was a (<u>pleasant</u>, dull) winter afternoon. The sun cast a (soft, ~~feeble~~) glow on the (white, ~~pale~~) landscape.

While the dictionary meanings of *soft* and *feeble* are close in meaning, the connotations of *feeble* don't fit the controlling idea *pleasant*. Likewise, *pale*, which means whitish, has *unpleasant* connotations.

1.   Phillipa Marlow, private eye, glanced up to see a rather (sinister, appealing) figure enter her office. He was (obese, plump); his (graceless, awkward) body filled the doorway. He had tiny, (half-closed, squinty) eyes like a scared (rat's, fieldmouse's). Even at this distance, his skin appeared (creased, wrinkled), as though he had slept in it badly. Fittingly, his hair was (wild, mussed) and stood up in stiff (spikes, cowlicks). When he spoke, his voice was (high, shrill) and had a nasal (twang, whine). Phillipa shook his hand. The palm was (moist, clammy), his grip (hard, firm). Phillipa wanted to (help, get rid of) him.

2.   Ms. Joan Bagley has asked me to recommend her for a place in your graduate program. I (can, cannot) do this wholeheartedly. Ms. Bagley is (intelligent, clever). She is (ambitious, driven). At the same time, there is about her a definite (inwardness, self-centeredness). She seems to (weigh seriously, brood over) the problems in her field of study. Though most of her work is (traditional, derivative), she can produce work of remarkable (originality, eccentricity). In short, I think she is one of the (most distinctive, oddest) graduates of this college in years.

CONCISENESS

Along with exactness, you should be aiming for conciseness in your writing. That is, you don't want to use more words than you have to to achieve your purpose. Using too many words leaves your readers feeling that you are not quite in control of your writing, or even worse, that you are wasting their time by not getting to the point.

Look at these sentences. Which version is more concise?

A. Food technologists have radically altered the diet of the average American. In fact, they have almost done away with *real* food. Milk shakes may have no milk. Hamburgers may have no meat.

B. People who work in food technology have radically and drastically altered or changed the dietary habits of the average member of the American public. As a matter of hard fact, these food scientists have almost completely more or less done away with anything that might resemble *real, true, natural, honest-to-goodness* food that people can eat. Milk shakes don't often deserve the name because they aren't made with milk anymore. Also hamburgers have been designed to be made without meat.

Paragraph B shows several of the problems that can lead to wordiness. For one thing, the writer has frequently used a phrase where one word would have conveyed exactly the same information: *people who work in technology* instead of *technologist, dietary habits* instead of *diet.* Second, the writer here has repeated herself in several places: *radically and drastically; altered or changed; real, true, natural, honest-to-goodness.* Nothing is gained by this unnecessary repetition.

In writing, more words are not necessarily better than fewer words. What matters is not so much the number of words as the fact that each word does its fair share of work in the sentence or paragraph.

Exercise D

Revise each of the following sentences to make it more concise.

1. In the movie it shows how the two little young children who are twins were affected by a divorce their parents got.

_____

_____

_____

2. The driver of the car, which was a rusty Pinto, neatly executed an escape only seconds before the car started burning with flames.

_____

_____

_____

3. There are three responsibilities that I perform every Saturday during the morning.

_____

_____

_____

4. Whatever the course I am taking, it always seems necessary for me to involve myself in a considerably large amount of writing.

_____

_____

_____

5. The motion to elect a vice-chairman failed due to the fact we didn't have a quorum at the meeting.

_____

_____

_____

6. Frequently and several times I made an attempt to contact you because I
   have to ask you to write a note for me about my absence.

   _____

   _____

   _____

7. Long-range forecasts trying to predict the weather in advance of when it
   happens are always risky and uncertain things to try to do.

   _____

   _____

   _____

8. Some years ago, the collection of stamps from many countries in an
   album used to be a hobby that even children in school could participate
   in and be a part of.

   _____

   _____

   _____

9. Many students who have graduated with a Ph.D. from a graduate school
   will find it very difficult or discouraging to find a job in the field of teaching.

   _____

   _____

   _____

10. The "Big Band" sound associated with the music of the '30's and '40's is
    making a return to a comeback in popularity among some of the musi-
    cians who are young in today's society.

    _____

    _____

    _____

11. The very first electoral vote in the history of the United States for the last 200 years ever cast for a woman of the female sex was given to Theodora Nathan, a candidate representing the Libertarian Party, in the year 1976, during the Bicentennial.

12. Many people who live in American society at the present time and age do not look with favor on the practice of censoring books that students in schools can read from libraries operated by public school systems.

Exercise E

The following paragraphs contain many examples of wordiness. Rewrite the paragraphs using the fewest possible words. Be ruthless.

I am writing this letter to answer your letter written on the 25th of January. You made a request for information concerning the dimensions in size of our newest unit most recently produced for sale. The unit we are speaking of is five feet in length, two feet in width, and four feet tall in height. It should be observed that this unit under discussion will fit into most storage areas in most places. It was our purpose when we designed the unit that it should fit in these areas. It is the smallest of the units offered for sale at the present point in time, and it is our opinion that we can be proud, and justifiably so, of this product of ours. It is our hope and expectation that you will find it likable. (136 words)

The purpose of this handbook is to give you guidance through the days, which are difficult, of your first time on the campus of a college like ours. Most people who are entering freshmen have the experience of a nervous state during this time period. One of the reasons why this is so is because they have not developed familiarity with the design and layout of the campus. It is to help them develop this familiarity that in this handbook it contains maps of the campus. Another of the reasons is the one that exists because they lack sureness concerning the procedures to be followed for registration. The handbook contains a list of the procedures to be followed for registration, as well as a list of offices of the administration, and a list of the groups on campus which exist to be of use. (144 words)

EDITING

In the revision process, you are looking for ways to clarify your ideas through improved unity, coherence, and word choice.

In the editing process, which should be the last step before preparing a final copy, you are looking for errors that may distract your reader from your idea.

Misspelled words, sentence construction errors, or improper punctuation can give your reader a negative impression of a piece of writing. These errors may be so annoying to a reader that he or she will not really pay attention to your carefully organized, well-supported, beautifully worded paper.

So teach yourself to recognize the errors you know you are prone to, and check your writing very carefully for those kinds of mistakes.

limonene 821 **line**

lim·o·nene (lim′ə nēn′) *n.* [< ModL. *Limonum* (< Fr. *limon*, LEMON) + -ENE] any of three isomeric terpenes, C₁₀H₁₆, present in many plant products such as lemon peel, orange oil, pine needles, peppermint, etc.

li·mo·nite (lī′mə nīt′) *n.* [< Gr. *leimōn*, meadow, orig., low ground (for IE. base see LIMB¹) + -ITE¹] a brownish, hydrous ferric oxide consisting of several minerals: an important ore of iron —li′mo·nit′ic (-nit′ik) *adj.*

Li·mou·sin (lē′ moo zan′) region & former province of WC France: chief city, Limoges

lim·ou·sine (lim′ə zēn′, lim′ə zēn′) *n.* [Fr., lit., a hood: from the costume worn in LIMOUSIN] 1. a former kind of automobile with a closed compartment seating three or more passengers and the top extended forward over the driver's seat 2. any large, luxurious sedan, esp. one driven by a chauffeur ☆3. a buslike sedan used to carry passengers to or from an airport, train station, etc.

limp¹ (limp) *vi.* [ME. *lympen* < OE. *limpan*, to befall, occur (in a specialized sense, to walk lamely), akin to MHG. *limpfen*, to walk with a limp, OHG. *limfan*, to befall, happen < IE. *lemb*- < base *leb*-, to hang down, be limp, whence L. *labor*, *limbus*] 1. to walk with or as with a lame or partially disabled leg 2. to move or proceed unevenly, jerkily, or laboriously, as because of being impaired, defective, damaged, etc. —*n.* a halt or lameness in walking —limp′er *n.* —limp′ing·ly *adv.*

limp² (limp) *adj.* [< base of prec., akin to MHG. *lampen*, to hang limply] 1. lacking or having lost stiffness or body; flaccid, drooping, wilted, etc. 2. lacking firmness, energy, or vigor 3. flexible, as the binding of some books —limp′ly *adv.* —limp′ness *n.*

limp·et (lim′pit) *n.* [ME. *lempet* < OE. *lempedu* < ML. *lempreda*, limpet, lamprey: cf. LAMPREY] any of several varieties of mostly marine, gastropod mollusks, with a single, low, cone-shaped shell and a thick, fleshy foot, by means of which it clings to rocks, timbers, etc.

lim·pid (lim′pid) *adj.* [Fr. *limpide* < L. *limpidus* < OL. *limpa*, *lumpa*, water: see LYMPH] 1. perfectly clear; transparent; not cloudy or turbid [*limpid* waters] 2. clear and simple [*limpid* prose] —lim·pid′i·ty, lim′pid·ness *n.* —lim′pid·ly *adv.*

☆limp·kin (limp′kin) *n.* [LIMP¹ + -KIN: from its walk] a raillike wading bird (*Aramus vociferus*), found in Florida, Central America, and the West Indies

Lim·po·po River (lim pō′pō) river in SE Africa, flowing from South Africa into the Indian Ocean: c. 1,000 mi.

limp·sy, limp·sey (limp′sē) *adj.* -si·er, -si·est [Dial.] limp, as from exhaustion or weakness

lim·u·lus (lim′yoo ləs) *n.*, *pl.* -li′ (-lī′) [ModL., name of the genus < L. *limulus*, dim. of *limus*, sidelong (see LIMES) + -OID] *same as* HORSESHOE CRAB

lim·y (lī′mē) *adj.* lim′i·er, lim′i·est 1. covered with, consisting of, or like birdlime; sticky 2. of, like, or containing lime —lim′i·ness *n.*

lin. 1. lineal 2. linear

lin·ac (lī′nak) *n.* *shortened form of* LINEAR ACCELERATOR

lin·age (lī′nij) *n.* 1. the number of written or printed lines on a page or in an article, advertisement, etc. 2. payment based on the number of lines produced by a writer

lin·al·o·ol (li nal′ə ōl′, -ōl′; lin′ə lōōl′) *n.* [< MexSp. *linaloa*, an aromatic Mexican wood (< Sp. *lináloe* < L. *lignum aloës*: cf. LIGNALOES) + -OL¹] a terpene alcohol, C₁₀H₁₇OH, in several essential oils, used in perfumery

linch·pin (linch′pin′) *n.* [ME. *lynspin* < *lyns* (< OE. *lynis*, linchpin, akin to G. *lünse* < IE. base *elei*-, to bend, whence ELL, Sans. *āṇih*, linchpin) + *pin*, PIN] a pin that goes through the end of an axle outside the wheel to keep the wheel from coming off

Lin·coln (liŋ′kən) 1. [after Pres. LINCOLN] capital of Nebr., in the SE part: pop. 150,000 2. *same as* LINCOLNSHIRE 3. city in Lincolnshire, England: pop. 73,000 —*n.* a breed of sheep with long wool: orig. from Lincolnshire

Lin·coln (liŋ′kən), Abraham 1809–65; 16th president of the U.S. (1861–65): assassinated —☆Lin·coln·esque (liŋ′kə nesk′) *adj.* —☆Lin·coln·ian (liŋ kō′nē ən) *adj.*

Lin·coln·i·an·a (liŋ kō′nē an′ə, -än′ə) *n.pl.* [LINCOLN + -IANA] books, papers, objects, etc. having to do with Abraham Lincoln

Lincoln Park city in SE Mich.: suburb of Detroit: pop. 53,000

Lin·coln·shire (liŋ′kən shir′) county in NE England, on the North Sea: 2,272 sq. mi.; pop. 513,000

Lincoln's Inn *see* INN OF COURT

☆lin·co·my·cin (liŋ′kō mī′sin) *n.* [(*Streptomyces*) *lincoln*(*ensis*), the bacteria from which derived (isolated from a soil sample collected near Lincoln, Nebr.) + MYC- + -IN¹] an antibiotic drug, C₁₈H₃₄N₂O₆S, used in the treatment of various bacterial diseases, esp. those resistant to penicillin or those involving an allergy to penicillin

Lind (lind), Jenny (born *Johanna Maria Lind*; *Mme. Otto Goldschmidt*) 1820–87; Swed. soprano: called the *Swedish Nightingale*

Lin·da (lin′də) a feminine name: see BELINDA

lin·dane (lin′dān′) *n.* [after T. *van der Linden*, Du. chemist (20th c.) who isolated the isomer + -ANE] an iso-

meric form of benzene hexachloride, used as an insecticide

Lind·bergh (lind′bərg, lin′-), Charles Augustus 1902–74; U.S. aviator: made first nonstop solo flight from New York to Paris (1927)

Lin·den (lin′dən) [from its *linden* trees, brought from Germany] city in NE N.J.: pop. 41,000

lin·den (lin′dən) *n.* [ME., *adj.* < OE. < *lind*, linden, akin to G. *linde*: popularized as *n.* via G. *linden*, pl. of *linde*: prob. < IE. base *lento*-, flexible, yielding, whence LITHE] any of a genus (*Tilia*) of trees of the linden family, with dense, heart-shaped leaves, widely cultivated throughout the North Temperate Zone: the American variety is also called BASSWOOD —*adj.* designating a family (Tiliaceae) of chiefly tropical trees including the lindens and jutes

Lind·say (lin′zē, lind′-), (Nicholas) Va·chel (vā′chəl) 1879–1931; U.S. poet

☆Lin·dy (Hop) (lin′dē) [after C. A. LINDBERGH'S ("*Lindy's*") transatlantic "*hop*" [*also* l- h-] a lively dance for couples, popular in the early 1930's

line¹ (līn) *n.* [ME. *line*, merging OE. *line*, a cord, with OFr. *ligne* (both < L. *linea*, lit., linen thread, n. use of fem. of *lineus*, of flax < *linum*, flax)] 1. *a*) a cord, rope, wire, string, or the like *b*) a long, fine, strong cord with a hook, sinker, leader, etc. used in fishing *c*) a clothesline *d*) a cord, steel tape, etc. used in measuring or leveling *e*) a rope, hawser, or cable used on a ship *f*) a rein: *usually used in pl.* ☆2. *a*) a wire or wires connecting stations in a telephone or telegraph system *b*) the whole system of such wires *c*) effective contact between stations [hold the *line*, please] 3. any wire, pipe, system of pipes or wires, etc. for conducting water, gas, electricity, etc. 4. a very thin, threadlike mark; specif., *a*) a long, thin mark made by a pencil, pen, chalk, etc. *b*) a similar mark cut in a hard surface, as by engraving *c*) a thin crease in the palm or on the face 5. a mark made on the ground in certain sports; specif., *a*) any of the straight, narrow marks dividing or bounding a football field, tennis court, etc.: often used in combination [*sideline*] *b*) a mark indicating a starting point, a limit not to be crossed, or a point which must be reached or passed ☆6. a border or boundary [the State *line*] 7. a division between conditions, qualities, classes, etc.; limit; demarcation 8. outline; contour; lineament 9. [Archaic] [*pl.*] lot in life; one's fate 10. [*usually pl.*] a plan of construction; plan of making or doing 11. a row or series of persons or things of a particular kind; specif., *a*) a row of written or printed characters extending across or part way across a page ☆*b*) a row of persons waiting in turn to buy something, enter a theater, etc.; queue *c*) an assembly line or a similar arrangement for the packing, shipping, etc. of merchandise 12. a connected series of persons or things following each other in time or place; succession [a line of Democratic presidents] 13. *same as* LINEAGE¹ 14. the descendants of a common ancestor or of a particular breed ☆*a*) a transportation system or service consisting of regular trips by buses, ships, etc. between two or more points ☆*b*) a company operating such a system *c*) one branch or division of such a system [the main *line* of a railroad] *d*) a single track of a railroad 16. the course or direction anything moving takes; path [the *line* of fire] 17. *a*) a course of conduct, action, explanation, etc. [the *line* of an argument] *b*) a course of movement 18. a person's trade or occupation, or the things he deals in [what's his *line*?] ☆19. a stock of goods of a particular type considered with reference to quality, quantity, variety, etc. 20. *a*) the field of one's special knowledge, interest, or ability *b*) a source or piece of information [a line on a bargain] 21. a short letter, note, or card [drop me a *line*] 22. a single metrical unit consisting of a specified number of feet; verse of poetry 23. [*pl.*] all the speeches in a play; esp., the speeches of any single character 24. [Colloq.] persuasive or flattering talk that is insincere 25. [*pl.*] [Chiefly Brit.] a marriage certificate: in full, **marriage lines** 26. *Bridge* the horizontal line dividing trick scores from honor scores ☆27. *Football a*) *short for* LINE OF SCRIMMAGE *b*) the players arranged in a row on either side of the line of scrimmage at the start of each play 28. *Geog.* an imaginary circle of the earth or of the celestial sphere, as the equator or the equinoctial circle 29. *Math. a*) the path of a moving point, thought of as having length but not breadth, whether straight or curved *b*) such a path when considered perfectly straight 30. *Mil. a*) a formation of ships, troops, etc. in which elements are abreast of each other *b*) the area or position in closest contact with the enemy during combat *c*) the troops in this area *d*) the officers in immediate command of fighting ships or combat troops ☆*e*) the combatant branches of the army as distinguished from the supporting branches and the staff 31. *Music* any of the long parallel marks forming the staff 32. *TV* a scanning line —*vt.* **lined**, **lin′ing** 1. to mark with lines 2. to draw or trace with or as with lines 3. to bring or cause to come into a straight row or into conformity; bring into alignment (often with *up*) 4. to form a line along [elms *line* the streets] 5. to place objects along the edge of [*line* the walk with flowers] ☆6. *Baseball* to hit (a pitched ball) in a line drive —*vi.*

fat, āpe, cär; ten, ēven; is, bīte; gō, hôrn, tōōl, look; oil, out; up, fur; get; joy; yet; chin; she; thin, *then*; zh, leisure; ŋ, ring; ə for *a* in *ago*, *e* in *agent*, *i* in *sanity*, *o* in *comply*, *u* in *focus*; ' as in *able* (ā′b'l); Fr. bâl; ë, Fr. coeur; ö, Fr. feu; Fr. mon; δ, Fr. coq; ü, Fr. duc; r, Fr. cri; H, G. ich; kh, G. doch. See inside front cover. ☆ Americanism; ‡foreign; *hypothetical; < derived from

Spelling

14

In writing, one of the most important impressions you want to create for your reader is the feeling that you are in control. No matter how exact or how concise your word choices, the impression of being in control of your material can be destroyed by a series of misspelled words. One spelling error might be overlooked, but a pattern of poor spelling can make even a sympathetic reader doubt the value of your ideas. Therefore you need not only to choose the correct word for each writing situation but also to edit carefully for correct spelling.

USING THE DICTIONARY

The most useful, all-around tool in editing is the dictionary. It helps with spelling, pronunciation, grammar, word choice, defining, and understanding.

To get the most use out of any tool, you have to know how to handle it. In the case of the dictionary, you must first be able to find the word you want and then understand the information the dictionary is giving you.

Finding the Word

When you use a dictionary to look up a word in a book you are reading, there is no problem finding the word. However, often when you are writing, you use the dictionary to find words you have seen or heard but do not know how to spell. You can do two things: (1) get yourself a "bad speller's dictionary" listing many of the common misspellings in alphabetical order with the correct spelling after, and (2) learn the commonly confused letters and sounds.

The same sound can be produced by different combinations of letters. For instance, suppose that you are looking up the spelling of a word that means "a severe inflammation of the lungs" and sounds like *newmonya*. If you look under *n* in the dictionary, you won't find the word. But what other letter combinations also have the sound of *n?* *kn, gn,* and *pn.* Therefore you should look under each of these combinations until you find the word you want: *pneu mó nia.*

Here are some of the most common sound combinations. You can use these to help you look up words in the dictionary.

	a–consonant–silent *e*	name
	ai	laid
ā (long *a*, says its own name)	*au*	gauge
	ay	play
	ea	steak
	ei	veil
	ey	grey
	e	she
	e–consonant–silent *e*	Pete
	ea	team
ē (long *e*, says its own name)	*ee*	feed
	ie	believe
	(c) *ei*	receive
	ey	key
	eo	people
	oe	amoeba
	i–consonant–silent *e*	fire
	y	cry
ī (long ī, says its own name)	*ie*	tie
	ei	height
	ai	aisle
	igh	high
	uy	buy
	o	no
	o–consonant–silent *e*	note
ō (long ō, says its own name)	*oa*	boat
	ow	flow
	oe	foe
	ough	dough
	eau	bureau

	oo	cool
	ew	blew
$\overline{oo}$	*ue*	clue
	eu	maneuver
	u–consonant–silent *e*	rule
	ui	suit
	o	move
	oe	canoe

	u–consonant–silent *e*	mule
ū (long ū,	*ou*	you
says its	*ew*	few
own name)	*eau*	beauty
	eu	feud
	iew	view
	yu	yule

	a	above
ə(uh)	*e*	agent
schwa - used	*i*	busily
in unaccented	*o*	bottom
syllables	*u*	circus
	ou	curious

	k	kill
	c	car
k	*cc*	account
	ch	character
	ck	back

	s	see
	c	city
s	*ps*	psychology
	sc	scene

	sh	shine
	ci	special
sh	*sci*	conscious
	ch	machine
	ce	ocean
	ti	nation

Exercise A

Using the sound lists above and your own knowledge of letter combinations, find the correct spelling of each of the following words in a dictionary.

1. sī kō′ sis
   a severe mental disorder _____

2. snēk
   to go in a stealthy way _____

3. rak′ it
   a loud noise
   _____

4. rān
   the time when a king or
   queen occupies the throne
   _____

5. brō shoor′
   a pamphlet
   _____

6. nok
   to strike with the fist
   _____

7. mor′ fēn
   a medicine used to dull pain
   _____

8. hā′ dā
   the period of greatest success
   _____

9. lav′ a tor ē
   a room with equipment for
   washing
   _____

10. fō′ bē a
    a fear with no basis in
    reality
    _____

Spelling Variations

Obviously, when your dictionary search has been successful, the spelling of the word is in front of you in dark type. Sometimes you will find the dictionary giving you more information than you expected: a word may be given with several spellings. For example, the sample dictionary page shows two spellings for a word meaning limp or tired out: *limpsy* and *limpsey*. Either spelling is correct. In most dictionaries, the first spelling given is the more commonly used.

Exercise B

What are the other accepted spellings of these words?

1. chiseled _____

2. catalog _____

3. theater _____

4. judgment _____

5. Halloween _____

Syllables

When you find a word in a dictionary, it is usually broken up by dots. These dots show where the word may be divided when the whole word won't fit on the end of a line. For example, if you had to split the word *linchpin*, you could do it only between the *h* and the *p: linch-pin*. These divisions can be a help in learning to spell the word.

Exercise C

Where you can divide the following words?

EXAMPLE:
Lincolniana *Lin-coln-i-an-a*

1. judgment _____

2. prophet _____

3. California _____

4. Roosevelt _____

5. clinker _____

Pronunciation

After the word has been given in dark type, most dictionaries give the pronunciation in parentheses. For example, look at the word *limy* on the sample dictionary page. In parentheses, you are told the pronunciation is *lī′ mē*.

The accent (′) shows you which syllable receives more force in saying the word. The symbols above the *i* and *e* indicate specific sounds. The key to the pronunciation symbols is at the bottom of the sample dictionary page. There you are shown the symbol in a common word in which the sound appears. For instance, the sound indicated by *ē* is the sound of the first *e* in *even*.

Exercise D

Use the pronunciation key at the bottom of the sample dictionary page. For each symbol, write in the word the dictionary uses to give you the sound.

EXAMPLE:

ô *horn*

1. zh _____

2. u _____

3. ä _____

4. ī _____

5. ō _____

When you check the pronunciation of some words, you will find several pronunciations given. All are correct. For example, there are three correct ways given on the sample dictionary page for the pronunciation of the unusual word *linalool.*

Exercise E

Look up the following words in the dictionary and give the pronunciations listed.

EXAMPLE:

calm *käm   kälm*

1. recondite _____   _____

2. harass _____   _____

3. tomato _____   _____

4. nauseous _____   _____

5. almond _____   _____   _____

Parts of Speech

The dictionary also tells you whether the word is a noun, a verb, an adjective, or some other part of speech. For example, the *n.* placed after the pronunciation of the word *linden* on the sample dictionary page means *linden* is a noun. Recognizing these abbreviations is useful because many words can play several parts. Thus, finding the precise form of the word you are looking for often means checking for the abbreviations. For example, the word *line* on the sample page is used both as a noun (*n.*) and a verb (*vt.* and *vi.*). The definitions are grouped after each abbreviation.

Exercise F

Using your own dictionary, give the full term represented by the following abbreviations.

EXAMPLE:

n.   *noun*

1. *adj.*   _____

2. *prep.*   _____

3. *pron.*   _____

4. *interj.*   _____

5. *adv.*   _____

Exercise G

List the parts of speech given in the dictionary for each of the following words.

EXAMPLE:

line   *n., vt., vi., adj.*

1. round   _____

2. hallo   _____

3. clean   _____

4. without   _____

5. yesterday   _____

Meanings

Finding the meanings of words is the basic use of the dictionary. Most words have several meanings, all closely related, but with shades of difference. It is important to check all the meanings until you find the one which explains the word in the context you are reading. For instance, if you were looking for the meaning of *line* in the sentence "She came from a great line of champions," you would have to look under the meanings until you came to number 14: *the descendants of a common ancestor or of a particular breed.*

Exercise H

Look up the italicized word in each sentence and give the definition which best fits the context.

EXAMPLE:

It was a *limp,* dog-eared copy of "Hamlet."
flexible, as in the binding of some books

1. He wanted his coffee *black.*

   _____

2. The committee finally got down to the *core* of the issue.

   _____

3. He made the base sentence the *focus.*

   _____

4. The police were in *hot* pursuit.

   _____

5. The *proof* of the pudding is in the eating.

   _____

Usage Labels

Dictionaries also label certain meanings of words if they are specialized or particular to a certain dialect of English. For example, in the sample dictionary page, definition number 24 of *line*—as it would be used in the sentence "She handed him a *line* about her last job"—is labeled [Colloq.], meaning *colloquial* or informal. These labels may help you choose your words with greater precision.

Exercise I

Using your own dictionary, find the meanings of the following terms.

1. Colloquial [Colloq.] _____

_____

2. Slang _____

_____

3. Archaic [Arch.] _____

_____

4. Obsolete [Obs.] _____

_____

5. Dialect [Dial.] _____

_____

Exercise J

Find the meaning given for the italicized words in the following sentences. Put the usage label accompanying that meaning in the blank.

EXAMPLE:

He had a smooth *line. Colloquial*

1. He got some more *ammo* and continued firing. _____

2. I have a *boon* to ask of you. _____

3. Anne decided to *perk* some more coffee. _____

4. Then she *rustled* up some pancakes. _____

5. He was drowned in the *crick.* _____

Word History

Dictionaries also give the history of the word: they tell you what it meant in the past and what languages it came from. (You will find a section in the front of most dictionaries explaining the symbols used in the word histories.) For example, the sample dictionary page gives the history of *line* in brackets after the pronunciation. The word came from a merging of the Middle English *line* with the Old French *ligne*. Both these words came from the Latin *linea*, which meant "linen thread" and derived from *linum*, which meant "flax," the plant which gives us linen.

Learning the history of a word often makes the word easier to remember. Paying attention to word histories will gradually deepen your knowledge of the language you speak and write.

Exercise K

What unusual meanings did the words below have in the past?

EXAMPLE:

line   *linen thread*

1. hour   _____

2. brawn   _____

3. window   _____

4. daisy   _____

5. hypocrisy _____

Exercise L

What languages produced the following words?

EXAMPLE:

linalool   *Mexican Spanish*

1. dandelion   _____

2. coleslaw   _____

3. maroon   _____

4. Los Angeles _____

5. pajama   _____

> ### What's in the Dictionary
>
> Spelling
> Syllabication
> Pronunciation
> Parts of Speech
> Meanings
> Usage Labels
> Word History

IMPROVING YOUR SPELLING

If you are a poor speller, you may get very discouraged sometimes because you think you can't spell *anything*. But that's not the case. Most people have definite patterns to their misspelling. They miss the same words over and over, or they make the same kinds of mistakes.

The way to overcome this spelling problem is to recognize what words or what spelling patterns give you trouble by keeping a list of words that you misspell. When you get a paper back from your teacher, write down any words that are marked for spelling. In one column, put down the word the way you spelled it. In another column, write the correct spelling. When you have a dozen or so words, study your list to see if there are any patterns of spelling that regularly give you trouble. For instance, look at this list:

Incorrect Spelling	*Correct Spelling*
terrable	terrible
refussing	refusing
planed	planned
evidince	evidence
occured	occurred
hopping	hoping
returnible	returnable
dependibility	dependability
acceptence	acceptance
riden	ridden
terreble	terrible
ocurred	occurred

What spelling problems seem to give this student trouble? One is that she misses the *i, e,* or *a* at the end of several words: return*a*ble, terr*i*ble, evid*e*nce, accept*a*nce, depend*a*bility. Another is that she isn't sure when to double the consonant: ri*dd*en, refu*s*ing, pla*nn*ed, ho*p*ing, o*cc*u*rr*ed.

Here is another list. Can you spot any problem areas for this student?

Incorrectly Spelled	*Correctly Spelled*
aventure	adventure
strat	straight
almos	almost
moshun	motion
minature	miniature
piture	picture
suppose	supposed
Wensday	Wednesday
there	their
sucseed	succeed
recieve	receive

This student seems to spell by pronunciation. He leaves letters out because he doesn't hear those letters when he says the word: a*d*venture, straig*ht*, pic*t*ure. Sometimes, he doesn't choose correctly between two possible spellings for the same sound: mo*tion*, rec*ei*ve, th*eir*.

If you are lucky, you will notice some patterns in the words you have trouble spelling, and then you can train yourself to watch out for those trouble areas or those specific words that always give you problems.

Improving Your Spelling

1. Keep a spelling list.
2. Break words into syllables.
3. Memorize the four spelling rules.

However, even if you don't discover a pattern, there are some ways you can improve your spelling.

Spelling Cards

First, make a 3 × 5 card for each word whose spelling gives you trouble. Tape these cards to your bathroom mirror or on the cover of a notebook or on the bulletin board next to your phone, anywhere that you will see them every day.

Practice a few words as you brush your teeth, or wait for class to start, or talk on the phone. Just seeing the words correctly spelled will help them to stay in your memory, but spelling them out loud or copying them a few times will help even more. Every three weeks or so take down some old cards and put up some new ones.

Syllables

Second, get into the habit of breaking words down into syllables. The dictionary will show you the syllables in a word. Every word is a combination of vowel sounds (*a, e, i, o, u,* and sometimes *y*) and consonant sounds (all the other letters). Each syllable in a word contains one vowel sound and usually one or more consonant sounds. It is easier to spell a word if you break it into syllables and can hear more easily the separate sounds of each part of the word. The words below are divided into syllables:

> sep a rate
> Feb ru ar y
> ad ven ture
> min i a ture
> ter ri ble
> ac cep tance
> oc curred

Seeing and hearing the syllables of words can help you spot the part of the word that's giving you trouble. Many people, for example, have trouble remembering the first *a* in separate. You can handle a trouble spot like this by thinking of some memory trick such as, "there's *a rat* in the middle of separate," or by making a card with *sep a rate* written on it and studying it for a few weeks until you have mastered that word, or by using a dictionary to check your spelling of that word whenever you use it.

Breaking a word into syllables can also help you see if there is a root part of the word to which some prefix or suffix has simply been added. In the box are some examples of words that are generally in the same family.

Related Words

Prefix	Root	Suffix
pro	ceed	ing
ex	ceed	
suc	ceed	ed
pro	claim	
re	cla(i)m	ation
dis	claim	er
in	duc(t)	tion
pro	duc(t)	tiv ity
pro	duc(e)	er
con	duct	

Recognizing a familiar part in an unfamiliar word may help you to spell the unfamiliar word correctly.

Studying the syllables in a word can also help you overcome the problem of leaving out letters. You can train yourself to see and/or hear all the letters. For example, if you had made a study card for *Feb ru ar y,* you could probably spell the word easily by concentrating on the sounds that are frequently lost in pronunciation: Feb *ru* ar y.

Spelling Rules

Third, there are some fairly reliable spelling rules. Memorizing these rules can cut down on the number of individual words whose spelling you have to memorize.

1. Use *i* before *e*
    Except after *c,*
    Or when sounded as *a,*
    As in *neighbor* and *weigh.*

    EXAMPLES:

    re ceive   re lief
    con ceive   be lieve
    de ceive   be siege
    Exceptions (No rule is perfect!)
    leisure, neither, weird, height

(handwritten margin notes: ceize, pateince, s, truly, malicious, lovable)

2. Words ending in silent *e* usually drop the *e* before adding a vowel suffix. The *e* remains with a consonant suffix.

EXAMPLES:

hide	+	-ing	=	hiding
name	+	-ed	=	named
desire	+	-able	=	desirable
drive	+	-er	=	driver
name	+	-less	=	nameless
care	+	-ful	=	careful
sincere	+	-ly	=	sincerely
amaze	+	-ment	=	amazement

Exceptions

judge	+	-ment	=	judgment
argue	+	-ment	=	argument
true	+	-ly	=	truly
peace	+	-able	=	peaceable
courage	+	-ous	=	courageous

and other soft *c* and *g* words with *a, o,* or *u* suffixes

3. In a word ending with consonant–*y*, change the *y* to *i* before adding any suffix that doesn't begin with *i*.

EXAMPLES:

worry	+	-ed	=	worried
worry	+	-ing	=	worrying
lonely	+	-ness	=	loneliness
try	+	-ed	=	tried
try	+	-ing	=	trying
study	+	-ous	=	studious
silly	+	-ness	=	silliness

Never use [handwritten]

4. Words of one syllable or accented on the last syllable which end in a vowel–consonant pattern double the final consonant before adding vowel suffixes. The doubled consonant keeps the vowel sound short.

apostrophe for plural [handwritten]

EXAMPLES:

slip	+	-ed	=	slipped
plan	+	-ing	=	planning
occur	+	-ence	=	occurrence
hid	+	-en	=	hidden
jam	+	-ed	=	jammed
permit	+	-ing	=	permitting

Exercise M

Suffixes

-ed
-ing
-ous
-able
-ible
-ness
-ance
-ence
-ment
-ly
-less

To each word given below, add as many of the suffixes in the box as you can. What spelling rules can you use for each word? Check the dictionary for each.

EXAMPLE:

manage	+	-ed	=	managed	Rule 2
manage	+	-ing	=	managing	Rule 2
manage	+	-able	=	manageable	Rule 2 (Excep.)
manage	+	-ment	=	management	Rule 2

1. move
2. happy
3. grieve
4. prefer *red*
5. equip
6. commit
7. stop
8. fit
9. transfer
10. steady

happily happiness

prefference double the final consonance when accent on the last syllable

memo

EASILY CONFUSED WORDS

In some cases, what looks like a misspelling is really a confusion between two similar words. Look at the following list. If any of these pairs of words give you trouble, make study cards for them or try to find some memory trick to help you remember the difference between them.

1. ac CEPT
   (to receive)

   He accepted the reward.

   No one except his mother came.

   ex CEPT
   (to exclude)

2. af FECT
   (to influence)

   Her life affected us all.

   The effect was tremendous.

   The doctor effected her recovery.

   ef FECT
   (a result; to bring about)

3. cite   site   sight
    (to summon or quote)   (place)   (the power to see;
                                              something seen)

She cited the line from the play to prove her point.

The site for the new bank is on the corner.

The sight of the accident victim made me sick.

4. DES ert   *(also ab*   des SERT
    (a hot, dry place)   (a sweet served after a meal)

Camels live easily in the desert.

I rarely eat desserts.

5. here   hear
    (in this place)   (to sense with the ears)

I have lived here for forty years.

You hear with your ears.

6. it's   its
    (it is)   (belonging to it)

It's a shame you didn't win.

Our team has lost its standing.

7. new   knew
    (not old)   (to know in the past)

Her new car got better mileage.

I knew him before he was famous.

8. passed   past
    (went by)   (a time before the present)

I passed the house several times.

In the past, women were not allowed at this school.

9. PRIN ci pal   PRIN ci ple
    (most important;   *two meanings*   (a fundamental law)
    head of a school)   *is your pal*   *not the same*

His principal reason for becoming a principal was to make
more money.

Religion gives us an ethical principle to guide our actions.

10. right   rite   write
    (just; correct;   (a ceremony)   (to make letters)
    that which is due to
    anyone)

    You're right; it is your right to have an attorney present.

    Funeral rites help us to deal with death.

    He could write a very effective letter.

11. scene   seen
    (a sight; part of a play)   (observed)
    I have never seen such a beautiful scene.

12. their   there   they're
    (belonging to them)   (in that place)   (they are)

    Their houses all looked alike there.

    They're conformists.

13. two   too   to
    (2)   (also; excessive)   (toward; for)

    Too has too many o's.

    Zoo too has too many o's.

    The two words sound alike to many people.

14. your   you're
    (belonging to you)   (you are)

    You're very possessive of your belongings.

15. whose   who's
    (belonging to whom)   (who is)

    Who's to say whose way is best?

Exercise N

Choose the correct word for the blanks in each sentence below.

(two, too, to)   1. I ordered _____ boxes _____ be sent

                           _____ my house _____ .

(affect, effect)   2. What _____ will this test have on my class

                           grade? It will not _____ your grade too
                           much.

(here, hear)   3. Can you _____ me in _____ ?

(new, knew)   4. He _____ this group when their act was

_____ .

(scene, seen)   5. That _____ was the clumsiest one I have

_____ in some time.

(your, you're)   6. If _____ a police officer, let me see

_____ identification.

(principal, principle) 7. A basic _____ of good writing is to empha-

size the _____*pa(*__ idea.

(there, there, they're) 8. _____ the children learn to read _____

letters before _____ five years old.

(accept, except)   9. Everyone _____ Don will be there to

_____ the award.

(its, it's)   10. _____ very difficult to hold _____ keel

steady in a heavy wind.

EDITING PRACTICE

Circle any misspelled words in the following paragraphs. Then rewrite them, correcting any spelling errors. Use your dictionary to check yourself.

1.   You're environment as a riter can be a principle ingrediant of your sucess. Too write, you should chose an amosfere of quite, away from the distracshuns of telvision and children. You should have the rite tools, two. Your sure to need plenty of stationary, pens or pensils, and a good dictionery. You shoud have a comftable chair, a large, flat writting surfice, and a good lite. If you have the write conditions, you can help yourself achieve excellance as a writer.

2.   Its know suprise to me that you one the gold metal. After seeing what occured during the figir skatting competision, I new you wood win. Beleive me, I was so proud of you're preformance. Your rythm and controll couldn't help but effect

the judges. Their can be no arguement that youre the best in your catagory. The other too skaters don't posess half your lovlyness on the ice. I relize you had to work long hours to succede. So please except a personnel word of congradulations from me on this happyest of occassions. Its a privledge to know you and be your freind.

Problems
in Sentence
Construction

15

In the editing process, you should be checking for errors in sentence construction that may confuse or distract your reader. In this chapter you can review some of the most common sentence problems and their solutions.

SENTENCE FRAGMENTS

(See also page 10).

A sentence expresses a complete idea by showing a subject involved in some action. A fragment is an incomplete idea that has been punctuated as if it were a sentence.

FRAGMENT	For instance, if the tulips die.
FRAGMENT	To the moon.
FRAGMENT	Backing up slowly.

A fragment can be corrected either by attaching it to an existing sentence or by rewriting the fragment so that it has its own subject and its own verb.

FRAGMENT	When I am near Orlando. I will visit Jodie.
EDITED	When I am near Orlando, I will visit Jodie.
EDITED	I am near Orlando. I will visit Jodie.
FRAGMENT	Smiling broadly. Bruce walked down the aisle.
EDITED	Smiling broadly, Bruce walked down the aisle.
EDITED	Bruce smiled broadly. He walked down the aisle.

Exercise A

Edit the following groups of words so that there are no sentence fragments.

1. José has opened the city's first Spanish restaurant. Near the old market. Another new eating place has also opened this week. An English-style pub.

_____

_____

_____

2. Letter writing is a lost art. In today's society. Everyone uses the telephone. Which is faster. But not as permanent. As a letter.

_____

_____

_____

3. In a recession. People have less money to spend. Forcing them to watch every penny carefully.

_____

_____

_____

4. Huge theme parks in many areas of the country. Provide a family with varied entertainment. Reasonably priced.

Huge theme parks in many areas of the country, provides

a family with resonally prrced, varied entertanment

_____

5. After studying Greek for three semesters, Liz attempted to read Aristotle in the original language, Not succeeding very well...

_____

_____

_____

6. Advertisers don't always sell a product. On its own merits, Appealing ~~in-stead~~ to people's vanity. *[handwritten: instead they make them]*

_____

_____

_____

7. Alan spends a lot of time with his children: ~~Helping~~ them with their homework, And playing games with them. *[handwritten: He helps]*

_____

_____

_____

8. Martha's car was an ancient blue Dodge. Its chrome pitted and rusty. Its upholstery torn and stained. *[handwritten: Which   was   And   was]*

_____

_____

_____

9. The booby (boo-bee) is a tropical seabird, Who is clumsy on land, But graceful in the air.

_____

_____

_____

10. Since it *was* opened, The Katherine House has sheltered over 300 battered women *and* their children, *Providing* them with temporary housing and counseling.

_____

_____

_____

SUBJECT–VERB AGREEMENT
(*See also pages 63–70.*)

In order to avoid confusing your reader, you have to be sure that subjects in your sentences are matched by their verbs. A singular subject needs a singular verb, and a plural subject needs a plural verb.

Most of the time, agreement is no problem since the form of the verb is usually exactly the same whether it is singular or plural.

Problems with agreement can occur only when the verb is in the present form or the has-or-have-plus-participle form. These verb forms have two endings, one with an -s (for *he, she,* or *it* subjects) and one without (for all other subjects.) For instance:

> Jane writes. (*singular*)
> Jane and Bill *write*. (*plural*)
> Jane *has* written. (*singular*)
> Jane and Bill *have* written. (*plural*)

When the subject is obviously singular or plural, and it occurs in its usual position at the beginning of the sentence, you should have no trouble using the correct singular or plural verb.

Exercise B

In each sentence below, label the subject as singular or plural, then make the verb agree with the subject by choosing a verb form ending in -s or one without the -s.

EXAMPLES:

(develop)   McDonnell Douglas Corporation *has developed* a new insulation system for tankers carrying liquefied natural gas.

(find)   Readers *find* our coverage thorough.

(prosper)*ed*   1. Mr. Knoll _____ since his defeat.

(decide)*d*   2. The new chairperson _____ when the meeting will be held.

(make)*s*   3. Aluminum _____ new cars lighter.

will (cost)   4. Two new stereos _____ over $1,000.

are (want)*ing*   5. The investors _____ a reasonable profit.

(guarantee)   6. Banks _____ a steady rate of interest.

(blame)*s*   7. Lucy _____ Charlie Brown for her trouble.

(give)   8 This hotel *is giving* _____ fine service.

will (save)   9. Our experts _____ you money.

(chop)*s*   10. Stan _____ the onions very fine.

There are a few situations where you may have trouble recognizing the subject or recognizing whether it is singular or plural. These are the situations you need to watch out for in editing your writing.

1. Subjects joined by *and* are plural. However, singular subjects followed by *as well as, together with,* or *in addition to* do *not* become plural.

> The necklace *and* the bracelet (*plural*)
> The necklace *as well as* the bracelet (*singular*)
>
> The knight *and* his lady (*plural*)
> The knight *together with* his lady (*singular*)
>
> Tennis *and* soccer (*plural*)
> Tennis *in addition to* soccer (*singular*)

2. Subjects joined by *or* and *nor* are considered separately. The subject closer to the verb determines whether the verb should be singular or plural.

Mr. Owens or his *sons* (*plural*)

The sons or *Mr. Owens* (*singular*)

A horse or *two cows* (*plural*)

Two cows or *a horse* (*singular*)

The Chase Building nor the *Merritt Building* (*singular*)

The Merritt Building nor the *Chase Building* (*singular*)

3.   Prepositional phrases after the subject do not change the subject.

The *son* of the immigrants (*singular*)

Some *presents* for his daughter (*plural*)

A *painting* with over a hundred colors (*singular*)

The *ringing* of the bells (*singular*)

Twelve *airlines* in our region (*plural*)

4.   *Here* and *there* are not subjects. These words signal a delayed subject with which the verb must agree.

There is a *wealth* of information (*singular*)

There are a dozen *ways* (*plural*)

Here comes the *bride* (*singular*)

Here come the *bridesmaids* (*plural*)

5.   These subject pronouns are always singular:

another	everybody	no one
anybody	everyone	nothing
anyone	everything	one
anything	much	somebody
each	neither	someone
either	nobody	something

Everything is wonderful (*singular*)

Neither fights as well (*singular*)

Anyone gets a refund (*singular*)

6.   These subject pronouns are always plural:

both	few
many	several

Few claim victory (*plural*)

Several agree (*plural*)

Many know (*plural*)

Both cry (*plural*)

7. These subject pronouns may be either singular or plural, depending on what is being discussed:

all   any   enough
most   none   some

All of his writing is (*singular*)

All of the eggs are (*plural*)

Some of the dress has (*singular*)

Some of the trains arrive (*plural*)

None of the cake remains (*singular*)

None of the cakes remain (*plural*)

8. Some subjects, called *collectives*, may appear to be plural but are considered singular in most cases. Collective nouns are nouns like *team, herd, troop, audience, group*, and *jury*, in which a number of individuals are considered as one unit. These nouns require a plural verb only when the members of the unit act as individuals rather than as part of the unit. (This happens rarely.)

The jury disagree on the verdict (*plural*)

The jury agrees on the verdict (*singular*)

The herd stampedes across the prairie (*singular*)

The team have their uniforms cleaned (*plural*)

The audience cheers that scene (*singular*)

Exercise C

Edit the following sentences so that the verbs agree with the subjects. Cross out any incorrect forms; write correct forms above them.

1. Everybody need love.

2. Jane Fonda and Robert Redford star in that film.

3. Michael, as well as his brother, attend Middle States University.

4. Several bottles of expensive perfume stands on the counter.

5. The green pencil or the red ones sell for 49 cents.

6. Neither my car nor my husband's car starts in cold weather.

7. Here lie the body of the Unknown Soldier.

8. Nothing grows in that barren soil.

9. The deans or the president welcomes the incoming freshmen.

10. The audience stamps its feet and whistles whenever Julia comes on stage.

11. There waits challenges unknown to most Americans.

12. Smith, together with James, represents the 33rd District.

13. A dancer in elegant clothes glides majestically around the floor.

14. Either the ski team or the skaters win a gold medal every winter.

15. Few realizes the dangers of sports.

16. Full-sized cars and compact cars fights for the consumer's dollars.

17. The attractions of the quiet island offers an incredible vacation.

18. The troop spends the income from the candy sale on community service projects.

19. The managers and the clerical staff receives a cost-of-living increase every year.

20. Some of the ornaments is broken.

21. Neither newspapers nor radio dominate the entertainment field any more.

22. Coffee, as well as delicious cakes, completes my favorite dinner.

23. Here goes our finest gourmet chefs.

24. All of the meat simmers in the broth for 40 minutes.

25. The dictionary, with its thousands of entries, explain the meaning of every word in the language.

PRONOUN REFERENCE

(*See also pages 153–55.*)

A pronoun is a word that stands for a noun. For example:

Mary Lou bought a car, and she paid for it in cash.

In this sentence, *she* stands for **Mary Lou,** and *it* stands for *car.*

Confusion arises for your reader when it is not clear what word the pronoun refers to, as in this sentence:

UNCLEAR REFERENCE   When Mike saw the thieves shoot at the policemen, he ran toward them.

Does *them* mean *thieves* or *policemen?*
In editing this sentence, you might write:

EDITED   When Mike saw the thieves shoot, he ran toward the police.

or

EDITED   Mike ran toward the thieves when they shot at the policemen.

PRONOUN AGREEMENT
(See also pages 155–160.)

If a pronoun refers to a specific person, place, or thing, it must match the noun that it refers to. A singular noun (*chair*) requires a singular pronoun (*it*). A plural noun (*chairs*) requires a plural pronoun (*they, them*). A feminine noun (*Rachel*) requires a feminine pronoun (*she, her*). A masculine noun (*Grover*) requires a masculine pronoun (*he, him*). Nouns of indefinite gender (*the producer, the owner*) can use masculine or feminine pronouns (*he, him, she, her*).

Exercise D

Using the list of pronouns below, show which ones would match each of the following nouns or groups of nouns.

Singular	*Plural*
I, me	we, us
you	you
he, she, it, him, her	they, them

1. Professor Alden _____

2. two dozen cookies _____

3. a counterfeit diamond _____

4. St. Elizabeth Ann Seton _____

5. the children _____

6. Rob and I _____

7. a bottle of ink _____

8. my mother _____

9. you and the captain _____

10. the bantam rooster _____

11. Dr. Chin _____

12. Rachel and John _____

13. the new dean _____

14. a wheel of cheese _____

15. you and Marlene _____

16. the neighbors and I _____

17. a gang of thieves _____

18. Rupert _____

19. his plane _____

20. the dancer _____

Exercise E

Edit the following sentences to correct any errors in the use of pronouns.

1. Neither the Joneses nor the Smiths liked his trip to Mexico.

_____

_____

2. Celia gave her mother her favorite quilt.

_____

_____

3. No one wanted their picture taken.

_____

_____

4. The electric company and the water service raised its rates this year.

_____

_____

5. The saleswoman offered us an unbelievable discount. We immediately accepted their proposal.

_____

_____

6. The company moved their office to Maclean. Ms. Campbell told the reporters that they would have better facilities for research there.

_____

_____

7. His bookshelves were crowded. They were piled up sideways and half falling off the edges.

_____

_____

8. If an accused person needs a lawyer, they can get them from the Public Defender's Office.

_____

_____

9. All the girls must pay her deposits before leaving on her trip.

_____

_____

10.   Carol wrote Nancy to ask if she could come a few days early.

_____

_____

Exercise F

Rewrite the following paragraphs to correct any errors in subject–verb agreement or pronoun agreement.

1.   Membership in the State Consolidated Drivers' Clubs now offer unbelievable benefits. First of all, the entire family are covered by one low fee of $12.50. And that's just the beginning. The club reimburses drivers up to $50 if them have to call a tow truck. The club pay for emergency travel expenses, and they offer a reward for information on cars stolen from members. A member also get discounts on car rentals, hotel accommodations, and meals if they travel within the state. Most of these benefits is available only to Consolidated members. Smart Homestate drivers belongs to Consolidated.

2.   My new Camaro with their streamlined body is the sharpest-looking car on the block. Its glossy, metallic paint and gleaming chrome makes them sparkle when the sun hit it. Another feature that sets off the car are his magnificent spoilers. Then there is her classy mag wheels. Inside, the camel-colored upholstery, as well as the sleek console panel, looks luxurious. All of these features shows why my car is the star of the neighborhood.

ADJECTIVE AND ADVERB FORMS

Adjectives

You use adjectives to describe a subject or other noun more precisely. In editing, you should be sure you have used the correct form of the adjective.

Most adjectives can take more than one form to show different degrees of the quality they describe. For instance, to show that one test has more difficulty than another, you might say:

This test was harder than the first one.

Or, to show that one bicycle was more recently acquired than another, you might say:

My bike is *newer* than yours.

This form of the adjective is called the *comparative* because it is used to compare two people or objects. The word *than* appears after the comparative form.

There is also a *superlative* form of the adjective for use when you want to compare more than two people or objects. For example:

This story is the *hardest* one in the book.

or

My bike is the *newest* one on the block.

Notice that the word *the* usually appears in front of the superlative form of the adjective.

Here is how you construct the comparative and superlative forms of adjectives.

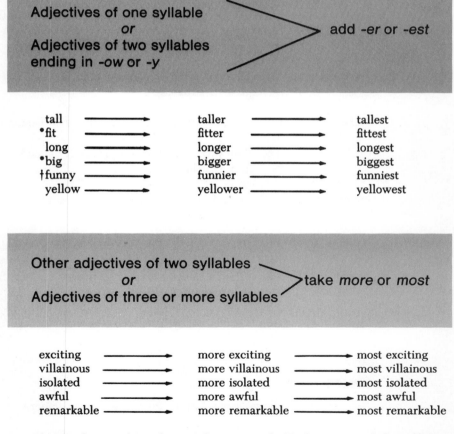

Adjectives of one syllable
or
Adjectives of two syllables ending in -ow or -y
> **add -er or -est**

tall	taller	tallest
*fit	fitter	fittest
long	longer	longest
*big	bigger	biggest
†funny	funnier	funniest
yellow	yellower	yellowest

Other adjectives of two syllables
or
Adjectives of three or more syllables
> **take *more* or *most***

exciting	more exciting	most exciting
villainous	more villainous	most villainous
isolated	more isolated	most isolated
awful	more awful	most awful
remarkable	more remarkable	most remarkable

* Most adjectives that end in a single consonant double the consonant before adding -er or -est.

† Change the -y to -i before adding -er or -est.

A few adjectives have their own unique comparative and superlative forms:

good   ⟶   better   ⟶   best
bad   ⟶   worse   ⟶   worst
little   ⟶   less   ⟶   least

Exercise G

For each sentence below, supply the correct form of the adjective: simple, comparative, or superlative.

(sturdy)   1. This oak tree looks _____ than the one in back.

(early)   2. Please reply at the _____ possible date.

(clever)   3. Your baby announcements are _____ .

(elaborate)   4. The company is planning a _____ retirement party this year than last.

(hot)   5. Cleo's curry is the _____ dish I have ever tasted.

(serious)   6. The Jaffe case will be the _____ one the committee has had this year.

(complicated)   7. Sexual intimacy makes a relationship _____ than it was before.

(big)   8. The _____ health care problem today is cost.

(good)   9. Clark's offers _____ tractor service facilities than any other dealer in town.

(disturbing)   10. Drug use by preteenagers has become a _____ problem.

Exercise H

Edit the following paragraphs for any errors in adjective form.

1.   Senta is one of the abler swimmers in the state. Her backstroke is the most fast of anyone's on her team, and her free-style is even fastest. Still, it is her but-

terfly that is the impressivest. In that stroke, she excels. She has the most great extension with her arms of any recent member of the team, and her dolphin kick is powerfuller than any other swimmer's I have seen. Unfortunately, her breast stroke is not very good. In fact, her whip kick is the ridiculouser exhibition of co-ordination ever performed in water.

2.   Peter thought things would get gooder after the first of the year, but they seemed to go from bad to badder. His financee found someone more good. He had had only a little money; now he had more little. He had hoped for a gooder job; instead, he lost his old one. If things didn't take a turn for the more good by June, he was moving to California. This was certainly the most baddest year of his life.

Adverbs

Like adjectives, adverbs may take different forms to show the degree of the quality involved. For instance, if you want to say that one student worked with more care than another, you could say:

> Jennifer did the assignment *more carefully* than Judi.

If you want to say that Jennifer used more care than anyone else, you could say:

> Jennifer did the assignment the *most carefully* of anyone.

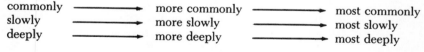

In general, *-ly* adverbs form the comparative and superlative by using *more* and *most*.

commonly	→ more commonly	→ most commonly
slowly	→ more slowly	→ most slowly
deeply	→ more deeply	→ most deeply

A few adverbs use *-er* and *-est* to form the comparative and the superlative.

fast	→ faster	→ fastest
late	→ later	→ latest
near	→ nearer	→ nearest
far	→ farther	→ farthest

Some adverbs have special forms for the comparative and superlative.

well	→ better	→ best
badly	→ worse	→ worst

Exercise I

In each sentence below, supply the appropriate form of the adverb: simple, comparative, or superlative.

(frequently)   1. According to the police, murders occur _____ during the early morning than at any other time.

(suspiciously)   2. The man who acted _____ of all was Mr. Greene.

(energetically)   3. Linda and Paul danced _____ than Peggy and Ed.

(artistically)   4. However, the poster designed _____ of the whole group was Sheri's.

(accurately)   5. This map shows the soil conditions _____ than the one put out by the Department of Agriculture.

(badly)   6. No man has ever behaved _____ to a woman than Hamlet behaved toward Ophelia.

(monotonously)   7. Dr. Hermann lectured _____ on the development of the printing press.

(strategically)   8. The _____ located island in the Pacific was Hawaii.

(fast)   9. The new train covered the distance two hours _____ than the old one.

(well)   10. Allen loved Cissie _____ of all his sisters.

Exercise J

Edit the following paragraph for any errors in adverb form.

The trip ended more badly than it had begun. The raft moved toward the opening in the rocks rapidlier than they had thought it would. The guide standing on the large rock near the shore motioned to them to paddle strenuousliest on the left side. They tried to. But the current was carrying them definitelier to the right. The guide gestured franticlier. It was too late. They were caught most completely in the current and their raft capsized more fast than anyone could yell, "Person overboard!"

Confusion of Adjectives and Adverbs

Many times, you can't tell whether a word is an adjective or an adverb just by looking at it. While it is true that many adverbs end in *-ly,* the word *early* can be an adjective as well as an adverb. And words like *better, fast,* and *worst* can also be either adjectives or adverbs.

When you are editing, you need to look at how the word is used in the sentence in order to choose between the adjective form and the adverb form. For instance, look at these two sentences:

> The Sioux are *independent.*
> The tribe responded *independently.*

Independent in the first sentence describes *Sioux. Independent* functions as an adjective telling *what kind* of people the Sioux are. In the second sentence, *independently* tells *how* the action or responding took place.

Which of the following two sentences contains an adverb?

> He is a really good sprinter.
> His talent is real.

In the first sentence, *really* tells *how* good. *Really* is an adverb. *Real,* in the second sentence, tells *what kind* of talent. *Real* is an adjective.

Exercise K

Supply the correct adjective or adverb form for each of the following sentences.

(loud)   1. The radio is playing too _____ .

(quiet)   2. This dishwasher is guaranteed to run _____ .

(bad)   3. Bill has very _____ handwriting.

(agile)   4. Charlie is an _____ skier.

(bitter)   5. The coffee tasted _____ .

(sad)   6. Marlene certainly looked _____ last night.

(sad)   7. She smiled _____ at her friend.

(strange)   8. The room seemed _____ empty.

(diligent)   9. A dozen soldiers searched the area _____ for the missing keys.

(clear)   10. The sky looked _____ this morning for the first time in weeks.

(brave)   11. Under pressure, Rich acted _____ .

(practical) 12. When solar energy becomes _____ , it will change our lives.

(frequent)   13. Supermarkets _____ offer inexpensive store brands.

(peaceful)   14. The river ran _____ by our house.

(peaceful)   15. The river seemed _____ as it ran by our house.

Exercise L

Edit the following paragraph for correct use of adjective and adverb forms.

Brian arrived at the gym prompt at 5:30, feeling tiredly. He quick changed clothes, putting on a workout suit that was fresh washed and a pair of newly sneakers. Then, he went upstairs and did a strenuously workout. Thursdays, he always worked his chest and arms. He did several sets of bench presses, raising and lowering the bar careful with completely concentration. After several other chest exercises, he blasted his biceps with super sets of curls. These helped his growth tremendous. Incredible, he had gone from a 16-inch to a 19-inch arm in just two months of real intensely exercises. Finished, he took a warmly shower and was on his way home by 7:30. After his workout, he felt total well.

MISPLACED MODIFIERS
(See also pages 46–49.)

You choose modifiers to clarify or describe a particular word in a sentence. In order to avoid confusing your reader, you should be sure that the modifier is as close as possible to the word it describes.

MISPLACED	Look for problems in every sentence with spelling.
EDITED	Look for spelling problems in every sentence.
EDITED	Look for problems with spelling in every sentence.
MISPLACED	Covered with onions and mushrooms, Ron makes the best hamburger in town.
EDITED	Ron makes the best hamburger in town, covered with onions and mushrooms.
EDITED	Ron's hamburger, covered with onions and mushrooms, is the best one in town.

DANGLING MODIFIERS
(See also pages 113–15.)

Your reader will get very confused if your sentence has a modifier that has nothing to describe.

DANGLING	Many community colleges offer on-the-job training while taking regular classes. (Who is taking classes?)
EDITED	Many community colleges offer on-the-job training to *students* who are taking regular classes.
EDITED	Many community colleges offer *students* on-the-job training as well as regular classes.
DANGLING	In order to be a doctor, long years of training are necessary. (Who wants to be a doctor?)
EDITED	If *someone* wants to be a doctor, long years of training are necessary.
EDITED	In order to be a doctor, a *person* needs long years of training.

Exercise M

Edit the following sentences so that all modifiers are clearly related to the words they describe.

1. Filling out the application, my head began to ache.

   _____

2. The museum is presenting an exhibit for students in the main gallery on French Impressionism.

   _____

3. John could see the excited crowd flying into the airport.

   _____

4. We sat through a movie that was boring because of Jill's request.

   _____

5. Bewildered by their new surroundings, we rushed to greet the refugee family.

   _____

6. Singing in the shower, the glass became fogged up.

   _____

7. To open the package, the side of the box had to be ripped off.

   _____

8. The man decided to take another bus with the umbrella and briefcase.

   _____

9. Sitting on the beach, several dolphins leaped from the water.

   _____

10. Freshly painted, the sailor admired the deck of the ship.

   _____

SHIFTS IN VERB TENSE

(See also pages 160–64.)

You can confuse your reader if you set up a certain time frame in your sentence and then don't follow it. In editing, check your verbs for consistency.

SHIFT	Ellen *left* for St. Louis, but suddenly the car *breaks* down.
EDITED	Ellen *left* for St. Louis, but suddenly the car broke down.
SHIFT	The new advertising campaign *will cost* half a million dollars. However, it *was* worth the money.
EDITED	The new advertising campaign *will cost* half a million dollars. However, it *will be* worth the money.

SHIFTS IN POINT OF VIEW

(See also page 164–65.)

Your reader can easily become confused if you keep moving the focus from *I* to *you* to *he* in your sentences. In editing, make sure your sentences keep the same point of view.

SHIFT	*I* like going to a school where *you* have small classes.
EDITED	*I* like going to a school where *I* have small classes.
SHIFT	A *student* preparing for the test should realize that *you* will be graded on your punctuation and spelling.
EDITED	A *student* preparing for the test should realize that *she* will be graded on *her* punctuation and spelling.

Exercise N

Edit the following sentences for shifts in verb tense or point of view.

1. We start when we were infants to shape your adult personality.

_____

_____

2. Peterson owned the only car dealership in town until Ryan opens one in the fall.

_____

_____

3. If you buy a wood-burning stove, a family can usually lower its heating costs.

_____

_____

4. Phil and Tom have agreed to plow the garden after the ground thawed.

_____

_____

5. Credit cards often encourage people to spend more money than you have.

_____

_____

6. Sprays that are intended to kill weeds were dangerous to children and pets too.

_____

_____

7. We have ordered the most advanced computer system a person can afford.

_____

_____

8. The county road crews will work day and night so the roads were cleared.

_____

_____

9.   There is no reason why anyone should buy "blind." You had expert con-
     sumer advice written every year.

     _____

     _____

10. The best history teacher I ever had was Mrs. Donaldson. You can always
     count on her for unusual facts.

     _____

     _____

PASSIVE VERBS

A sentence can be written so that it emphasizes action being done (*active*) or
action being received (*passive.*)

ACTIVE	Henry baked a cake.
PASSIVE	A cake was baked by Henry.

(For the formation of the passive verb, see pages 404–8.)

In most sentences, the active verb is more effective than the passive.
Sentences with an active verb tend to be shorter and more direct. However,
there are some times when you will want to use the passive verb. In editing,
check any use of the passive verb to be sure it is appropriate.

Suppose, for instance, that you do not know who performed a certain action. You could write an active sentence such as:

Someone stole the diamonds.

But that sentence would just emphasize your lack of knowledge. A passive
sentence like

The diamonds were stolen.

would probably be more effective since it puts emphasis on what you do know.

Or, suppose that you know who performed an action, but you do not
want your reader to know. For instance,

Bathing suits are not permitted in this restaurant.

If you are the owner of the restaurant, this use of the passive may keep you
from having to deal with complaints. However, readers may be suspicious of

the passive that is used to conceal. Such use of the passive is frequent in bureaucratic and governmental writing where no one wants to assume responsibility for an action.

Finally, the passive verb can help you put emphasis on a certain idea. This sentence, for instance,

> The teacher distributed the grades.

puts emphasis on the teacher by making her the subject. This passive sentence,

> Grades were distributed by the teacher.

puts emphasis on the grades by making them the subject. Which sentence you would use would depend on whether you were writing primarily about the teacher or primarily about grades.

Exercise O

Rewrite each of the following sentences, changing active verbs to passive and passive verbs to active. In some sentences, you must supply a doer for the action. Be prepared to explain when you might choose one sentence or the other as most appropriate.

1. That bill will be introduced by Senator Cade next week.

     _____

     _____

2. The children were lined up on the parking lot.

     _____

     _____

3. I will hand out the souvenirs after the ceremony.

     _____

     _____

4. You must turn in an expense voucher.

     _____

     _____

5. The opening hymn is sung by the congregation.

_____

_____

6. My brother has broken the vase.

_____

_____

7. Seventeen rooms have been prepared.

_____

_____

8. Maureen saddled the pony.

_____

_____

9. Interest rates have been raised dramatically.

_____

_____

10. A lifeguard needs at least 40 hours of training.

_____

_____

EDITING PRACTICE

Edit the following paragraphs for problems in sentence construction that may confuse or distract a reader from the ideas being presented.

1.   On the Fourth of July, we are going on a picnic. This was our family's favorite way to celebrate the holiday. At first, a decision could not be made about where to go. You usually prefer to go to the beach. Or a wooded park would be perfect. I

don't like the beach because you always get messy. They chose the beach in spite of me. Next, you have to decide what to eat. We packed a basket of chicken, some salad, some lemonade, and we also took a chocolate cake. Piled with all that food, we could hardly fit our bathing suits, towels, and sports equipment into the car. You need the sports equipment for all the games they play at the beach. My father and uncle like surf-fishing. He says we could also play water polo. My sister and I prefer touch football, volleyball, or just playing tag in the sand. My mother and aunt walk miles along the beach collecting shells. She has found some unusual shells during these walks. We have a goodly time at picnics. After a full day driving slow home, a pleasantly exhaustion is felt by everyone.

2.   College is a lot differenter than high school. For one thing, it was more harder to get in. To be considered for college, the SAT must be taken. After being accepted, the classes are also much harder. My English teacher only said that we would have to write a theme on the first day of class every week in our notebooks. Then she didn't remind us until she had collected the notebooks. Since then I have followed the instructions faithfully given by each professor. I handed him a report for chemistry class which I had recently read. In history, we had a week just to read a book that was 400 pages in small type long. Then a teacher tells you to expect a test next time. Recovering from the first week of classes, the whole weekend went by too fastly. You just have to adjust to the difference between high school and college.

Punctuation

16

Punctuation is an important way that you help your readers keep their focus on your main ideas. In editing, check to see that your punctuation clarifies rather than confuses.

> **Definition of a Sentence**
>
> A group of words that expresses a complete idea with
> a SUBJECT
> and a VERB showing past, present, or future time
> > not introduced by a SUBORDINATION SIGNAL

BASIC SENTENCE PATTERNS

Following is a list of the common sentence patterns and their punctuation. These will each be discussed individually.

Sentence.
1. Sentence?
   Sentence!
2. Sentence; sentence.

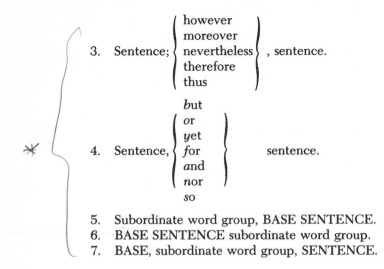

3.   Sentence;
$\left\{\begin{array}{l}\text{however}\\\text{moreover}\\\text{nevertheless}\\\text{therefore}\\\text{thus}\end{array}\right\}$
, sentence.

4.   Sentence,
$\left\{\begin{array}{l}\textit{but}\\\textit{or}\\\textit{yet}\\\textit{for}\\\textit{and}\\\textit{nor}\\\textit{so}\end{array}\right\}$
sentence.

5.   Subordinate word group, BASE SENTENCE.
6.   BASE SENTENCE subordinate word group.
7.   BASE, subordinate word group, SENTENCE.

Pattern 1

A sentence by itself begins with a capital letter and ends with a period, a question mark, or an exclamation point. In all of the basic patterns, a question mark or an exclamation point could be substituted for the period.

> She can make it.
> Can she make it?
> She made it!

IMPORTANT: A subordinate word group (that is, any word group that does not fit the definition of a sentence) by itself should not be punctuated like a sentence. (See Chapter 1.)

Confusing	*Corrected*
If I had a dime.	She asked if I had a dime.
Running swiftly.	Running swiftly, I caught the train.

Pattern 2

Two or more sentences joined without any coordination signal must be linked by a semicolon (;). Never use a comma in this pattern. (See Chapter 3.)

> Lois brought the sandwiches; Herb picked up the beer.
> Bees produce honey; wasps produce nothing.
> NEVER: Bees produce honey, wasps produce nothing.

Pattern 3

Two sentences joined by a linking adverb (*however, thus,* etc.) are punctuated with a semicolon placed after the first sentence and a comma placed after the adverb. This is simply a variation of pattern 2, except for the comma after the adverb. (See Chapter 3.)

> I enjoy hot weather; however, I dislike the humidity.
> She missed half the semester; consequently, she must repeat the course.

Pattern 4

Two sentences joined with a coordination signal should be linked with a comma. An easy way to remember the coordination signals is by the first letters, which spell *boy fans:* *b*ut, *o*r, *y*et, *f*or, *a*nd, *n*or, *s*o. (See Chapter 3.)

> Greg was tired of small-town life, so he moved to Chicago.
> Harry must buy back the check, or the store will prosecute him.

Pattern 5

When a sentence starts with a subordinate word group, a comma is a useful way of marking the end of the subordinate word group and the beginning of the base sentence. The marker helps signal the reader that the central idea in the sentence is coming. (See Chapter 4).

> If you will have a seat, the doctor will see you soon.
> Even though wages stayed low, prices continued to climb.

Pattern 6

On the other hand, no punctuation is required when the subordinate word group follows the base sentence since the subordination signal by itself tells the reader the base sentence is finished. (See Chapter 4).

> He had his first accident when he was sixteen.
> Casey would waltz while the band played on.

Pattern 7

When a subordinate word group interrupts the flow of the sentence, you should surround it with commas. (See Chapter 4).

Agnes, who was nobody's fool, called the police immediately.

The Rams, even without their first-string quarterback, won easily.

Exercise A

Edit the following sentences for correct punctuation. Use the list of sentence patterns to help identify the appropriate pattern, and write the number of the pattern in the space provided.

EXAMPLE:

_____ Is Mary driving or will Ted bring her?

__4__ Is Mary driving, or will Ted bring her?

__5__ 1. Even though he reads slowly, Sam loves long novels.

__4__ 2. Montreal is a beautiful city, but the winters are too cold for me.

__4__ 3. Three of my checks bounced, because I didn't get to the bank on time.

__3__ 4. Anna married Karenin; however, she loved Vronsky.

__2__ 5. Small-town life has its pleasures; it also has serious drawbacks.

__5__ 6. Lying peacefully in its green valley, the village had remained undisturbed for centuries.

__5__ 7. Carlisle wants that report by Thursday, and you had better get it to him on time.

__3__ 8. Body-building is not an Olympic sport; nevertheless, it has a worldwide following.

__5__ 9. As he was dying, the great poet asked for more light.

__7__ 10. Detroit, the auto capital of the United States, is also an important cultural center.

COMMA SPLICES AND RUN-ON SENTENCES

If you fail to show with your punctuation where one idea ends and another begins, you run a great risk of confusing your reader. Sentences are the basic units of thought in writing, so sentences must be clearly marked.

COMMA SPLICE	The woods were filled with snow, the snow was filled with children.
RUN-ON	The woods were filled with snow the snow was filled with children.
EDITED	The woods were filled with snow. The snow was filled with children.

EDITED	The woods were filled with snow, and the snow was filled with children.
EDITED	The woods were filled with snow; the snow was filled with children.
COMMA SPLICE	Dying of cancer is often lonely and painful, hospices can help.
RUN-ON	Dying of cancer is often lonely and painful hospices can help.
EDITED	Dying of cancer is often lonely and painful. Hospices can help.
EDITED	Dying of cancer is often lonely and painful, but hospices can help.
EDITED	Dying of cancer is often lonely and painful; hospices can help.

Exercise B

Edit the following sentences so that one sentence is correctly separated from another.

1. Margaret slipped, ~~and~~ she injured her back.
2. The Congo flows into the Atlantic, ~~and~~ the Nile empties into the Mediterranean.
3. Arthur sent out three hundred applications, but he got no job interviews.
4. *When* The going gets tough, the tough get going.
5. Myra had an awful experience, *is* She hasn't been the same ~~since~~.
6. Rhett loved Scarlett, *but* she thought she loved Ashley.
7. India plowed into the Asian continent *and as a result,* the Himalayas were formed.
8. The Industrial Revolution enriched Europe, *but* it created huge social problems too.
9. Timbuktu *which* is on the Niger River ~~it~~ was once the greatest city in Africa.
10. Linda worked hard, *so* she deserves her success.

COMMAS

The basic function of the comma is to separate. As you can see from the sentence patterns shown at the beginning of this chapter, commas may separate two or more equally important ideas, or they may separate a more important idea from a less important one used as an introduction or an interrupter.

Commas with Coordinate Ideas

A series of coordinate (equally important) adjectives should be separated by commas.

> The room was small, stuffy, and crowded.
> The stuffy, crowded room made me feel sick.

You can tell adjectives are coordinate if you can reverse their order:

> Joe was an ambitious, hard-working, and honest businessman.
> Ellen was an honest, hard-working, and ambitious businesswoman.

In a sentence where you cannot reverse the order, no commas are used:

> Four tall trees / tall four trees

Tall and *four* are not really coordinate adjectives here. They do not modify the same word. *Tall* modifies *trees*, but *four* modifies *tall trees*.

Commas are used only where the adjectives are coordinate. Here are other examples of commas with a series of coordinate ideas:

> *Ronda, Margo, and June* made the team.
>   coordinate subjects
> Fred *dusted, straightened, and vacuumed* the living room.
>   coordinate verbs
> My favorite cities are *Boston, Atlanta, and Denver.*
>   coordinate complements
> Jim hunted ducks *in the fields, by the pond, and on the river.*
>   coordinate modifiers
> *The prince owed everyone money, and he had no way to pay*
>   coordinate   sentences
> *his debts.*

Although the comma before the *and* in a series is sometimes omitted, that comma can make a significant difference in the meaning of a sentence.

> Warren ordered a green sweater, a case of champagne, a
> car with cut-velvet upholstery, and a radio.

Without the last comma, it is not clear whether Warren ordered a car and a radio separately, or a car with a radio in it.

Sometimes, as the examples following show, the comma may be even more significant, a matter of millions of dollars in investments, or even of life and death.

Renegade comma stirs
legal debate in county

By KATHERINE WHITE

*Baltimore County Bureau
of The Sun*

What's in a name, or a comma? In Baltimore county government circles, quite a bit.

The fate of a controversial shopping center, the proposed Franklin Mall in Reisterstown, has teeter-tottered for the past several weeks on either side of a comma in a local law. Everyone involved, from the Planning Board to the County Council to the county solicitor, has had a different view of what a single sentence really means— and what various people intended it to mean at various times.

The county leaders are not alone in their confusion, however. A survey by *The Sun* of local language experts and nationally known authorities on English usage resulted in only one clear conclusion: If words could kill, the poorly written sentence in question might have taken its revenge on public officials in Towson.

Leading off the consultants in *The Sun*'s informal survey was Edwin New-man, an NBC correspondent and the author of "Strictly Speaking" and "A Civil Tongue." He said the sentence in question "is so incompetently written, I can't tell what they mean, but they have managed to be fairly confusing."

Richard Mitchell, an English professor at Glassboro State College in New Jersey, the editor of "the Underground Grammarian," as well as the author of "Less Than Words Can Say," was aghast.

"Good God!" was all he could say at first. He paused a moment and then summoned his courage to comment, "The sentence is terrible! Either it has too many commas or not enough. . . . The person who wrote it should be castigated."

The troublesome section of the law establishes exemptions to new development rules contained in the county's growth management ordinance. A subparagraph of the law outlines those rules, but concludes with a sentence that is supposed to enlighten the reader about which properties are exempt from the rules. That sentence reads as follows:

"This subparagraph does not apply . . . to any development in a CCC [community core commercial] district, CSA [commercial support area] district or RAE [residential apartment-elevator] zone in a town center. . . ."

Does that mean properties in all three districts are exempt? Or only if those zones—or just the last two of them—are also located in a town center? Or does it only exempt the last zone if it is in a town center? Such is the stuff of which legal— and language—debates are made.

Dr. Mitchell said the sentence "is as much a problem in logic as a problem in grammar. . . . Why there isn't a comma after CSA I can't imagine."

He called the situation an interesting example of what "those damn teachers" tell their students today: "That little things like punctuation don't matter. Go with what makes you feel better."

Baltimore *Sun*, January 20, 1980.

Parker fate tied to comma

By SCOTT LEBAR

Staff Writer

William Joseph Parker's life may be hanging by a comma.

After all the arguments on the constitutionality of the death penalty are voiced, Prince George's County Circuit Court Judge Howard S. Chasanow will be left with the new Maryland statute and its punctuation in deciding the fate of 28-year-old Parker.

A critical phrase in the law has drawn careful examination since Parker's conviction last week of the first-degree felony murder and second-degree rape of 13-year-old Elizabeth Archard.

That phrase may be missing the comma that could send Parker to jail instead of the gas chamber.

Under the new law, a person convicted of first-degree murder committed with any of 10 so-called "aggravating circumstances" is eligible for the death penalty.

Parker's conviction falls under the 10th circumstance: "The defendant committed the murder while committing or attempting to commit robbery, arson, or rape or sexual offense in the first degree."

Parker's attorney, Fred W. Bennett, said he will file his arguments next week claiming the death penalty is not only a disproportionate punishment for Parker's conviction, but that the conviction does not fall in this category because Parker was found innocent of first-degree rape. If the law was to apply to all rapes, Bennett argues, a comma would have followed the phrase "or rape." And according to several defense attorneys, the confusion caused by a missing comma is enough to prevent a man's being put to death.

That decision rests with Chasanow, who has not yet scheduled a sentencing hearing for Parker. By law, the judge's decision is automatically reviewed by the Court of Appeals.

But the St. Mary's County jury's verdict has already generated concern about the wording of the law.

"We're curious ourselves," said Assistant Attorney General Deborah Handel, who heads the criminal appeals division. "We're aware the question has been raised . . . and we'll be checking that."

Chasanow, who is regarded as scholarly and sensitive judge, has not contacted her office. But her interest was aroused when she heard the verdict and became aware of the possible ambiguity of the law.

"That's the $64 question," she said. "It's up to the Court of Appeals to make that determination."

Annapolis *Evening Capital*, May 16, 1979.

Exercise C

Edit the following sentences to make the coordination of parts clear to the reader.

1. The trees bushes and shrubs need pruning.
2. Frannie bought hamburger noodles and cheese.
3. Rising from behind the hill glinting through the trees illuminating the world, the sun appeared.
4. Cautiously with great precision and with infinite patience, Sergeant Godovsky disarmed the bomb.
5. Prudence washed her hair put it up in rollers and went shopping.
6. None of the children wanted to go to a movie visit a museum or have dinner with their grandmother.

7. Dorothy,the scarecrow,and the tin woodman were afraid of lions tigers and bears.
8. This detergent comes in small size,medium size and giant economy size.
9. We had scrambled eggs,buttered toast,and bacon.
10. The receiver picked the pass out of the air,avoided three tacklers and scrambled into the end zone.

Commas with Subordinate Ideas

Subordinate ideas need to be separated from the main idea in two situations. The first is when the subordinate idea precedes the main idea.

> *Jim,* Marian called.
>
> *After the show,* we had dinner.
>
> *Marching down the street,* the circus was a child's dream come true.
>
> *To win the contest,* Joel spent hours rehearsing his speech.
>
> *Filled with anger,* the prisoners refused to speak to the warden.
>
> *When the ballots were counted,* Teresa won.

The second situation calling for a comma is when the subordinate idea interrupts the main idea.

> I think, *Dorothy,* that you should go home.
>
> Mei Ling, *the hostess,* told us to be seated.
>
> Joshua, *despite his quick temper,* is generous.
>
> The answers, *however,* may not be the same.
>
> Their faces, *scrubbed and shining,* were angelic.
>
> The prisoners, *filled with anger,* refused to talk to the warden.
>
> That book, *if you want my opinion,* is dull.

In both situations, you use the commas to be sure that your reader is aware of what is the most important idea in your sentence—the base sentence. In a case where you begin with the base sentence and follow it with a less important idea, it is not usually necessary to separate the ideas with a comma.

> Theda will return your call *when she gets home.*
>
> Money is not that important *anyway.*

Note that sometimes a subordinate idea in the middle of a sentence is *not* an interrupter; it is an important part of the main idea. For instance:

> Any student *who doesn't study* deserves to fail.

Here, the idea *who doesn't study* is necessary to the meaning of the sentence and should not be cut off from the main idea by commas.

Uses of the Comma

To separate coordinate ideas:

> Baltimore is Maryland's biggest city, but Annapolis is the state capital.

> Kateri Tekawitha was a Mohawk, a martyr, and possibly a saint.

To separate subordinate ideas from the base sentence:

> A native of the Northeast, Georgia O'Keefe is the unrivalled painter of the Western landscape.

> Georgia O'Keefe, a native of the Northeast, is the unrivalled painter of the Western landscape.

Exercise D

Edit the following sentences, using commas to keep the reader's attention focused on the main idea.

1. Whenever Chloe gets a vacation the airlines go on strike.
2. Let's eat Granma!
3. I think however you may want to replace your engine.
4. My sister Louise who was married yesterday went to Bermuda for her honeymoon.
5. With only seconds to go in the fourth quarter Jabbar shot from down court and hit.
6. I believe your honor that my client is innocent.
7. David Sterling my best friend in high school married Karen my old girl-friend.
8. Once I started the paper was easy to write.
9. The neighbors you know the ones I mean just bought a Mercedes.
10. From playing Monopoly my favorite game I learned how to become a business tycoon.

Exercise E

Edit the following sentences for appropriate use of commas.

1. The ladies of the Elks prepared a magnificent feast that included spinach salad, quiche, roast beef, potatoes and ice cream with chocolate sauce.

2. You were hired to cook, Miss Genderson, not to dispense advice to the lovelorn.

3. *Meetings and Conventions,* a trade publication, estimates that American corporations and organizations held over 757,000 meetings last year.

4. As new car prices escalate, more people are learning to repair their old cars.

5. Fire, especially in the dry season, is a great danger to animals who live in the forest.

6. The lake was filled with fish, and deer roamed the nearby woods.

7. The Board will consider a tuition increase, limitation of enrollment, and state funding for new buildings.

8. The Dean read the names, handed out the diplomas, and congratulated the students.

9. General Murchison ordered jeeps, amphibious vehicles, and tanks into the war zone.

10. My preference, Dr. Fernando, is to postpone the surgery.

11. They watched the tennis match with interest, although neither had seen a game before.

12. Lynn, who was my roommate for four years, is now the sales manager.

13. Oliver set out on a fine spring Tuesday, to propose to Nellie.

14. Wordsworth, urged the use of ordinary, everyday language in poetry.

15. Hayden's service was prompt, but his merchandise was inferior.

16. The car which is parked in the driveway has just been repaired.

17. The car which is parked in the driveway has just been repaired. The other one still needs a new battery.

18. Elated at her success, Tess hugged everyone in the room.

19. Under the bed, piles of unwashed socks moldered undisturbed.

20. My daughters, hot and sweaty, lounged on the porch after the game.

21. I really think ladies and gentlemen, that a taste for Mozart is easily acquired.

22. Having carefully prepared the slides in advance, Greg completed the demonstration in less than ten minutes.

23. The chairmen who agreed with the Speaker, sat on one side of the aisle.

___ 24. Most women characters on television are simpering docile clowns.

25. In some elementary schools, teachers spend <u>less</u> than half of each class-room hour actually teaching.

APOSTROPHES

The apostrophe is used mainly in two situations: to show possession and to show that a letter has been left out of a word.

In this sentence,

Carla's decision was irrevocable.

the apostrophe and the *s* show that the decision belongs to Carla. Singular nouns of more than one syllable that end in an *s* and plural nouns that end in *s* show the possessive with the apostrophe alone.

Dickens' book	*Keats's* book
students' tests	*student's* test
critics' reviews	*children's* gifts
buses' turn signals	*bus's* turn signal
girls' drawings	*girl's* drawing

Apostrophes also show that a letter has been left out. For instance, instead of writing *do not,* you frequently use the less formal version, *don't.* The apostrophe shows that the letter between *n* and *t* has been omitted.

Exercise F

What letters have been left out in each of the following words?

EXAMPLE:

haven't = have not

  1. I'll =
 *2. it's =
 *3. you're =
  4. didn't =
  5. she's =

  * Watch out for these words. They are easily confused with the possessive forms, which do not have apostrophes.
    Its means belonging to it. (*its cave*)
    Your means belonging to you. (*your sweater*)
    Their means belonging to them. (*their house*)

6. wouldn't =
7. we're =
8. you've =
9. they'll =
10. hadn't =
11. I'm =
12. he'd =
*13. they're =
14. I've =
15. can't =

Exercise G

Edit the following sentences for appropriate use of apostrophes.

1. I have never met Jeans mother, but I cant help feeling I know her since Jean hasnt stopped talking about her all year.
2. The Farmers house couldnt go another winter without its exterior being painted.
3. Medusas ugly face turned people to stone.
4. Although she was dying, the most comforting presence in the house was hers.
5. Its a shame that they wouldnt spend an hour with their daughters teacher.
6. Samuel didnt even hesitate in his passage from the Torah; he read the Hebrew flawlessly.
7. Solomons temple, with its rich furnishings, took years to build.
8. In the game of checkers, Aunt Frances couldnt be beat.
9. When you have arthritis, you can usually tell when its going to snow; youre warned by a certain feeling in your bones.
10. Its not hard to predict what hell do in a crisis; hell ask his wifes permission to act.

EDITING PRACTICE

Edit the following paragraphs for appropriate punctuation.

1. Roberta Turner
    Superintendent of Schools

    Dear Ms. Turner,

    Discipline problems on the countys school buses are getting out of hand. When students shout run and throw books the drivers cant maintain safe conditions. As a driver I dont feel that the school system supports the drivers. Were expected to maintain order yet we have no power to suspend disruptive students from the bus. If we fill out the school systems report forms on such students its often three or four weeks before we get any response. Ms Turner Im afraid that well have a major accident on one of our buses unless your office begins to take the discipline problem seriously. Your the only one who can help.

Sincerely,

Frank Borden
Driver

2.   Square dancing which many people associate with the West requires a quick mind as well as quick feet. First of all there are 150 basic moves in the square dancers repertory and these moves can be combined into many patterns like ''load the boat'' ''peel the top'' and ''relay the deucy.'' Once the steps have been learned its practice perseverance and concentration that dancers need to respond to the callers voice without missing a beat. Even advanced dancers cant follow without hours of practice and memorization. So square dancing isnt just good physical exercise its also good mental exercise.

Checklist for Revising and Editing

1. Does the paragraph have a topic sentence that clearly states the subject and the controlling idea?
2. Is the topic sentence appropriate to the audience and purpose?
3. Does every supporting sentence relate directly to the subject and controlling idea?
4. Are there enough supporting details to make the point convincingly? Are the details factual and concrete?
5. Are the supporting details arranged in a logical order?
6. Is the strategy of development suited to the subject, audience, and purpose?
7. Are there transitions or other signals to show connections between ideas?
8. Is there a concluding sentence which restates the main idea?
9. Are less important details in subordinate parts of the sentence? Are more important details emphasized by the sentence structure?
10. Is there some variety in sentence patterns?
11. Is each word as precise as possible? Is the language suited to the audience and purpose?
12. Have any doubtful words been checked in the dictionary for spelling and/or meaning?
13. Has every sentence been checked for structure problems that could confuse a reader?
14. Does the punctuation help to focus the reader's attention on important ideas? Is every punctuation mark there for a definite purpose?
15. Has someone else looked at the first draft of this paper?

Appendix:
Verbs

Verbs are the heart of language. They show people or objects involved in action: physical (running, singing), mental (thinking, observing), or just the action of existence (being, feeling).

Using verbs well can add a great deal to your flexibility as a writer. Verbs can do tremendous work for you if you know how to use them skillfully.

VERB FORMS

One of the first things you have to understand about verbs in order to use them effectively is that they have several different forms. Every verb, in fact, has three basic forms: the *present* form, the *past* form, and the *past participle* form, each used to indicate a different time for the verb.

For instance, here are the three forms of the verb *walk:*

Present	*Past*	*Past Participle*
(Today I) walk	(Yesterday I) walked	(For years I have) walked

Notice that the past is formed by adding *-ed* to the present and that the past participle looks like the past.

Exercise A

Using the pattern shown above, write out the three forms of these verbs.

Present	*Past*	*Past Participle*
1. deliver		
2. hypnotize		

Present	*Past*	*Past participle*
3. plant		
4. rub*		
5. try*		
6. cook		
7. play		
8. open		
9. start		
10. watch		

Most English verbs are regular in the way they form their basic parts. All you have to watch out for with these regular verbs is an occasional spelling change like doubling the final consonant (as in **rubbed**) or changing *y* to *i* (as in **tried**).

IRREGULAR VERB FORMS

There are some verbs which do not follow the *-ed* rule. For instance, the verb *sing* has as its three forms:

Present	*Past*	*Past Participle*
sing .	sang	sung

Look at these other irregular verb forms:

think	thought	thought
come	came	come
go	went	gone
write	wrote	written

As you may have suspected already, there is really no substitute for just plain memorizing the irregular verb forms. However, you are probably already familiar with a number of those forms, especially if you are a native speaker of English. Test yourself with the list below by covering up the second and third columns. Check off the ones you know and then concentrate on memorizing the rest. It is often helpful to say the three parts out loud while you are memorizing them.

Present (Today I—)	*Past* (Yesterday I—)	*Past Participle* (For years I have—)
(be) is, are, am	was, were	been
beat	beat	beaten
begin	began	begun
bite	bit	bitten
blow	blew	blown

* Watch out for spelling change.

break	broke	broken
bring	brought	brought
burst	burst	burst
buy	bought	bought
choose	chose	chosen
come	came	come
do	did	done
draw	drew	drawn
drink	drank	drunk
drive	drove	driven
eat	ate	eaten
fall	fell	fallen
fight	fought	fought
find	found	found
fly	flew	flown
forget	forgot	forgotten
freeze	froze	frozen
give	gave	given
go	went	gone
grow	grew	grown
hang (suspend)	hung	hung
have	had	had
hide	hid	hidden
hold	held	held
know	knew	known
lay	laid	laid
lie	lay	lain
lose	lost	lost
ride	rode	ridden
ring	rang	rung
rise	rose	risen
run	ran	run
see	saw	seen
send	sent	sent
set	set	set
shake	shook	shaken
shine	shone	shone
show	showed	shown
shrink	shrank	shrunk
sing	sang	sung
sink	sank	sunk
sit	sat	sat
slide	slid	slid
speak	spoke	spoken
spend	spent	spent
spin	spun	spun
stand	stood	stood
steal	stole	stolen
stick	stuck	stuck

strike	struck	struck
swear	swore	sworn
swim	swam	swum
swing	swung	swung
take	took	taken
teach	taught	taught
tear	tore	torn
throw	threw	thrown
wear	wore	worn
weave	wove	woven
win	won	won
write	wrote	written

Whenever you are doubtful about the form of a verb, look up the word in the dictionary. It will show you all the forms of an irregular verb. If the dictionary shows only one form of the verb, that means the verb is regular and forms the past and past participle parts in the regular way, by adding -ed.

VERB TENSE

One of the most important uses of the three different verb forms is the formation of different tenses. *Tense* is the quality of a verb that shows *when* an action takes place. English has six main verb tenses: *present, past, future* (the simple tenses) and *present perfect, past perfect, future perfect* (the perfect tenses).

There are some verb forms that do not show time—for instance, *to cry* or *crying.* When you are constructing a sentence, you must include a verb that shows time. A verb that has tense is one of the requirements for a complete sentence.

Present Tense

You use the present tense when you want to talk about action that is going on now or when you are talking about things that are always true. For example:

One hundred centimeters *equal* one meter

The present tense is formed by using the first or present form of the verb. For instance, the verb *write,* with all its possible subjects in the present tense, looks like this:

I write	we write
you write	you (pl.) write
he, she, it writes	they write

Notice that there is a change in the verb when its subject is a *he*, a *she*, or an *it*. In that case, the present tense verb adds an *-s*.

Exercise B

Try writing out all the present tense forms of the verb *show*.

I _____   we _____

you _____   you (pl.) _____

he, she, it _____   they _____

The verb *fall:*

I _____   we _____

you _____   you (pl.) _____

he, she, it _____   they _____

The verb *talk:*

I _____   we _____

you _____   you (pl.) _____

he, she, it _____   they _____

Exercise C

Fill in a present tense verb for each subject below. Remember to add an *s* to the verb if the subject is a *he*, a *she*, or an *it*.

1. Robert _____.

2. The horses _____.

3. You and Sharon _____.

4. Laurie and I _____.

5. The light _____.

6. Two men _____.

7. Stella _____.

8. That station wagon _____.

9. My roommate and I _____.

10. The choir director _____.

11. Dr. McKenna _____.

12. Her hair _____.

Exercise D

Write a summary of the plot of a TV show you have seen recently. Tell the story in the present tense. Circle all the present tense verbs in your story.

Past Tense

You use the past tense of the verb to show that an action was completed at some time before now.

The past tense is formed by using the second form of the verb. For instance, the verb *write* looks like this in the past tense:

I wrote	we wrote
you wrote	you wrote
he, she, it wrote	they wrote

The verb *look:*

I looked	we looked
you looked	you looked
he, she, it looked	they looked

Notice that all the forms of the verb are the same in the past tense.

Exercise E

Write out the past tense for each of these verbs:

1. *show*

I _____   we _____

you _____   you _____

he, she, it _____   they _____

2. *fall*

I _____ we _____

you _____ you _____

he, she, it _____ they _____

3. *begin*

I _____ we _____

you _____ you _____

he, she, it _____ they _____

4. *lie* (to recline)

I _____ we _____

you _____ you _____

he, she, it _____ they _____

5. *go*

I _____ we _____

you _____ you _____

he, she, it _____ they _____

Exercise F

Underline all the verbs in the following paragraph; then rewrite the paragraph, changing the verbs from the present tense to the past tense.

Steve is determined to become a professional singer. He gets up early every morning and jogs because he wants to increase his lung capacity. Exercise helps him with breath control. Then he attends voice and music classes for four hours. In the afternoon, he practices in his studio. He warms up by singing scales. Then he rehearses some songs he already knows. Finally, he works on a new piece. While he eats dinner, he listens to recordings of famous singers. Almost every night, he either performs somewhere himself or goes to listen to another singer perform. Steve spends every minute of the day working toward his goal.

Your new paragraph should begin: When he was younger, Steve

Exercise G

Underline all the verbs in the following paragraph; then rewrite the paragraph, changing the verbs from the past tense to the present tense. (Watch out for the -*s* on the verb if the subject is a *he,* a *she* or an *it.*)

Twenty years ago, Frenchman's Point was an inexpensive place to live. Houses sold for under $10,000, and interest rates on mortgages were low. A family of four could easily eat for $50 a month. Food cost even less if the family had a garden, which most families did. Since the weather rarely became cold, people spent very little on heat. The simple life there demanded only simple clothes, so not much money had to be spent on finery. The most expensive entertainment was a 50-cent movie and a 10-cent soda. The people of Frenchman's Point lived well without much money.

Your new paragraph should begin: Even today, Frenchman's Point

Exercise H

Choose any ten irregular verbs from the list on page 376–78. List the present forms here:

1. _____   6. _____

2. _____   7. _____

3. _____   8. _____

4. _____   9. _____

5. _____   10. _____

Now write a short story in which you use each of these verbs at least once in the past tense. Circle each past tense verb in your story.

Future Tense

You use the future form of the verb to show that an action is going to take place at some time after the present moment: next hour, next day, next week, next year, and so on. For example:

I *will bring* the dessert.
Mark *will report* you to the dean.

The future tense is formed by using the present form of the verb with the helping verb *will*. Here is the verb *write* in the future tense:

I will write   we will write
you will write   you will write
he, she, it will write   they will write

Here is the verb *begin* in the future tense:

I will begin   we will begin
you will begin   you will begin
he, she, it will begin   they will begin

Notice that the form of the verb is exactly the same no matter what the subject is.

Exercise I

Using the verbs above as models, write out the future tense of the following verbs.

want

I _____ we _____

you _____ you _____

he, she, it _____ they _____

show

I _____ we _____

you _____ you _____

he, she, it _____ they _____

talk

I _____ we _____

you _____ you _____

he, she, it _____ they _____

Exercise J

Underline all the verbs in the following paragraph. Then rewrite the paragraph, changing the verbs to the future tense.

Two years ago, I began at the bottom of the field of journalism. I started out selling advertisements for a small weekly paper. At the same time, I asked the sports editor to let me cover some high school games. Gradually, I worked my way up to college games. Then a job as a reporter opened up at a paper in the next town. I grabbed it. Soon, I wrote half the stories in the paper. However, I wanted more money. So I moved to a daily paper as the police reporter. I did such good work that I quickly received a raise. Finally, I made the big time: The *Washington Post* offered me a job!

Your new paragraph should begin: Two years from now, I

Review: The Three Simple Tenses

	I called	I call	I will call
TIME	←──before now	now	after now ──────→
	past tense	present tense	future tense

The three simple tenses place action in three broad categories of time. Action which is happening now is shown by the present tense. Action which happened before now is shown by the past tense. Action which will happen at some time after now is shown by the future tense.

Exercise K

Identify the tense of the verb in each of the following sentences. Then rewrite the sentence using the verb tense indicated in parentheses. How does the meaning of the sentence change when you change the tense of the verb?

1. Pat satisfied the requirements.   (future)

2. The contractor prepared his bid.   (present)

3. Those children will require some assistance.   (past)

4. Everyone watches the conductor.   (past)

_____

5. Margie will graduate in December.   (present)

_____

6. Walter reported the news.   (future)

_____

7. Bob grows huge tomato plants.   (past)

_____

8. Is this correct?   (past)

_____

9 She struck the chord loudly.   (future)

_____

10. The committee sends monthly reports.   (past)

_____

11. Our house stood in Crofton.   (future)

_____

12. That man ran for governor in every election.   (present)

_____

13. We will swim for an hour a day.   (past)

_____

14. The council resolved several issues.   (present)

_____

15. Pepe feels strange in that class.   (past)

_____

16.   The Board passed the resolution.   (future)

_____

17.   Four scouts will become Eagles.   (past)

_____

18.   Snow filled the woods.   (present)

_____

19.   I expect to stay healthy.   (past)

_____

20.   No one will give up her lunch hour.   (present)

_____

21.   The Puritan writers use much symbolism.   (past)

_____

22.   The oak tree shaded the back porch.   (future)

_____

23.   Skateboarding will require protective equipment.   (present)

_____

24.   Rita finds the matching sock.   (future)

_____

25.   My sons will smile angelically into the camera.   (past)

_____

Present Perfect Tense

What is the difference between these two sentences?

I *sang* for ten years.
I *have sung* for ten years.

The first sentence uses a past tense verb to tell the reader that although you had a singing career at some time in the past, your singing career is now over. The second sentence tells the reader that your singing career began ten years ago and still continues now.

What is the difference between these two sentences?

The Pirates *won* the pennant.

The Pirates *have won* the pennant.

The first sentence tells the reader that the winning took place sometime in the past. The second sentence, using the present perfect tense, indicates that the winning has just taken place, in the very recent past.

The *present perfect* tense, then, is used to show actions that are not going on simply in the present; such actions have some relationship to the past too. Either the action began in the past and is still going on, or it has been completed so recently that it might almost be considered as a present action. The present perfect tense is formed by combining the past participle form of the verb with the present form of the verb *have*.

Here is the verb *write* in the present perfect tense:

I have written   we have written
you have written   you have written
he, she, it *has* written   they have written

The verb *look:*

I have looked   we have looked
you have looked   you have looked
he, she, it *has* looked   they have looked

Exercise L

Using these two verbs as models, write out the present perfect tense of the verbs below. (Notice the change in the helping verb (has) when the subject is *he, she,* or *it.*).

begin

I _____   we _____

you _____   you _____

he, she, it _____   they _____

talk

I _____   we _____

you _____   you _____

he, she, it _____   they _____

show

I _____   we _____

you _____   you _____

he, she, it _____   they _____

fall

I _____   we _____

you _____   you _____

he, she, it _____   they _____

go

I _____   we _____

you _____   you _____

he, she, it _____   they _____

Exercise M

In each of the following sentences, supply the appropriate form of the verb, past tense or present perfect tense. Be prepared to explain your choice.

(fear)   1. From that day on, I _have feared_ dogs until I reached adulthood.

(build)   2. Mr. Crosby _built_ our house two years ago.

(swallow)   3. Rover _have swallowed_ a bone. We must get him to the vet's.

(go)   4. You just missed Pat. She _went_ to work.

(speak) 5. Ms. Jordan _have spoken_ for an hour. I am getting bored.

(hate) 6. When we moved to Chicago, we _____ hated _____ living in the city.

(love) 7. Ever since we moved to San Francisco, we _have loved_ living in the city.

(spend) 8. Before entering medical school, my sister _____ spent _____ three years in the Navy.

(grow) 9. For the last twelve years, the farmers around here [have been growing] _____ grew _____ only one kind of corn, Silver Queen.

(teach) 10. Professor Dalton _have taught_ mathematics here for so long that he is practically a legend.

(teach) 11. Professor Abbott _____ taught _____ history here for so long that she was practically a living history book.

(look) 12. By the end of the day, my grandmother _____ looked _____ out that window a hundred times.

(submit) 13. The contractor _have submitted_ an estimate. But his bid is far more than we can afford.

(draw) 14. The architect _____ drawed _____ a plan. But last year's committee found her design much too elaborate.

(eat) 15. Ever since they were children, Sarah and Michael _have been eating_ nothing but oatmeal for breakfast.

(drink) 16. When we were young, we never _____ drank _____ coffee.

(cover) 17. So far, our insurance policy _have covered_ all our losses. But the repairs aren't finished yet.

(evaluate) 18. The supervisor _have evaluated_ all the library employees just this week.

(win) 19. My father's pickles _____ have won _____ the first prize at the county fair every year except last year.

(increase)   20.   Since the new sales campaign began in July, our orders

have increased by 20 percent.

(increase)   21.   During the last sales campaign, our orders ___increased___
by 20 percent.

Exercise N

Underline all the verbs in the following paragraph; then rewrite the paragraph, changing the verbs to the present perfect tense.

You ruined my life. I gave up my acting career for you. I put you through medical school. I stayed home to raise your children. I did without new clothes so that you could dress well. I entertained your smart friends even though they made fun of me. You never considered my feelings. You never gave me any money of my own to spend. You made me ask you for every small thing I needed. You expected a hot meal and a sexy come-on every evening. You were an unfeeling wife, Marsha. That's why I left you.

Your new paragraph should begin: For fifteen years, you

Past Perfect Tense

Look at the verbs in these two sentences:

$$\overset{1}{\text{Margaret \textit{left}}} \text{ the office and } \overset{2}{\textit{returned}} \text{ an hour later.}$$
$$\text{Margaret } \overset{2}{\textit{returned}} \text{ an hour after she } \overset{1}{\textit{had left.}}$$

In each sentence there are two actions. In the first sentence, the actions are mentioned in the order in which they occurred. First she left; then she returned. Therefore, both verbs are in the past tense. However, the second sentence presents the second action first and then the first. In order to make the time sequence perfectly clear, the second sentence uses the past perfect tense, *had left*.

Here is another example:

$$\overset{1}{\text{The children \textit{picked}}} \text{ two quarts of strawberries and } \overset{2}{\textit{ate}} \text{ them}$$
for dessert.

$$\text{For dessert, the children } \overset{2}{\textit{ate}} \text{ the two quarts of strawberries}$$
they $\overset{1}{\textit{had picked.}}$

The past perfect tense is also used to emphasize that one action was completely finished before another action started. For instance:

> As the electrician *repaired* the washing machine, sparks *shot* out.
>
> After the electrician *had repaired* the washing machine, sparks *shot* out.

These two sentences present different sequences of action. In the first, the repairing and the shooting are going on at the same time. In the second, the repairs are finished before the sparks start shooting out. This second case is where the past perfect tense is needed.

Here is another example of that use:

> Cinderella *had scrubbed* the kitchen floor when her fairy godmother *arrived*.
>
> Cinderella *scrubbed* the kitchen floor when her fairy godmother *arrived*.

Which sentence indicates that Cinderella finished her work before her fairy godmother got there?

The past perfect tense is formed by using the past tense of the helping verb (*had*) with the past participle form of the main verb. The verb *write* looks like this in the past perfect tense:

I had written	we had written
you had written	you had written
he, she, it had written	they had written

The verb *show:*

I had shown	we had shown
you had shown	you had shown
he, she, it had shown	they had shown

Exercise O

Using the above verbs as models, write out the past perfect tense of the verbs below:

fall

I _____   we _____

you _____   you _____

he, she, it _____   they _____

talk

I _____   we _____

you _____   you _____

he, she, it _____   they _____

begin

I _____   we _____

you _____   you _____

he, she, it _____   they _____

go

I _____   we _____

you _____   you _____

he, she, it _____   they _____

lay

I _____   we _____

you _____   you _____

he, she, it _____   they _____

Exercise P

In each of the following sentences fill in the appropriate form of the verb. Be prepared to explain your choices.

(say)   1. Suddenly I remembered what the coach _had said_ about bunting.

(close)   2. Louise _closed_ her briefcase and left the room.

(close)   3. Louise left the room after she _had closed_ her brief-case.

(paint) 4. Jeff __had painted__ the whole porch by the time Vance arrived.

(call) 5. Since they __had called__ us, we picked them up at the train station.

(call) 6. They __called__ us, so we picked them up at the train station.

(read) 7. Tom __read__ the chapter and made some notes on it.

(read) 8. Because Tom __had read__ the chapter, he passed the test.

(read) 9. Tom made notes on the chapter which he __read__.

(pack) 10. Celia __had packed__ the suitcase almost two weeks before we left.

(have) 11. When the salesman left, Mr. and Mrs. Murphy __had__ two solid hours of high-pressure tactics.

(see) 12. Since someone __had seen__ the thief, the police were able to solve that case.

(bake) 13. I __baked__ the cake, and my sister frosted it.

(bake) 14. My sister frosted the cake which I __had baked__.

(pass) 15. The lead car __passed__ the halfway mark before the last car started.

(forget) 16. After Sheila had mailed all her Christmas cards, she realized that she __had forgotten__ zip codes on the envelopes.

(snow) 17. Even though it __snowed__, we played that game.

(buy) 18. My wife made me return the golf clubs which I __bought__ the day before.

(receive) 19. Since the patient __received__ two units of morphine already, I did not prescribe any further medication.

(hang)   20.   Doris _____ the picture in the den, but later she moved it to the living room.

Exercise Q

Underline all the verbs in the following paragraph; then rewrite the paragraph, changing the verbs to the past perfect tense.

Fred prepared the house for his guests. He picked up all the old newspapers and dirty clothes in the TV room. Then he vacuumed the whole downstairs. In the kitchen, he put all the dirty dishes in the dishwasher and wiped down the counters, the stove, and the table. He swept the floor; he even scrubbed and waxed it. He cleaned up the bathroom; he wiped all the fixtures with soapy water, polished the mirror, and scrubbed the floor. He laid out fresh towels. Finally, he set vases of flowers throughout the house. The house had never looked so nice.

Your new paragraph should begin: By the time we arrived, Fred

Future Perfect Tense

Look at these two sentences:

I *will save* a thousand dollars.

By the end of the summer, I *will have saved* a thousand dollars.

In the first sentence, the future tense indicates that the saving will be done at some indefinite time in the future. In the second sentence, there is a definite time in the future by which the saving will have been done. You use the *future perfect tense* in a case like this where an action will be completed at some specific time in the future.

Here is another example of that use:

I *will accumulate* ten days of sick leave.

Before the summer, I *will have accumulated* ten days of sick leave.

The future perfect tense is formed by using the future tense of the helping verb (*will have*) with the past participle of the main verb. Here is the verb *write* in the future perfect tense:

I will have written   we will have written
you will have written   you will have written
he, she, it will have written   they will have written

The verb *show:*

I will have shown   we will have shown
you will have shown   you will have shown
he, she, it will have shown   they will have shown

Exercise R

Using the verbs above as models, write out the future perfect tense for the following verbs.

buy

I _____ we _____

you _____ you _____

he, she, it _____ they _____

lay

I _____ we _____

you _____ you _____

he, she, it _____ they _____

begin

I _____ we _____

you _____ you _____

he, she, it _____ they _____

fall

I _____ we _____

you _____ you _____

he, she, it _____ they _____

go

I _____ we _____

you _____ you _____

he, she, it _____ they _____

Exercise S

Underline all the verbs in the following paragraph; then rewrite the paragraph, changing the verbs, if appropriate, to the future perfect tense.

I will live through that Civil Service Exam. I will get up early, and I will eat a good breakfast. I will spend at least two hours reviewing the chapter on postal regulations. I will remember to put an extra pencil in my pocket. I will leave the house by 12:30. I will arrive in plenty of time. I will read each question carefully. I will follow all instructions to the letter. I know* I will pass. I think* I will score high. I hope* I will be chosen for the job.

Your new paragraph should begin: By this time next month, I

Exercise T

In each of the following sentences, supply the appropriate form of the verb, future tense or future perfect tense. Be prepared to explain your choice.

(drive)   1. By the time I get to Evanston, I _will have driven_ 2,000 miles.

(receive)   2. She ___will___ not _have received_ your letter before Tuesday.

(buy)   3. Everyone in the class _will buy_ his or her own subscription to *Newsweek*.

(give)   4. When I agreed to marry him, he _____ me a huge diamond ring.

(dress)   5. The children _will have dressed_ in their costumes when the principal arrives.

(make)   6. Harry _will make_ his second million on the sales of that record.

(lose)   7. The library _will lose_ over 2,000 books by the end of the semester.

(pay)   8. Since no one will volunteer for the extra duty, the home office

                   will pay someone to attend the meeting.

(apply)   9. We expect that several women _will apply_ for this job by the time the deadline arrives.

(see)   10. On graduation day this year, our college _will have seen_ 23 classes leave its campus.

* This verb stays in the present tense.

Review: Simple Tenses and Perfect Tenses

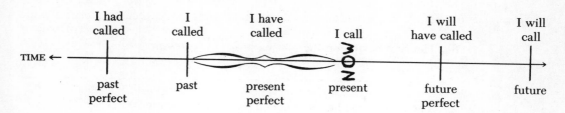

While the simple tenses show broad categories of time, the perfect tenses help to place actions more specifically within those time periods of past, present, and future. The past perfect shows a definite time in relation to the past. The present perfect shows a definite time in relation to the present. The future perfect shows a definite time in relation to the future.

Exercise U

Identify the tenses of the verbs in the following sentences. Rewrite the sentences, changing the verb tense as indicated. How does the meaning of the sentence change when the tense of the verb is changed?

1. Sandra applied for the manager's job.   (future)

   _____ will apply _____

2. I prepared an estimate.   (past perfect)
   had

   _____

3. The ship needs some repairs.   (past)

   _____ need _____

4. We will advertise the sale.   (past perfect)

   _____ had advertised _____

5. You have received several promotions.   (past)

   _____

6. The general signs all the recommendations.   (future perfect)

   _____ will have signed _____

7. They will have elected the president by then.   (past perfect)

   had (written above "will have")

_____

8. Henry reported on the marina project.   (present)

   reports

_____

9. The committee has announced its choice.   (present)

   announces

_____

10. We will not discuss the matter.   (present perfect)

   have discussed

_____

11. The auditor made an error.   (past perfect)

   had

_____

12. Mr. Lopez became the advisor.   (future)

   will become

_____

13. Such drastic action seems unnecessary.   (past)

   seemed

_____

14. We will resolve several issues.   (present perfect)

   have resolved

_____

15. I tried again.   (future perfect)

   will have

_____

16. His new novel, *Sirens,* appeared in February.   (future)

   will appear

_____

17. Not many secretaries have studied computers.   (present)

   studies

_____

18. You have been helpful.   (past perfect)

   had

_____

19. Our office was on Rowe Boulevard.   (future)

   _____ *will be* _____

20. The courthouse had disappeared by 1950.   (past)

   _____

21. The injury seemed accidental.   (past perfect)

   _____ *had* _____

22. Many dealers arrange financing.   (future)

   _____ *will* _____

23. Letter writing has become a lost art.   (past)

   _____ *became* _____

24. Historic Centerville restored the house.   (future perfect)

   _____ *will have* _____

25. Cable television expanded its service by 70 percent.   (present perfect)

   _____ *have* _____

THE VERB "TO BE"

One verb in English deserves special attention, the verb *to be*. Not only is it used very frequently, but it is extremely irregular in the way it forms tenses.
   Look at the following table, which shows the verb *to be* written out in six tenses.

	Present		*Present Perfect*
I am	we are	I have been	we have been
you are	you are	you have been	you have been
he, she, it is	they are	he, she, it has been	they have been

	Past		*Past Perfect*
I was	we were	I had been	we had been
you were	you were	you had been	you had been
he, she, it was	they were	he, she, it had been	they had been

Future

I will be   we will be
you will be   you will be
he, she, it will be   they will be

Future Perfect

I will have been   we will have been
you will have been   you will have been
he, she, it will have been   they will have been

Because this verb is used so much and because it has so many different forms, it would be a good idea to memorize this table so you will always know the form you need.

Linking Verbs

One important use of the verb *to be* is as a link between ideas. In this use, the verb *to be* is the main verb in the sentence. For example,

Margie *is* our representative.
or
Rich *was* angry last night.

There is a certain identity between *Margie* and *representative* and between *Rich* and *angry*. Thus, the verb *to be* is called a *linking verb*. It is almost like an equals sign between ideas, showing their close relationship.

Some other verbs can also function as linking verbs: *act, appear, become, feel, look, remain, seem, smell, sound,* and *taste*. For instance,

Millie *acts* fearless.

I *felt* sick.

Jan *will become* the captain.

Notice that in each of the examples above, you can substitute a form of the verb *to be* for the linking verb:

Millie *is* fearless.

I *was* sick.

Jan *will be* the captain.

You have to be careful with this second group of linking verbs, though, because sometimes they are not linking verbs. In

I *felt* a hand on my shoulder.

felt is not a linking verb. *Hand* is not the same as *I*. You also cannot substitute any form of the verb *to be* for *felt* in this sentence.

<blockquote>I *was* a hand on my shoulder.</blockquote>

doesn't make any sense.

Exercise V

Write ten sentences in which you use linking verbs At least five of these should use verbs other than *to be*. Circle the linking verb in each sentence. Can you tell what tense each verb is in?

Progressive Verbs

Another use of the verb *to be* is as a helping verb. *To be* can be used, for example, with an *-ing* form of another verb. Do you notice any difference in meaning between these two sentences?

<blockquote>She *calls* the restaurant for a reservation.
She *is calling* the restaurant for a reservation.</blockquote>

In both sentences, the action is taking place in the present, but the second sentence, with the verb *is calling*, gives more of a sense of the action being in progress at the present moment. This form is called the *progressive* form. The progressive form can be used with any tense of the verb *to be*.

PRESENT:	They [*are*] *walking* to the store.
PAST:	Shelly [*was*] *taking* notes.
FUTURE:	I [*will be*] *sending* you a catalog.
PRESENT PERFECT:	Dad [*has been*] *suffering* from these headaches for years.
PAST PERFECT:	We [*had been*] *planning* to close the account anyway.
FUTURE PERFECT:	You [*will have been*] *receiving* the magazine for six months before you will have to pay for it.

Notice that in each case the helping verb establishes the tense of the verb. The *-ing* form does not have a tense.

The progressive form of the verb can be used whenever you want to emphasize the sense of an action actually being performed at a certain moment.

Exercise W

Write out the forms of the verbs indicated below.

dance	(present)	(present progressive)
I		
you		
he, she, it		
we		
you		
they		

bring	(past)	(past progressive)
I		
you		
he, she, it		
we		
you		
they		

send	(future)	(future progressive)
I		
you		
he, she, it		
we		
you		
they		

claim	(present perfect)	(present perfect progressive)
I		
you		
he, she, it		
we		
you		
they		

invite	(past perfect)	(past perfect progressive)
I		
you		
he, she, it		
we		
you		
they		

select   (future perfect)   (future perfect
                                                        progressive)

I
you
he, she, it
we
you
they

Exercise X

For each of the following sentences, supply an appropriate form of the verb indicated. In the blank, give the regular verb form. Then rewrite the sentence using the progressive form. Be prepared to explain if one form seems more effective than the other.

EXAMPLE: (send)

Yesterday, I *sent* you the report.

Yesterday, I was sending you the report.

(dress)   1. I __am dressed__ . I will be ready in a minute.
                      (ing)

_____

_____

(talk)   2. They ___talked___ so loudly that no one could hear the
              music.   are talking

_____

_____

(sing)   3. Gene ___sings___ now; after him comes the magic act.

                  is singing

_____

(shop)   4. You___shopped___ here for years. Why do you want to go to
              a different store?

                      have shopped

_____

(plan)   5.   Dad _____ plans _____ this surprise for six months before their anniversary.

_____ is planning _____

_____

(write)   6.   Last year, Phillip _____ wrote _____ in his journal every day.

_____ was writing _____

_____

(teach)   7.   Next month, she _____ for 30 years.

_____

(try)   8.   Operator, I _____ this number for half an hour.

_____

(watch)   9.   While we _____ that show, I'll set your hair for you.

_____

(make)   10.   As soon as Maripat _____ enough money, she moved into her own apartment.

_____

Passive Verbs

The verb *to be* can also be used as a helping verb with the past participle. Notice the difference between these sentences:

Barry *selects* a representative.

A representative *is selected* by Barry.

The first sentence uses the present tense verb. In this sentence the subject, Barry, is performing the action of selecting. In the second sentence, Barry is still doing the selecting, but he is not placed as the subject of the sentence. In a sentence where the subject is not the doer of the action, the verb *to be* is used as a helping verb with the past participle. When the subject is not the doer of the action, the verb is said to be *passive.*

The passive can be used in any verb tense. Here are some other examples of the use of the passive.

ACTIVE:	Mike *made* some spaghetti.
PASSIVE:	Some spaghetti *was made* by Mike.
ACTIVE:	Someone *built* this monument in 1853.
PASSIVE:	This monument *was built* in 1853.
ACTIVE:	The teacher *will distribute* the grades.
PASSIVE:	The grades *will be distributed* by the teacher.
ACTIVE:	Greed *has ruined* many lives.
PASSIVE:	Many lives *have been ruined* by greed.
ACTIVE:	The Board of Trustees *prohibits* smoking.
PASSIVE:	Smoking *is prohibited.*

Exercise Y

Write out the active and passive forms of each verb below.

fill (present tense)

	Active	Passive
I	_____	_____
you	_____	_____
he, she it	_____	_____
we	_____	_____
you	_____	_____
they	_____	_____

place (past tense)

	Active	Passive
I	_____	_____
you	_____	_____
he, she, it	_____	_____
we	_____	_____
you	_____	_____
they	_____	_____

guide (future tense)

	Active	Passive
I	_____	_____
you	_____	_____
he, she, it	_____	_____
we	_____	_____
you	_____	_____
they	_____	_____

shoot (present perfect tense)

	Active	Passive
I	_____	_____
you	_____	_____
he, she, it	_____	_____
we	_____	_____

you _____   _____

they _____   _____

Exercise Z

Rewrite each of the following sentences, changing active verbs to passive and passive verbs to active. Does one version of the sentence seem better to you than the other?

1. The committee rejected the mayor's recommendation.

    _____

    _____

2. The fire killed two residents of the nursing home.

    _____

    _____

3. The first kilometer has been completed by the swimmers.

    _____

    _____

4. By children, "spaghetti" is often pronounced "pasketti."

    _____

    _____

5. The manufacturer had promised a refund within 48 hours.

    _____

    _____

6. The fruit was delivered on Monday.

    _____

    _____

7. Someone started the ecology movement in the 1960's.

_____

_____

8. The teams will end the soccer season in two weeks.

_____

_____

9. Sheila had knitted Bob's sweater as a gift.

_____

_____

10. For twenty years, we have sought peace.

_____

_____

Index